Ms M Roberts
24 York Road
Sale
Cheshire
M33 6UU

"AND THE 1 PLAYS ON"

The Biography of Ernie Waites M.B.E.

as told to
WALLY LINDSAY

THIS IS A TRUE STORY
In the early chapters some licence has been taken in describing characters and to produce a coherent narrative based on available information but all relevant facts, such as names, dates and locations are, as for as known records permit, substantially correct.

"AND THE BAND PLAYS ON"

Published by Wilshere Publications
14 Hayling Road, Sale, Cheshire

First published 1994

Copyright © W. A. Lindsay 1994

All rights reserved
This book is sold subject to the condition that it shall not,
by reason of trade or otherwise, be lent, re-sold, hired out,
or otherwise circulated without the publisher's prior consent
in any form of binding or cover other than that in which it is published
and without a similar condition including the condition being imposed
on a subsequent purchaser.

ISBN 0 9522931 0 2

Printed in Great Britain by
SANKEY LORD LTD.
Nelson, Lancashire

"AND THE BAND PLAYS ON"

ACKNOWLEDGEMENTS

Every effort has been made to record events as accurately as possible and to include all who have played a significant part in Ernie's life. Time, however, does dim memory and if, in spite of all our endeavours, someone has been omitted or some event mistakenly attributed, may we offer our apologies and give the assurance that a correction will be made in any subsequent editions.

We wish to record our thanks to the many people who have assisted in the production of this biography, particularly:

Mr. Richard Percy for supplying photographs of old Scarborough.

Mr. Brian Berryman for confirming historical details of Scarborough Old Town.

Mr. Bob Donnelly for extensive photographic assistance.

Mr. Frank Hall for the photograph of H.R.H. the Prince of Wales.

Mr. Ivor Hurst J.P. for his encouragement and for patiently proof reading the final manuscript.

CHAPTER ONE

To the other occupants of the compartment the girl by the window appeared to be reading but although her eyes were scanning the magazine she was completely unconscious of any meaning of the words. Her mind was in no condition to accept any input, nothing seemed able to penetrate the turmoil churning in her mind. Her thoughts were flitting from what could have been, what was, and, for fleeting horrifying moments, what might be. She laid the book in her lap and closed her eyes but was unable to find respite in rest - a luxury she had not enjoyed for over three weeks now - all she had had were restless periods of semi-sleep punctuated by spells of panic and despair.

A sudden puff of black smoke from the engine drifted past the window and her attention was drawn to the passing countryside. How different this landscape was from the industrial grime she had passed through the previous day; she could even imagine she was back home crossing the fields of Kerry. The journey across Ireland to Dublin and the choppy crossing to Holyhead had been made in a state of mental apathy but now, as the train neared Scarborough, the trepidation welled up again.

She glanced round the carriage. All six seats were occupied and the string racks above them were loaded with cases - her contribution was merely a canvas valise which easily contained all her possessions. The framed prints of railway scenes fixed above each seat meant nothing to her and would not have registered even if they did. She examined the faces of her fellow travellers and was somehow relieved to see they showed no interest in her, but why should they? Here she was a stranger amongst strangers; none would offer sympathetic platitudes, none turn their backs and, most comforting of all, none would expound bigoted contentious comment. There was some consolation in loneliness, she was away from it all now and the Irish Sea between her and the home she had left under a cloud of ignominy. She was on her own. She was Kathleen O'Brien. She was seventeen. She was pregnant.

She looked down at her magazine, still open at the same page as when she had left York, and, for once, some words registered - "Talking Pictures!". Films that had sound! She thought of the converted Parish Hall at home where she and Terry had been enthralled by the flickering escapades of Charlie Chaplin accompanied by the continuous tinny outpourings of an out-of-tune piano. It was after one of these shows that her nightmare had begun; they had gone back to the hotel and, somehow, she had ended up in his bed. It had been no violent explosion of passion, more the experimentation of forbidden affection, the first sexual experience for either of them. Terry! The tears welled as she tried to expunge the memory. This child she was carrying was his and he would never know it or even see it. Terry was the son of the owner of the hotel at which she had worked as a chambermaid since leaving school, he, too, was seventeen and over the past year they had grown very fond of each other, to the mutual displeasure of both families -Terry's family were Protestants. When her condition was made known the response from both sides had been immediate and unanimous - they should both leave the area before anyone in the little community became aware; arrangements were hastily made for her to "take a holiday" to an aunt in England and he was being shipped off to a distant member of the family who had emigrated to America a generation ago.

She was so absorbed in her thoughts she never realised the train had stopped until passengers began reaching for their luggage. She waited for the last to leave before she made her way to the ticket barrier. There she found herself alone, the throng of travellers had quickly dispersed and it was clear that no one had come to meet her. She deliberated for a few minutes and then realised she had to find her own way to Aunt Frances'. She rummaged in her purse for the scrap of paper with the address and found it beneath the coins- three shillings and eight pennies, all that remained from the money Terry's father had reluctantly given her for her fare. She decided she could afford a penny for a cup of tea and headed for the refreshment room.

Clasping the cup of hot tea she delighted in the warmth flowing into her hands and tried to imagine what Auntie Frances would be like. She did not remember her, but knew she was a year older than her mother and had left Ireland when she was sixteen to go into service in Scarborough. She had married someone called Tom before the war and had been home to Ireland only once, in 1918. Since then the only contact had been by irregular infrequent letters and she had realised, even as a child, that there was some long standing family disagreement. Her stomach began to turn again -none of this augured well for her acceptance of an enforced and burdensome guest. She found she couldn't drink the tea, left it on the table and walked out into the street.

Outside, dwarfed by the station colonnades, she sat on a low wall and took her first sight of her new home. The late September sun was trying to force its way through the watery clouds and the first drops of rain were beginning to fall. There seemed to be bustle everywhere, so different from the quiet little village she had left. Five roads met here; open-topped trams rattled to and fro emblazoned with advertisements for everything from Allenbury's Pastilles to the Pleasure Park, parents were shepherding children across the roads and motor cars were challenging the carthorses for space. A delivery boy went by, the huge basket on the front of his cycle loaded with packets, and gave her an admiring glance causing her to redden and look away. She saw a policeman approaching (she was still amused by his tall helmet, so different from the flat caps of the Garda) and she stopped him,

"Can you direct me to Princess Street?" she asked. He thought for a moment before replying,

"Aye lass," he said, "it's up by the Castle. Bit far to walk mind, take the tram yonder."

She crossed the road, boarded a tram and gazed with interest at the shops and buildings she passed; the Pavilion Hotel, Maypole's Dairy and the wonder of the enormous frontage of Rowntrees Store. Perhaps, she thought, one day she might find happiness here. This was a holiday town, larger than anything she had ever experienced, famous for its spas and leisure facilities - surely there was something here, somewhere. She almost forced an anticipatory smile when, suddenly somehow, the vista changed. She had left the town centre and now saw drab buildings and unpainted ware-houses opposite a harbour where women were gutting fish. The tram stopped and she alighted. The anguish flooded back as she walked up the small hill, as the conductor had directed her, for the air of squalor was overwhelming. Just a few steps from the road she saw the sign "Princess Street" and inwardly groaned.

She was standing at the end of a narrow street of neglected houses of the Georgian era and disconsolately compared them to the village street she had left behind; gone were the cosy stone cottages, gone was the hard-packed trodden winding road bordered by wild grass verges, gone was the laughter and noisy banter from Riley's bar. Instead she saw these old houses whose doors opened directly to the uneven flagstones edging cobbles pockmarked with patches of crushed and flattened horse droppings. Along the street groups of ragged children were playing, skipping, spinning tops with little whips or rolling marbles in the gutters. A lamplighter was making his slow way along the street lighting the gas lamps with a long pole and chasing away two grubby urchins who were swinging round one of his charges on a length of rope tied to its projecting arm. She consulted her piece of paper once more and walked along the pavement. Passing the houses she realised that in the midst of this squalor there was obvious self-respect. The curtains, though tattered, were spotlessly clean, the knockers on the peeling doors scrupulously polished and every front step gleamed in the fading light. This was a place where poverty had found no victory; the threadbare jerseys of the youngsters were immaculately darned, the pavement outside each house individually swept and the glass in the decaying window frames shone defiantly. Then she was there. She closed her eyes, took a deep breath and exhaled with a long silent sigh. She knocked.

The door was opened by a gaunt woman who appeared to be in her fifties. Her own mother was thirty-six, could this really be her sister? The aunt she remembered from photographs had been a vivacious young lady who could have been her mother's twin; the only likeness she saw now was the colour of her red hair.

"Aunt Frances?" she asked warily, "I'm Kathleen."

There was no smile of welcome, no intimate embrace, just a despairing look of sorrowful resignation.

"Oh, are you now? Then I suppose you'd better come in."

Following the woman Kathleen found herself in a room where the woodwork was painted a dull brown and the floral wallpaper was peeling in several places. This was obviously the living area of the house, dominated by a huge cast-iron range with glowing coals behind the grate on its right hand side. To the left of the fire was an oven door and, on top, a kettle was boiling. The stone flagged hearth was bounded by a heavy iron fender and the whole array gleamed with polished blacklead. Above the fireplace was a large shelf covered by a worn embroidered scalloped cloth on which stood an ornate black marble clock surrounded by statuettes of Our Lady of Lourdes and St. Christopher and several small holy pictures. Incongruously, at one end, was a cylindrical box crammed with wooden spills. The centre of the room was taken up by a scrubbed wooden table and four painted chairs, in the small space between the table and the grate were two shabby Victorian armchairs above which a wooden clothes airer was suspended from the ceiling. Under the staircase, opposite a twelve paned sash window, was a black horsehair sofa and on the far wall, well away from the fire, a large chest of drawers. The wall above the drawers was occupied by a large ornately framed picture of the Sacred Heart. The printed oilcloth on the floor. worn brown in places, was almost completely covered by rugs made from strips of old clothing laboriously pegged into lengths of sacking. In the fading light the room created an atmosphere of murky foreboding.

Frances sat in one of the armchairs and indicated that Kathleen should use the other,

"Last time I saw you you'd have been about six years old. I wouldn't have recognised you, don't suppose you remember me?"

"No, Aunt, but I have seen your photographs."

"Taken when I was younger and full of high hopes! Those days have gone, lass. Let me give you some advice. Don't go getting ideas like I did about England being the land of milk and honey. It isn't, and I'm living proof of it. Came here expecting everything and look what I've finished up with - a bloody hovel!" She paused and wiped some imaginary spots from the pinafore that completely covered her clothing except for the hem of a woollen skirt. She was obviously a very unhappy woman but she sat with her head erect, her knees held tightly together and her back straight and proud. "Suppose I look a wreck compared to the women back home, don't I? Hope you didn't expect to come to a grand house like you see in the magazines. I did - now I live with the stink of fish, scraping to find the next meal for the kids. That's why I didn't write so often."

"It's no better at home," Kathleen said, "but did you ever consider going back?"

"Often, in the old days, but with the kids and Tom's pittance of a wage how could I? Anyway, Tom thinks Scarborough is heaven on earth, he'd never go to Ireland, and talking of Tom, I'd better warn you, he's not at all pleased about you coming here. Your father never asked us, you know, just a letter saying you were on your way. Tom was right mad, you can imagine."

The trepidation swelled up inside her again and her eyes filled with tears, "I didn't know, honest, and it was nothing to do with me, he just gave me some money and your address, told me to pack a bag and go."

Aunt Frances huffed. "Huh! Typical! Always was like that. Any sign of trouble, duck out and let someone else do the worrying......this time it's us."

Kathleen could restrain herself no longer. She cradled her head in her hands and felt herself suffocating as she gasped for breath between paroxysms of tears. Frances came to her, knelt by the chair and put an arm round her shoulder until the sobbing subsided.

"Nay, lass, I've nothing against you, poor kid," she said, pulling Kathleen's head on her shoulder, "come on now, will it help to tell me all about it before the kids come in and Tom gets home?"

That was all she needed. The crying diminished to a pitiable wimper and, constantly wiping tears with her handkerchief the whole story gushed out; the families' bitter condemnation of her friendship with Terry, the clandestine meetings which made the relationship flourish, the terrifying discovery of her pregnancy, the two weeks of utter panic she endured before telling her parents, the dismay at the complete lack of sympathy and the immediate banishment. Frances listened without interrupting the flow and, when Kathleen had finished, merely added,

"I think we both could do with a cup of tea." She got up, opened a cupboard by the side of the range and took out a chipped teapot and two cups. She spooned tea from a square tin caddy decorated with a picture of Edward VII into the pot and then filled it with water from the kettle.

"And sitting in the dark don't help," she added. Taking a spill from the box on the mantlepiece she lit it from the fire and used it to light the gas mantle on a bracket protruding from the chimney breast. The tone of the room seemed to change in the hissing light. She poured tea into the cups, added thick condensed milk from a jaggedly opened tin and handed one to Kathleen, there were no saucers and the tea tasted sickly sweet.

"Feeling better?"

"Yes......and thanks Auntie."

"Right, now come here and freshen yourself up before you face the terrors, it's time they came in."

She took Kathleen into the back room, "the scullery" she called it. This room was cold, the floor was of stone flags and the rough walls whitewashed. Under a small window was a stone sink some four inches in depth above which was a solitary brass tap. In the corner of the room was a brick built "copper" - rather like an oven but with an opening at the top covered by a wooden lid, below it was a grilled front which hinged open to allow a fire to be made. It was here that the weekly washing was boiled before being squeezed through the huge iron mangle standing by the side wall. Frances ran cold water from the tap into a chipped enamel bowl and added hot water from the ever-handy kettle on the grate. She gave Kathleen a towel and a large block of Sunlight soap and left her. As she rinsed her hands and washed the tear stains from her face she could hear her aunt at the front door shouting "David! ......Tommy!"

As she returned to the living room through the back door the two boys ran in from the front, each to receive a cuff round the head from their mother,

"Just look at the state of you! Straight through! Wash!" The boys, aged about twelve and ten, passed her without even an inquisitive glance.

By the time they came out of the scullery Frances had set four bowls and spoons on the table and was ladling out a thick soup-like concoction she had taken from the oven. Four hunks of bread, hacked from a cottage loaf were on a plate in the centre. The boys sat at the table and, for the first time, looked enquiringly at Kathleen.

"This is your cousin Kathleen, from Ireland, she'll be staying with us for a while," then, to Kathleen, "that's Tommy and that's David."

"Mum said you had three children."

"Oh, there's Bernadette, but she lives-in at the Pavilion, she's a kitchenmaid there."

The boys hadn't touched their food, they were sitting in silence. Frances nodded to the elder boy. They crossed themselves and he said grace. They grabbed their spoons and ate ravenously.

Kathleen tasted the food and, not even trying to guess what was in it, found it warm and satisfying. She was beginning to feel more comfortable until she recalled what her aunt had said about her uncle's attitude and the bread suddenly stuck in her throat,

"When will Uncle Tom be home?" she asked.

"A couple of hours yet, he doesn't finish work 'til seven and he'll call in at the "Leeds" on his way. Stop worrying, and eat your tea."

The meal was eaten accompanied by chit-chat conversation which took in the boys, their schooling and their pastimes. Kathleen, in turn, told them of village life in Ireland and was surprised at their genuine interest as well as their politeness. An acute intelligence belied their impoverished appearance and they were blessed with a dry Yorkshire wit. When the meal was finished they collected the crockery and, without any prompting, did the washing-up, refilled the faithful kettle and placed it back on the range. The next hour was spent in a mood of nervous apprehension. Frances and Kathleen sat in the armchairs exchanging stories while the boys, clearly aware of their anxiety but too well-mannered to enquire, sat at the table, one reading a well-thumbed copy of "The Magnet" while the other sorted a stack of dog-eared cigarette cards. Then Uncle Tom came in.

It would be more fitting to say he burst in. He had obviously been drinking and entered the room like the villain of a Victorian melodrama, the front door banging against the wall as he threw it open.

"The bastards have put us on short time again! Three bloody days a week from Monday....." He caught sight of Kathleen and paused enquiringly. Frances jumped up.

"This is our Kathleen .....you know, Bridie's girl."

"Mother of Jesus! That's all I bloody wanted! I've just found out we're on half bloody money from next week and now you tell me I've another sodding mouth to feed! Has dear bloody Bridie sent any money to keep her? You can bet your bleeding life she hasn't ...."

He was interrupted by Kathleen's collapse into another bout of uncontrollable despair, all the efforts of Frances to calm her became fruitless as she curled forward in the chair, shoulders heaving. Frances rapidly took control, she knelt by Kathleen's side again and embraced her, saying to the boys, quietly,

"Tommy, David, be good lads, go to your bedroom." Without any questioning they went upstairs, both giving a reproachful glance at their father as they passed him. He calmed down, at a loss to know what to do.

"Sit down, Tom," she said authoritatively, "She's here, though not of her own choosing. She's family .... and she's staying .... at least until I can find her somewhere more suitable. I'll get your tea."

That night was the most miserable one Kathleen could ever remember, even outstripping the night in Ireland when she had faced her father's wrath when she told him she was pregnant. Aunt Frances had made her a make-shift bed on the sofa but she could not sleep. Before she had left home her mother had unearthed a cheap brass ring and, for the sake of some idea of hypocritical propriety, had insisted she wore it on her third finger. Sitting on the sofa in the darkness her thoughts threw her back into the past, to Ireland, to home and to Terry. She twisted the ring on her finger and contemplated what could have been; it could have been a real one, his, and they could have been together, eagerly anticipating the arrival of their baby. She stroked her hands over her belly and the tears came again. She tugged the ring from her finger, threw it across the room, fell prone on the sofa and cried herself into merciful exhaustion.

She woke to the sound of the grate being raked out. Frances shovelled the ashes into a mis-shapen bucket and carried it outside. She returned with the bucket filled with coal and re-lit the fire. When the small iron door was closed over the grill there was a roar as the flames took hold and, within minutes, the welcome glow was once again in the room.

"What time is it?" Kathleen asked.

"Half past six. Thought I'd better get you up before the boys come down. Have you slept?"

"Yes, I can't understand it .... first real sleep I've had for weeks."

"You were worn out, lass. Come on, out of bed with you, let's see what today brings. I've had an idea ... do you fancy going back to work?"

"Oh yes! Nothing I'd like better, but how, where?"

"Leave it with me .... now get up! Tom will be down at seven but don't worry your head about him, he'll be sober this morning and a different man."

"You're sure?"

"I'm sure. Trust me, Kathleen, I've had sixteen years of it."

She went into the scullery and by the time she returned with a saucepan of water Kathleen had dressed, "Now get in there and get a wash, you'll have no chance when they arrive!"

Breakfast consisted of thick porridge made with water and the thick condensed milk. Tom and the boys were still eating theirs when Frances put on her coat.

"Right, I'm off to work, I'll be back about one, Kathleen, why don't you have a look round? The castle's worth seeing, so's the church."

There was an embarrassed silence after she left until Tom spoke,

"Sorry about last night."

"That's all right."

"No it's not," he said dejectedly, "I shouldn't get like that .... but what the hell can I do? We're existing, not living, what can I give my kids? What provider am I when my wife has to go out at this time scrubbing floors? And now we're all going on half time and half wages. What's going to happen to us? 'A land fit for heroes' they promised us .... and look what we've got. Dammit Kathleen, this is 1927, and you'd think it was still the time of Charles Dickens!"

Her antipathy of last night vanished and was replaced by sympathy. In place of the wretch fortified by drink she now saw a pitiful figure of despair, a proud man broken by circumstances. She did not know what to say and the brooding silence returned. The boys took the empty porridge bowls into the scullery.

"Fran's right," Tom said, "you should have a look round. Don't sit here, it'll drive you mad."

"What about the door? Is there a key?"

"No need for a key, leave it open, no one will come in round here .... not that there's much to take." He looked at the clock, "It's time I was off, see you tonight."

Wrapping a hand-knitted scarf round his neck and putting a cap on his head he left the house. It was noticeable he had no top coat. Kathleen was once again impressed by the two boys. They went into what was clearly an established routine; they banked up the fire, swept the hearth, and generally tidied the room before going off to school. Her own coat was hanging on the cupboard door. She put it on and walked out into the street.

Outside the house she could see the ruins of a castle looming above so she had no doubt as to what direction she should take. She knew she could not enjoy her situation but she did get some pleasure during the morning walk. She spent some time at the Norman ruins and then made her way to St. Mary's Church. In the graveyard she found the grave of Anne Bronte and stood there in meditation; she felt a strange affinity for the sisters and could well imagine herself as the tragic heroine of one of their novels.

She spent a pleasant hour investigating the old church and, deciding to find a different way back, went down the steps of Church Stairs Street. She was amused by the fact that she always seemed to be going up or down steep inclines, at home the roads were level and flat. To her surprise she found herself back in Princess Street, albeit at the other end from where she had entered it the previous evening. She decided to turn right. She looked at the street name to avoid getting lost and smiled, "St. Sepulchre Street". Was there a Saint Sepulchre? she pondered, she had never heard of him if there was. What would she find next, "Blessed Tombstone Gulch"? She didn't, but at the top of the road she saw a huge grey stone building which reminded her of the Grecian temples she had seen in history books at school, only this was not dedicated to Athene, large letters proclaimed it "MARKET HALL". She went inside.

There was nothing like this at home! It's cavernous interior echoed with the noise of shoppers patronising the myriad of stalls. It was a wonderland of working class commerce, selling everything from clothing to household needs. A large area was taken up with farm produce and it was at these stalls that she lingered, comparing prices of dairy goods with those at home. One thing was different. Alongside the fresh stocks there were boxes containing bruised fruit, semi-rotten vegetables and cracked eggs which were being sorted over and purchased at very low prices by the ragged customers. She wondered whether this was the way Aunt Frances had to scrimp and that gave her an idea. She bought fresh potatoes and vegetables and then made her way to the butchers stalls to buy mutton chops.

When she got back Kathleen found the saucepan empty and washed and realised the boys had been home to have last night's leavings for their lunch. By the time her aunt arrived home there was a real Irish stew bubbling in the saucepan on the range. This time it was Frances' turn to show emotion. She blinked to hold back tears, took her niece in her arms and said,

"Would you believe lass, that's the first meal I've not had to cook in sixteen years." Kathleen was embarrassed at the reaction to such a small gesture but her aunt continued with a smile "I'm wondering if I've done the right thing now."

"What do you mean?"

"Let's have a cup of tea."

Kathleen had quickly learned that in Yorkshire the ritual of a cup of tea seemed to preface every important announcement or accompany any discussion so she waited patiently while the brew was made, then, sitting in the armchairs by the fire her aunt explained.

"You know I clean at the Balmoral? Well, I've been there years now and one of my jobs is the manager's office. He trusts me, see, and I get on real well with him. Well, I knew that he has got a chambermaid's job going so this morning I mentioned you. Didn't tell you this morning, didn't want to build your hopes up, but he's going to see you, wants you there in the morning. If you get the job you can live in - better than making do on that sofa."

Kathleen beamed, then hesitated, "But what about...." she looked down at her stomach.

"Don't mention it unless he does, and I see no reason why he should. Worry about that later, most girls seem to leave within a year anyroads."

The next day Kathleen accompanied her aunt to work and followed her round the hotel as she cleaned, amusing herself by assisting with the dusting. Her interview with the manager was simple and she went home in light heart. She now had work, she was to start the next Monday and could move into the hotel on Sunday afternoon. Today was Saturday, she had only one more night to spend on the sofa.

CHAPTER 2

She first met Edith and Sarah socially at the end of her second week although she had noticed them even on the first day she started work. It would have been difficult not to notice them, they were two bubbly young women who worked as waitresses. They were day staff, seemingly inseparable, always ebullient and their ever ready smiles made them popular in the hotel with guests and staff alike. Her day off that week was Sunday and she was passing through the foyer on Saturday evening as they were going home.

"Goodnight." she said.

They turned and, as one, came towards her, hands outstretched. "Why, hullo," said the taller of the girls, "I'm Sarah, this is Edith. You're new here."

"Been here two weeks."

"Where are you living?"

"I'm living in, I've come from Ireland."

"What the dickens do you do with yourself for company in your time off?" Edith asked.

"Not much, my aunt is a cleaner here - that's how I found out about this job - she lives on Princess Street, I've been to see her once or twice, that's about all I could do - but I got my first pay yesterday so I am not so tied now. Can you recommend anywhere?"

"When's your day off?"

"Tomorrow."

"Sunday? That doesn't help, not much happens on Sundays in October." Edith said.

"Yes it does!" Sarah corrected her, "What about our weekly orgy?" Kathleen's eyes shot wide open. Edith laughed,

"She's on about our one night of extravagance," she said, "on Sundays our beloved husbands see their way to taking us out for a drink ... only one mind, but we look forward to it. Would you like to join us?"

"Oh, I'd love to .... but would they mind?"

"The men? Why, no! They leave us on our own anyway and go off playing dominoes."

"I've got a better idea," Sarah said, "You be ready for three o'clock and I'll come here for you, I'll take you home and you can have tea with us first." She turned to Edith, "And how about you and Bert? Let's make it a party!"

Little did Kathleen know that those few words were to change her life, the lives of her new-found friends and the future of her unborn baby.

She spent a happy afternoon with Sarah and her husband Charlie. Edith and

Herbert arrived at tea time and, although the meal was necessarily frugal, she experienced the most enjoyable time she had had in Scarborough. They were clearly suffering the same hardships as Aunt Frances but they faced life with a defiant cheerfulness that was infectious.

In the evening, at Herbert's suggestion, they went to the Black Swan. Kathleen had never been in a pub before but fortunately she looked older than her years and her presence was not questioned. After a short while the men left them to join a group of their cronies and while telling part of her story she learned the personal histories of her new friends. She felt she was not yet ready to tell them of her pregnancy and, not without a pang of deceit, stuck to the story of moving to go into service. To her great relief this was not questioned.

"Ah!" Sarah said, "So you **are** one of us!"

Kathleen looked at her quizzically.

"So did we," Edith explained, "we came here from Durham five years ago."

"We were sixteen," Sarah interrupted, "and ready to take on the world!"

"You came together?" Kathleen asked.

"Of course, we always seem to do things together. We saw no future in Durham so we decided to try here. Both went to the same school, grew up together we did, both got jobs as chambermaids at the Balmoral, both lived in until we got married."

Kathleen smiled, "Did you do that together?"

"Almost!", Edith said, "I beat her to it by six months."

"Charlie and Bert are old mates," Sarah added, "We used to go out as a foursome, still do, come to think of it, though not to the same places these days. There used to be real action on the Donkey Field, believe me."

"Donkey Field?" Kathleen queried.

"Peasholme Park, favourite spot for courting," Edith explained, "then Bert and I got married eighteen months ago and they got hitched last year."

"So you're due for the Donkey Field any day and wedding bells around 1931," Sarah laughed, "hope you're ready for it!"

"I bet there's someone waiting in the wings already for a bonny lass like you." Edith quipped and was surprised to see a sudden dropping of Kathleen's eyes. "Oh, sorry," she said hurriedly, "have I goofed again? So that's why you came, lass, he let you down, eh? Never you mind, there's plenty of time."

She realised immediately that she had said the wrong thing. Kathleen suddenly became a different girl, she seemed to be miles away and her eyes had grown sorrowful, she was clearly near to tears, Sarah hastily changed the subject.

"You should have been here a couple of months ago," she said, "to see the pageant."

Edith rapidly took her cue. "Aye, that were gradely -all about Scarborough over the years."

"A hundred years," Sarah added, " '1827 and 1927 SHAKE HANDS' they called it."

The words had fallen on deaf ears. Edith tried again, "Where did you say your aunt lives?" She knew the answer, it was all she could think of on the spur of the moment, but the direct question had its intended effect and attracted Kathleen's attention. She shook her head,

"Sorry, what did you say?"

"I asked you where your auntie lived."

"Princess Street."

"Not bad, those houses are they?"

"You think so?"

"Better than where we live." Edith said, relieved that they had regained her interest and had defused what appeared to be an awkward moment, "We're not far away from there but all we've got is one room in 'Blue Bell Mission', it's a home, of sorts, but the quicker we can get out the better. When we first got married we lived with Bert's mother in Longwestgate .... take my tip, lass, when your time comes don't live with in-laws, it's the only times me and Bert ever fell out, so we took anything that was going. Sarah and Charlie struck lucky finding their place."

The two older girls were careful not to re-introduce the subject of Kathleen's assumed wayward boyfriend. The men rejoined them, bought more drinks, and the evening ended with merriment and laughter. It was the first time Kathleen had laughed for over a month and she was grateful to her new companions. It was only when she was alone in her attic room later that she recalled the incident in the pub and, for the first time, seriously began to reflect on her position. Sooner or later she would have to seek medical advice, she would have to find somewhere to live when the baby was born, she would probably have to fall upon Aunt Frances again .... but how would Uncle Tom react? Fortified by the unaccustomed drinks she had consumed she managed to postpone the problems for another day. She had, at last, found friendship. She went to bed and enjoyed an intoxicatedly induced sleep.

Over the next weeks she grew more and more attached to Edith and Sarah and the long standing duo became a trio. Due to their guidance she got to know Scarborough and looked forward to the guided walks they arranged for her. They showed her the Japanese Gardens in Peasholme Park with its floating bandstand in the lake surrounded by gardens, they took sandwiches and thermos flasks and spent whole days at Oliver's Mount, a vantage point from which she could see all over the town but, most of all, she was fascinated by the long walk along the Victorian promenade of Marine Drive. She would spend hours there at Sandside, a bustling area of continuous activity where the sea itself was obliterated by the mass of hundreds of boats and drifters, mostly from Lowestoft, that packed the harbour. Columns of smoke from the funnels mingled with the towering masts in the sky while,on the jetties, using every inch of available space, bare-armed girls were gutting fish with the dexterity of a juggler.

By December her skirt waist was becoming uncomfortably tight. She had let out the seams but was now forced to fasten it with a large safety pin strained to its extremities. She went to see Aunt Frances and, over the obligatory cup of sickly tea, poured out her problems. Her aunt's advice was harsh but practical,

"Kathleen," she said, "you've more important things to worry about than your skirts. I've been watching you in the mornings, at work, and you really must face up to facts. You seem taken up by those two waitresses you've got pally with and you're forgetting time's going by, and fast! I've wanted to have a word with you but didn't want to interfere. Now you've come I'll have my say. First of all, what does your mother say? Have you heard from home?"

Kathleen looked downcast, "No," she said, "not a word."

"No, neither have we," Tom put in, "Bloody disgrace. He could have at least sent some money for you to live on, if it wasn't for us where would you be now? On the bloody street! Fine father he is........."

She realised Tom had been drinking again. Aunt Frances hastily interrupted "That's nothing to do with it...."

"Of course it bloody well is, how the hell....."

"Tom!" Frances adopted her authoritative tone and he knew it was time to let her speak, "First of all, seeing you're concerned most about it, clothes. Well, mine obviously won't fit you so you'd better see what you can find in town, there's loads of stalls down a side street by the market that sell second-hand stuff, and some of it's not bad if you look for it - and it's cheap. But have you thought about where the baby will be born? They certainly won't let you stay in the hotel...."

"And there's no way you can have it here." Tom added, stopping abruptly at Frances's withering look.

"We know that, Tom," she continued, "so you'd better get yourself down to the Parish Relief. You're going to need a midwife, baby clothes .....good God, girl, wake up!"

Tom came in again, "And what are you going to do with the little bugger when it's born? You can't take it home and we don't bloody want it!"

Kathleen knew she had made a mistake in coming in the evening, she should have waited for her day off and made an afternoon visit while Tom was out. But he had hit a nerve. The enormity of her predicament suddenly manifested itself and she, unwillingly, broke down again. Her memories of Princess Street would be branded for ever with misery.

She walked slowly back to the Balmoral in deep and troubled thought. Within weeks now her pregnancy would be obvious to everyone, she must do something before Christmas.

In a way, her problems began to sort themselves out. She found the stalls by the market and spent some of her precious savings on larger clothing. She wore one of her newly acquired dresses on their next weekly visit to the "Mucky Duck" (She had begun to use Herbert's name for the Black Swan). As they walked into the light of the pub Charlie said jokingly,

"Scarborough seems to suit our Kathleen, I'm sure she's put weight on!"

"Aye, it's the good food she's getting at the Balmoral, reckon we should all move in there!"

The men went to the bar for the drinks and the women to their accustomed seats in the corner. The first drink was consumed with their usual banter and, after fetching a second, the men followed their routine and adjourned to the dominoes.

"Do you know, Kathleen," Edith said, "I do think Charlie's right, you **are** putting on weight!"

Kathleen knew this was the time. The relief was noticeable as she let it all come out. She told the whole story; the families' hostility, her affection for Terry; their banishment. The girls listened with tenderness and sympathy.

"Why didn't you tell us before?" Edith said, "I could have lent you dresses - I'm bigger than you are, much to my dismay!"

Sarah was more down to earth. "Now, look," she said, "tomorrow afternoon I'll go to the Parish Relief office and find out a few things. Have you seen a doctor?"

"Not here, I saw one in Ireland when I found out...you know..."

Edith interrupted. "On your next time off I'll take you to our doctor, we're all on his panel. Meanwhile I reckon you should say nothing in the Balmoral, hang on as long as you can. With a bit of luck you should manage to January before you get too obvious."

"So you won't be going home for Christmas?" Sarah asked.

Kathleen shook her head slowly and sorrowfully. "No."

"Well, that settles that, you'll spend it with us."

"Oh, I can't."

"There's no 'can't' about it, you're not sitting in that attic all over Christmas. Edith and Bert always come to our place, they've no room, and you are joining us!"

"Have you thought what will you do when the baby arrives?" Edith asked.

"I've done little else! I can't take it home and I can't really keep it here, can I? I dread to think of him being branded illegitimate, what future would he have? I did think of pretending to be a war widow, but I'm much too young."

"You've made up your mind it's a **he** then?" Sarah joked.

"He or she, it's a terrible cross to bear through life. The doctor has suggested I have him adopted, but I'd always be worried as to what sort of people he was with. How would I find the right person?"

"Leave it for now," Edith said, "the men are coming back.... and don't take any more of their teasing about weight to heart, they don't mean anything. We'll put them in the picture in our own good time."

During the following week she made more progress than she could have dreamed of. Spurred on by the girls she saw a doctor, was relieved to get an excellent report and, through his guidance, made provisional arrangements for her confinement to take place at the infirmary wing of the Workhouse on Dean Road.

Christmas did not just come that year, it swooped down on her. It was when Sarah reminded her of her invitation that she realised it was only a week away. She spent her day off that week in the market and bought small presents for Aunt Frances, Uncle Tom and the boys but got more pleasure in seeking out gifts for her friends.

Charlie, too, visited the market, but he went late on Christmas Eve and, with many others, loitered around the stalls selling poultry watching the rows of plucked birds hanging on the rails dwindle in number as the more wealthy bought them. He knew that any still there at the end of the day would be sold off at bargain prices. It was eleven o'clock before the stallholder decided to close and there was a scramble by those who had waited patiently. He was lucky and, for his zealously guarded shilling, obtained a large, by then well-thumbed, chicken.

Kathleen went to Mass on Christmas morning and realised that, for the first time in her life, she could not take Christmas Communion. She had not been to confession for weeks; she could not, in her heart, confess to being sinful. She was sorry she was in this predicament but she could not be penitent for bearing Terry's child. That afternoon she walked through the light snow and, arriving at Sarah's, was greeted affectionately.

The house Sarah lived in was larger than Aunt Frances' but they occupied only the ground floor, upstairs was let to another family. There were three rooms downstairs; they lived in the back room and used the front as a bedroom, at the back, as in Princess Street, was the scullery. As Kathleen entered the living room she was astonished by the change since she had last visited. The room was welcoming and festive; paper chains were festooned across the ceiling and a Christmas tree decorated with tinsel and tiny candles stood proudly in one corner. The table, covered by a spotless cloth, was neatly set out, in the centre was a home-made cake dripping with icing and at each place lay a Christmas cracker. Saucepans were bubbling on the range and, from the oven, came the luscious aroma of roasting chicken. She handed her presents to Sarah who placed them, unopened, under the tree while Charlie poured glasses of sherry. It was obvious they had scrimped and saved for weeks for this one day.

Edith and Herbert arrived within half an hour and received an equally warm welcome; their presents went under the tree and Charlie replenished the sherry glasses. While joining in the chit-chat Kathleen's mind could not avoid going back to home; the scene would be similar except that there would be a goose in the oven, more people would be present and the table laden with more local produce. She killed her reminiscing and mentally rejoined the company, even more grateful for their hospitality.

The dinner was eaten with great frivolity, accompanied by Charlie's pride and joy, his gramophone. It stood on a small table with its large metal horn protruding into the room. He spent the meal time continually getting up to wind the motor and change the needle as the machine repeatedly ground out "Bye Bye Blackbird", "The Black Bottom", and "Ain't She Sweet", the only records he possessed.

After eating the Christmas pudding, pulling the crackers and donning the paper hats that were inside, the women cleared the table while the men, with much jocularity, washed up in the scullery. The gramophone was switched off and, while Charlie filled glasses at the sideboard, Sarah distributed the parcels that had collected under the tree. There was the usual banter as, one by one, they opened their presents; Charlie parading in a new cap, Bert modelling the cardigan that Edith had knitted without his knowledge, Sarah delighted with a bottle of "Phul-Nana" scent and Edith smiling with pleasure when she found a pair of brand new slippers. Then it was Kathleen's turn. Sarah first gave her a small packet from herself and Charlie. She took off the paper and opened a tiny cardboard box and, as she saw what it held, involuntary tears came to her eyes - it was a small brooch in the form of a shamrock. She pinned it to her dress and just said,

"Thank you, all of you." and wiped her eyes.

Sarah wondered if they'd made a mistake in their choice and added, hastily,

"And now the special', from Edith and Bert."

She lifted a huge parcel, wrapped in brown paper, and placed it on Kathleen's lap. Kathleen un-knotted the string and the paper fell off as the released contents expanded. On her knees she saw a full layette; baby clothes, tiny blue woollen coats and bonnets and, for some reason the most attractive of all, three pairs of bootees. One by one she held them up for inspection as the tears rapidly faded.

"Edith," she said, "you shouldn't have got all this, these must have cost a fortune!"

"Not at all," Edith replied, "I must be honest with you, Kathleen, they are not new."

"They look it."

"I know, that's why I bought them, it was a chance in a lifetime. I was in Addison's shop only last week and bumped into Cissie Mennell - you've met her, she lives in that house next to the school. Well, her baby is four months old now and it's amazing how quickly he's grown. She just happened to mention that she was going to sell them and I thought of you immediately. All we can hope is that you have a boy!"

Kathleen was excitedly rummaging through the pile, holding up first one item and then another when she said,

"There's too much here, Edith, surely."

"Nonsense - you enjoy them. They're good quality - and when your bairn's six months old you can pass them on to some other happy young woman."

Kathleen smiled.

"I'll do that, I promise," she paused and then added "and I know who I would like that to be."

"Oh, do you," Sarah laughed, "who?"

Kathleen looked down in embarrassment, wishing she had not made the remark.

"Come on!" Edith insisted, "Who?"

Kathleen looked her straight in the eyes,

"You," she said, "I've noticed how excited you've been about the baby - I only wish I could be so thrilled." She wrapped the paper loosely round the clothes, placed the parcel on the floor, rushed to Edith and threw her arms round her, "Yes, that's it!" she said, "I'm going to borrow these, and you must promise to take them back when your happy day arrives."

A sudden hush fell on the festivities and she realised that, somehow, she had said the wrong thing. Bert broke the spell,

"Hey! My glass is empty! And so is Kathleen's, come on Charlie, this **is** Christmas!" Things returned to normal and the party continued.

Sarah was required to work on New Year's Eve and so it was a foursome that settled in the Swan to prepare to welcome 1928. Kathleen was so accepted by now that when the men left them for the domino table she saw nothing odd in their behaviour, except, perhaps, that they had left earlier than usual. Very soon the topic of their conversation turned to Sarah and the disappointment of her missing the New Year celebrations. This time it was Edith who grabbed the opportunity to change the subject.

"Sarah will be fine," she said, "but how are you getting along?"

"Fine, thanks to you."

"I mean about plans for your little one, have you thought any more about adoption?"

"Lots, but I've no idea how to go about it, I'll ask the doctor next time I visit."

"You may have no need to," Edith said intriguingly, "do you remember how your little joke on Christmas Day fell on stony ground, you know, about me following you into mummyhood? Well, it will never happen, I'm afraid. We found out last year that Bert can't produce children. As you'll guess he's very upset about it, but I thought you deserved some explanation. Oh, we've come to terms with it, at least we had, until Christmas. I must admit you were right about me feeling a bit broody - Sarah's remarked on it too, and I've had a few little weeps .... until I thought.... Oh, hell! Kathleen, I can't beat about the bush like this .... I must be honest with you ....You'll have noticed that Bert and Charlie have gone off earlier than usual, well I asked them to leave us alone for a while ... . Kathleen, you said you'd consider having your young one adopted, can I have him?"

Kathleen had no need to consider. It was her answer! If she could not bring her child up herself she could see no one better to do it than this kind, thoughtful and caring girl she had grown to love. With eyes bright with relief she took hold of Edith's hands and said,

"Oh, yes, yes, yes ......and thank you!"

Edith stood up, "Bert! Charlie!" she called "Come back here, we've got something to celebrate. Happy New Year!"

January saw all three women in a state of bustling exhilaration. Baby garments and woollen blankets began to accumulate as every spare minute was taken up knitting and the bubbling rapport between Sarah and Edith grew greater as did the affection between Edith and Kathleen. At the end of the month they paid a visit to Richardson and Parker, a firm of solicitors, and the legal process for adoption began.

One thing only marred the beginning of the year; Kathleen's condition was now clear to everybody and, at the end of February, the hotel manager called her to his office.

"......so I hope you'll understand my position," he ended, "I've nothing against you personally, but you'll have to leave the hotel until after the baby is born. If you wish to return after the adoption there'll be a job for you but I'm afraid that, meanwhile, you must make other arrangements."

There was a serious meeting that weekend in the Mucky Duck as they considered the possibilities. Kathleen was most reluctant to approach Aunt Frances, Sarah was forced to eliminate Charlie's idea of putting a bed in their living room and they seemed to reach an impasse. Bert finally and firmly resolved the problem,

"There's only one thing we **can** do .... she's coming in with us!"

"But you've only one room." Charlie said.

"What of it?" Bert argued, "So I'll rig up a curtain across the corner and I'll borrow a camp bed. I'll manage there and Kathleen can share the bed with Edith."

"But......"

"There's no buts!" he insisted, "If I've got to wait for the arrival of my son, I'll wait in my own home ... in **his** home."

By early March Bert had made his arrangements and he called at the Balmoral to collect her and carry her valise. Over the months Kathleen had gathered that Edith and Bert were forced to live in poor accommodation and had prepared herself for the worst but as they turned into Cross Street even her most frightful speculations paled into insignificance. She now realised why they had never invited her to their home. Cross Street was dreadful; unlike her first impressions of Princess Street here she saw complete squalor, the buildings were derelict and a pernicious aura was evident even in the late afternoon. Blue Bell Mission, it appeared, was a hostel for the homeless, all sorts of down-and-outs used it, many staying only one night at the behest of the police. She began to have doubts about her decision to condemn her baby to this nadir of poverty.

They climbed the stone stairs, hollowed by generations of feet, to the room where the Waites existed (she could not contemplate the word lived and the door was opened by Edith. She found herself in a larger than average sized room that snubbed the locality. In spite of the remnants of paper on the damp walls, in spite of peeling paint and a sheet of cardboard in one window pane and in spite of the all-pervading smell of decay the room was homely. Edith kept it spotlessly clean and the glow from the grate was hospitable. The room was large enough to house a table and chairs as well as the double bed and, as Bert had promised, one corner of the room was curtained off by threadbare blankets nailed to a pole supported by the picture rail.

The next five weeks were lived in monotonous routine. Each morning, while

Edith raked out and relit the range, Bert would go off down the corridor with a large enamel jug and return with it full of water for them to wash in a bowl on the table, Edith would miraculously produce breakfast on the range and Bert would leave to work on his coal round. When Edith left for work Kathleen suffered intense loneliness. She was genuinely frightened to venture out alone and could only sit by the fire, knitting. As the days turned into weeks her doubts multiplied and she felt herself trapped in an impossible dilemma. If she allowed the adoption plan to go ahead her baby was doomed to this, if she changed her mind it had no foreseeable future whatsoever, and, in any case, the solicitors were already at work. She bore her doubts alone, she saw no way of confronting Edith about them without appearing ungrateful and disparaging. She was therefore elated when Bert arrived home on the third of May with a bottle of wine.

"Right!" he crowed, "We're having a toast! It's "Goodbye" to Blue Bell Mission!" Edith's face lit up and her mouth fell open,

"You mean.......?"

"Yes! I've found a lovely room near the Market Hall, near Boyes' Store, we can move in within the month!"

That evening was spent with great rejoicing and Kathleen felt a great weight lift from her mind. Whether the news or the merriment had any influence she could not tell but that night her labour pains began and she was rushed to Dean Road Workhouse. Her baby was born the next morning and she decided to call him Ernest Terence.

After two days it was found that, probably due to her poor diet over the last weeks, Kathleen was unable to feed the baby herself and he was put on a bottle. In a way she was relieved because, fighting her instinct, she was trying not to get too close to the child she was doomed to forsake. When the manager of the Balmoral was good to his word and offered her her job back at the hotel she accepted and returned to her attic room. Edith had, by now, given in her notice and devoted her days to caring for the baby, Kathleen visited the room at every opportunity to cosset and caress her son who was thriving in a make-shift crib, a pillow in what had been the bottom drawer of the sideboard.

After each visit, however, she found the parting to be more agonising and she knew she must make a final decision. She told Edith at the end of the month.

"I'm going back to Ireland."

Both Edith and Bert showed clear disappointment,

"Why? You know you're always welcome here, and everything will be much better when we move."

"I know, but I've been thinking and, believe me, it's not an easy decision.

We are due to sign the adoption papers next week and I don't think I could bear to meet you with Ernest in the street, I certainly couldn't face merely seeing him as a visitor. Anyway, you'll be his mother then and I want him to love you as such. Can you imagine the trauma he'll face when he grows older and we try to explain to him who I am? No, I'm letting my head rule my heart and going as far away as possible, though he, and you, will never be far from my thoughts." Her eyes filled with tears.

"Will you be going home?"

"I don't know. I've not made up my mind. I may go to Dublin and try to get work there. Then I'll contact home and see what the reaction is .... and then let things take their course. Quite honestly, I don't care what happens," she laid the baby tenderly in his drawer and rushed to the door, "I only know I can't bear to live like this!" With tears flowing down her face she ran out of the room.

The adoption papers were signed in the solicitors' office on Queen Street on the first of June and the following day Edith, Bert, Sarah and Charlie bid her a tearful good-bye at Scarborough Central. She had asked Edith if she could carry the baby to the station and she was still holding him as the guard was ushering the stragglers to board the train.

"You'll write, won't you?" Edith asked. Kathleen pondered for a while and then said tearfully,

"No .... I don't think so, let me go out of his life now, it's for the best." She kissed the baby, "Goodbye, Ernest," she said, "Be a good boy for Edi......for your mother......God bless you!"

She thrust the child into Edith's arms, boarded the train and slammed the door.

As the train drew away they could see her sitting by the window, her eyes scanning a magazine but they knew she was not reading.

CHAPTER THREE

On the afternoon of June 17th, Edith and Herbert met Charlie and Sarah Reynolds, all dressed in their Sunday best, at St. Mary's Parish Church for the baptism. It was a special occasion for them, not just because of the ceremony but because they were together again. Such meetings were now rare; gone were the Saturday evenings in the Black Swan as Edith's time was fully taken up with the baby. Charlie and Sarah, when asked to be god-parents, had suggested that the baptism should be delayed so they could save up to organise a christening party but Edith had insisted that it should take place immediately. In her mind there were over-riding reasons for this, she was convinced that Ernest's birth certificate was a millstone he would carry for life unless she did something about it, and as quickly as possible. Shame glared from the entries:-"Mother : Kathleen O'Brien", "Father :.......", nothing but a damning stroke of the pen. She was determined to mask this stigma and realised that, although the sacrament was taken sincerely, it also provided her answer. That afternoon, when they left the church, she possessed a certificate of baptism which named them as his mother and father. The first thing she did when she got home was to tear up the offending birth certificate and throw the pieces into the fire. From now on all that would be available would be an abridged birth certificate showing merely date of birth, and this baptismal document. She cherished that piece of paper and often took it from her box of valuables just to savour the words written on it: "Parents: Herbert and Edith Waites".

The following week Bert and Charlie loaded the contents of the Mission room on to the coal cart and they moved to their new home near the Market. This was a large front room on the first floor. On the ground floor was a communal scullery shared with the occupants of the other rooms. Here were the usual water tap, stone sink and brick built clothes boiler in the corner. The focal point of their own room was, naturally, the fireplace but this one was huge. The grate was in the centre with an oven on the left side and a boiler on the right which had a large brass tap. It soon took its place as the energy centre of the home: The flat iron would be heated on the coals and bread, pastry and meals cooked in the oven; toast would be made with a fork held before the grate and clothes would be dried on a folding wooden frame in front of the fire. Above all this was a large mantelpiece on which accumulated all their bric-a-brac; tin boxes of buttons, photographs, scissors, brushes, teapot and anything else that was needed to be at hand. It was here that they would sit in the evenings gazing into the hot coals creating pictures until the image was broken by a piece falling into the hearth.

The bed occupied the wall farthest from the fire and the table and chairs filled the centre. The floor was covered with worn out linoleum but they obscured this with home made clip mats. There was room, when the time came, for a second small bed.

The luxury for Edith, though, was the gas mantle which was fixed to a pipe coming down from the centre of the ceiling. The gas was turned on and off by two chains attached, one at each end of a brass bar above the light. It was with great delight that she packed away the oil lamp that had been their sole means of illumination in Blue Bell Mission.

Bert scoured the second-hand shops to pick up a pram and, from then on, every morning and afternoon Edith could be found proudly pushing it around the streets, mentally willing any friends and even passers-by to gaze inside. At night the pram was dragged up to the room where it doubled-up as a cot, the drawer having been relegated to its proper use. Life seemed idyllic.

Their euphoria, however, was short-lived. The rent for their room was higher than the tiny amount they had paid at the Mission, they no longer had Edith's wage and Herbert's coal round was not expanding, in fact, with the deepening recession it showed signs of contraction. As the weeks went by these problems, coupled with the additional expenses of the baby, eroded away their illusions of fulfilment. The spontaneous gaiety passed through a period of rugged stoicism and then finally turned into despair.

"What are we going to do, Bert?" Edith asked one evening as they ate their meal, "We just can't go on ...."

"Summat'll turn up," Bert replied, "I heard last week that Billy Sumner's thinking of packing his round in and going back to Barnsley, down the pit .... could be the making of us."

"I'm not talking about next month, or next week - it's now! Bert! Don't you realise, we're broke! I've got sevenpence in my purse, and the baby needs milk." Edith was beginning to tire of Herbert's Macawber-like outlook and tension was starting to stretch their once happy relationship. "I've made up my mind, I'm going back to work."

"You can't."

"Why not?"

"There's why not!" Bert pointed to the pram.

"Don't you think I've thought about that? I only need to work part-time, just enough to see us over, and I can get someone to look after Ernie while I'm out. It's not what I want, you know that, but it's the only way out."

"Someone to look after Ernie! Where are you going to find someone to look after a baby, for nothing?"

"I've found her. I had a word this morning and she's only too pleased."

"Who?"

"Amy."

Amy Waites was Herbert's sister, a prim maiden lady in her early twenties who was also one of the teachers at the Sunday School at Bar Street Church. She still lived with her mother in the little cottage adjoining Bert's coal shed and stable in Longwestgate and had doted on the baby since his arrival. When Edith had put the idea of baby-minding to her she had accepted effusively, secretly relishing the prospect of surrogate motherhood. Edith found a part-time job as a waitress at the Waverley Hotel near the station, an area which encompassed Bert's coal round, and he would often take the opportunity to call at the back entrance for a free cup of tea. The job, however, entailed her working every evening and some afternoons, so Amy soon became indispensable, happily washing nappies in the communal scullery, taking the baby out during the afternoons and generally preparing what meals she could in the home.

But unemployment was rising rapidly and, not of their own choice, people were buying less and less coal. Yet, though his round was diminishing Bert's time of arrival home got progressively later. He would come back, late and dirty, to find a meal of sorts awaiting him, his son tucked up in the pram and Amy ready to leave. Edith would get back nearer midnight after a long walk from the town centre to find the baby needing a change of nappy and her husband asleep in bed.

Day by day the wearisome routine went on. She would be up at six thirty, light the fire, wash and feed the baby, spread slices of Amy's home-made bread with dripping for their breakfast and pack similar sandwiches for Bert's lunch. He would tumble out of bed at seven, eat his breakfast in silence and go out of the house with barely a word. She then had the housework to squeeze in before her eagerly awaited daily rendezvous with Sarah and the soul saving hour of relaxation and gossip while pram-pushing.

By November she had grown disillusioned enough to air her concern to her friend,

"I don't know what's happening to Bert?" she said, "and I'm worried. I know things are not all that good with his job and he can't do all the things we planned .... perhaps that's affecting him .... perhaps he thinks he's a failure. I don't know, but he just doesn't seem interested. I hardly ever see him, the way our lives are going .... and from what I gather from Amy he's taken to stopping off at the Swan every night .... and that's something we just can't afford."

"Who's he drinking with? It's certainly not Charlie, when he's not at sea these days he's indoors."

"That's what I was afraid of, I know Bert - if he's started standing in that vault drinking on his own who knows what's going to happen?"

Sarah pushed along in silence for a while and then said,

"Look, kid, we've been pals all these years, do you mind if I tell Charlie what you've said? Perhaps if he had a quiet word with him .....?"

"Thanks, Sarah, I'd hoped you'd say that."

She arrived back at the house to find a large fall of soot on the hearth and the black dust had spread over the room. She was still cleaning it up when Amy arrived.

"Oh, so it's happened again!"

"Again?"'

"Aye, we had a fall last week. That chimney's going to catch fire any day now, then we'll have a right mess! Didn't Bert mention it?"

"Bert doesn't mention much lately."

"I asked him to get the chimney swept," Amy went on, "but all he said was 'It'll be all right' - I knew this would happen. What a mess! But leave it to me, you get off to work."

She put on her coat, took her handbag and left the house, not even realising she'd had nothing to eat since breakfast.

The next day she couldn't wait for her meeting with Sarah and had been waiting outside the Market for ten minutes before she saw her friend coming towards her.

"Did you tell Charlie?"

"Of course, and he's worried. He reckons Bert's in some kind of trouble .... he's not got involved with a bloody money-lender has he?"

"I don't think so, he's not that stupid, surely?"

"Anyway, Charlie says he'll go to go to the Mucky Duck himself tonight and if Bert comes in he'll tackle him. If anyone can do anything, Charlie can, so leave it for now. Have you made any arrangements for Christmas yet?"

"Christmas! I've not even thought about it. Good God, it doesn't seem a week since we were at your place with Kathleen .... I wonder how she's getting on? I wish she'd write ...."

"I often wonder that myself, perhaps she'll get in touch one day .... maybe Christmas will remind her. Charlie's busy making a rocking horse .....at least he says it's a rocking horse, looks more like a bit of wood on castors to me .... it's little Ernie's Christmas present! We're taking it for granted you and Bert will be over as usual."

"Thanks, Sarah, I hope we will .....I can always rely on you two, can't I?"

They walked on along Sandgate in silence. The two fun loving girls of the year before had matured into pensive and sober young women.

That evening Charlie Reynolds went to the vault in the Black Swan and found Bert already there, leaning on the bar with one foot on the brass rail, his left hand curled tightly round a pint glass. He was staring vacantly at an ashtray full of cigarette ends in front of him and making swirling patterns in the ash with the remnant of a yellowing Woodbine. He did not realise Charlie was there until a gnarled hand gripped his shoulder. He looked up and smiled cheerlessly,

"Charlie! What are you doing here? What're you having?"

Charlie restrained him from putting his hand in his pocket and said,

"I'm getting these."

When the beers had been delivered Charlie made his rehearsed explanation for his unaccustomed presence in the pub and then diplomatically steered the conversation to the real reason for his visit.

"I didn't expect you to be here," he said, "thought you'd be indoors with your pipe and slippers."

"What's the point?" Bert replied, "Edith's at work, all I've got at home is that bloody nagging sister of mine and a screaming kid. I come in here for some peace and quiet."

Charlie took his cue, glad that it had come so soon,

"What? Every night?"

Bert nodded disconsolately, "Aye, I suppose so."

"Come off it, Bert ....I've known you too long to believe that, what's wrong?"

"I've told you what's wrong, it's that bleeding kid. We've not been the same since he arrived. Edith's no time for me anymore."

"Don't be stupid, man, that's the way women are ... and it shouldn't be any other way."

"It's different for you, you don't know what it's like."

"I wish I did. You're lucky to have a son."

"Only on bloody paper ... every time I look at him I hear that bloody doctor telling me I wasn't a real man. And even if I was, what sort of man am I? Charlie, I'm going mad .... the coal round's falling apart, the rent arrears are piling up already and I haven't got two halfpennies to rub together."

"And spending what you **have** got in here helps, does it?"

"It helps me forget."

Bert was raising his glass to his lips. Charlie pressed on his arm and forced it back to the bar,

"Now, you listen to me ... we've been mates since we were kids .... and I wouldn't be a mate if I didn't say this. Stop feeling so bloody sorry for yourself, look what you've got ... a fine wife, a son - **your** son, bearing **your** name, and a business that could flourish if you put your mind to it. The money you're throwing away here could do a lot for all of them. Look at you, Bert, what are you doing to yourself, I bet you've not shaved for a week!"

To his relief Bert accepted his criticism passively and after another half hour of discussion, began to talk more optimistically and cheerfully. Bert surprised Amy that evening by arriving home before Ernie had been settled down for the night and, for the first time in weeks, held him in his arms while she cooked some chips for his supper.

Charlie's intervention seemed to have good effect. Bert spent time touring the streets around his stable before heading off towards the station and his banshee like call of "Cooooaaaaaal" did bring out the occasional housewife whose cellar was running desperately low. He started doing jobs at home again, he spent the whole of the following Sunday cleaning out his stable and repairing his cart, and the cobbler's last, unused for weeks, was put to good use repairing his well-worn boots. He even remembered the chimney. He bought an "Imp" block on his way home one evening, put it on the fire and covered the whole range with an old blanket, hanging it from the mantelpiece by weighting it with bricks. There was a roar from beneath the blanket as the block released its gases and a cascade of soot landed behind it. He labouriously cleaned up the mess and, with great satisfaction, told Amy on her arrival that the room was safe again.

By Christmas he had almost regained his self-respect and, for the first time, the annual dinner at Sarah's became an occasion centred on Ernie. Charlie, to everyone's relief, had allowed himself one luxury for Christmas - a new record. They were treated to endless renditions of "Old Man River".

It was not to last. Ernie was teething and early in the new year they began to suffer sleepless nights due to his continuous crying. Edith would sit at the end of the bed cradling him in her arms, frustrated with her inability to give comfort while Bert tossed and turned in bed blaming her for his lack of sleep.

"Can't you keep that bloody kid quiet? Isn't there owt you can give him?"

"There's probably plenty I could give him - if I had the money to buy it."

"So that's it .... bloody money again! I've not spent a penny on myself since before Christmas! What more can I bloody well do?"

And so it would go on, night after night, and the tense relationship deteriorated once again in bouts of silence and mutual recrimination. Everything came to a head one day in February when Bert arrived home unexpectedly, late in the afternoon. He slammed the door behind him, threw his leather headgear on the floor, sat on the bed and held his head in his hands. In spite of their rancour Edith was shocked at his obvious distress,

"What is it, Bert?"

"I'm finished." His head was rocking from side to side and for the first time in her life she saw tears running down his face. She was stunned by his frailty and instinctively ran to comfort him,

"For God's sake, Bert, what's happened?"

He calmed down. "You know most of my round's round the station, at least all my big deliveries are?

"Yes"

"Well, I went down there this morning and they're demolishing all round Westfield Terrace! You know they've been leaving the place for months, ever since they opened the new bridge ....that's why my round's been getting smaller.........now it's all gone. Building a new road. I've had it on my mind since New Year, but I thought I'd be all right if I took over Billy Sumner's round .... you know, him who was going back to Barnsley ......good area that .....all round Peasholme ...."

"Well?"

"He's not going. When I saw what was happening at Westfield Terrace I went straight to his stable .... and he's changed his mind. Said he decided in December, but I've not seen him."

It was Edith's turn to slump. She sat beside him on the bed and took his hands in hers,

"But you deliver to more places than Westfield Terrace".

"I know, but I usually spend all Wednesday there ... that's a whole day lost .... my best day ... and aren't things tight enough already .... and how much more are they knocking down?"

"What are we going to do, Bert?"

"I don't know, I just don't know."

They were still sitting in silence, and in semi-darkness when Amy arrived. Edith jumped up, took one look at the clock, grabbed her coat and rushed to the door,

"I'm late! That's all we'd need, for me to get the sack! See to Ernie, Amy, and get Bert's tea, will you?" She ran off down the street. Amy sensed something serious had occurred and was at a loss. She lit the gas.

"Fancy some toast, Bert?" She asked charily.

He took his cap from the hook behind the door,

"See to the kid," he snapped, "I'm going to the Swan."

Bert's wallowing in self-pity this time lasted for four weeks. This time it was his mother who pulled him back to face reality. Her landlord, who also owned the stable next door, mentioned to her that the rent was going deeper into arrears. One morning, as he arrived to collect his horse and cart, she was waiting for him.

".....and more than that," she concluded, "this was your father's stable all his life and he never owed a penny on it. We had our ups and downs, just like you're having, but we brought you up, and Amy, and Albert. I let you have it and what have you done? You're a disgrace to his memory! Pull your socks up, Bert .... or I'll sell the round to someone who's prepared to work on it."

It worked for a time, until, late in the year, Edith had to break more bad news. The Waverley was to become the next victim of the new road scheme, she had four week's work left.

The next two years were spent on the roller-coaster of Bert's inability to cope with the life of poverty. His periods of despair and escape to drink got progressively longer and the gaps of responsibility between them became correspondingly shorter. He maintained the rent on the stable at the expense of the rent on the room until, inevitably, the day came they were forced to leave.

Amy became his saviour on this occasion. She pleaded with her mother to give her brother one last chance and, for the sake of Edith and the child, room was made for them in their home. Edith was grateful but very perturbed, She felt they were living from one crisis to another and, on each occasion, it was only the intervention of a third party which dragged them back from disaster. She despaired at Bert's apparent inability to cope with life. They had lived in that cottage with his parents when first they were married and it invoked nothing but unhappy memories. She recalled the endless bickering, ill feeling and family squabbles. Yet in those days they had been a newly-married couple - now they were going back with a toddler.

They moved into the top back room of the cottage in Longwestgate just before Ernie's third birthday. Their furniture, for what it was worth, was stored in the adjoining stable and covered with empty sacks. After the demolition of the Waverley, Edith had found a job as a waitress at another hotel, but one which entailed her working every lunchtime and evening. Bert, mainly due to his mother's presence and driving, slowly rebuilt his business, but only by seeking trade in more remote areas, necessitating his working even longer hours also. With Amy living in the same house the welfare of the child fell more and more onto her shoulders.

Edith's only consolation during these unhappy years was her friendship with Sarah and they maintained the routine of regular meetings even during Sarah's pregnancy. When her baby was born, Charlie bought a second-hand push chair for Edith's use and the pram was passed on for the new arrival. Sarah had a son and he was named after his father. Edith's daily routine, however, meant that their daily meetings were confined to a brief hour each morning which they spent walking round the harbour with the children. She would prolong the outing as long as she could so as to spend as little time as possible in the confines of the house. In the afternoons things were very different. Amy had Ernie to herself and relished it; she would think nothing of pushing him all the way to Peasholme Park where he would revel in her undivided attention while he kicked his ball around to his heart's content, fed the ducks and, in summer months, listened to the band on the floating bandstand. This so intrigued Amy that she mentioned it to Edith one evening and suggested she should take him there to see for herself. A child of three was normally indifferent to a static band; Ernie had some strange and undefinable affinity with it and his little feet would beat in uncanny accuracy with the music. He seemed mesmerised; the ducks, his ball, playmates, all were ignored once the band started to play and it would be a very reluctant little boy who was unwillingly dragged home.

Adjoining the stable, on the other side from the house, were the railings surrounding the playground of Friarage School. This was a red brick building built early in the century and catered for all ages of children and the Infants' School stood just inside these railings. The front was built in a stepped formation which meant that one section butted out from the main building putting the three large windows it contained within feet from the road. Like all small boys Ernie loved throwing stones and one day, having been allowed to play outside the house, found some suitable projectiles in the gutter. The windows of the school were an irresistible target and he scored several satisfying direct hits. He was in the gutter, replenishing his arsenal when he heard a stern voice say "Boy!". He looked up at the woman towering over him. Miss Ford, a teacher wise in the ways of small boys, waited in silence, staring him in the eyes until, without a word being said, he dropped his stones back into the gutter. She then grabbed him by the scruff of the neck, dragged him into the building and, finger wagging to stress each word, threatened hell and damnation should he dare throw stones at her window again. Such was Ernie's introduction to education and the school he was to attend in the years to come.

CHAPTER FOUR

Amy's sudden death came as a shattering blow to the family. During the summer of 1932, she became very pale and seemed to have little energy. She had never been a robust girl and little notice was taken of her condition until one day when she fainted. She was on her feet almost immediately but, in falling, had hit her arm on the edge of the table. To everyone's surprise a massive bruise developed, far larger than anything they had experienced before. From then on, every little knock seemed to cause more bruising and Mrs. Waites became concerned. When she found blood on Amy's handkerchief she was very worried and asked where it came from. Amy opened her mouth and she was horrified to see her gums were bleeding. Amy was in the Workhouse infirmary that same afternoon and diagnosed as having acute anaemia. She had been ill for only five weeks when a policeman called at the house to call them to the hospital. When they got there they were too late, Amy had had a massive nose-bleed and had died. Ernie was told nothing except that "Auntie Amy has gone to live with Jesus" which he accepted without question. Winter was approaching so he did not miss the walks and trips to listen to the bands, and the only effect the tragedy had on his life was that his mother was now with him all day.

Luckily Edith's fears about the move to Longwestgate had proved to be unfounded. Their move, far from being difficult, turned out to be their deliverance. Amy had been a staunch ally as well as a keen and energetic child minder and, under his mother's influence Bert regained his self-regard. His improving coal business took him far across town but as the debts diminished his enthusiasm for work was rejuvinated. He found he could make up the shortcomings of his round by hiring himself and his horse and cart for other work. His mother, too, took a healthy interest in Ernie and the mischievous behaviour of the youngster became a tonic to the three women who nurtured him.

After Amy's death, Edith was forced to stop working and devoted her time to her son. Bert's income was by now just sufficient to maintain them, another factor which helped maintain his tenuous stability.

Ernie started school in the class of the formidable Miss Ford who remembered him from his marksmanship of the previous year. He, in turn, remembered their first encounter and maintained a healthy regard for her, being very careful not to solicit her wrath again. He was therefore a model pupil in her presence and learned quickly.

He still saw little of his father however. Bert would be out of the house before Ernie was awake and did not return until long after he was back in bed again. This was the one remaining defect that remained from the adverse days of the years gone by - Bert retained the habit of a nightly sojourn at the Black Swan before coming home. Edith made herself accept this as his way of life, he was not there drinking in a state of melancholy now, just enjoying his drink after a busy and dusty day. All that worried her was that, as the days went by, his stay there once again began to grow longer. She considered it prudent to bide her time before giving him unwelcome advice.

During the school holidays things were very different. Bert would take Ernie with him on his horse and cart delivering coal, moving furniture and mowing hay in the local fields. On the way home he would quite often stop at a cake shop and buy a currant square which Ernie would eat with great relish whilst seated on the cart as the horse made its cumbersome way back to the stable and home. On rare occasions, usually after much pleading, he would be allowed to sit astride the horse - this invariably resulted in his falling off, much to the amusement of the family.

Then school would restart and the man with the horse and cart who had been the creator of so much enjoyment would disappear from the boy's life again for months.

After eighteen months at Longwestgate they were out of debt and could start to look for a permanent home of their own. They found two rooms at 21A Cooks Row and moved in there in the summer of 1933.

Having two rooms was comparative luxury when compared with their previous homes. There was still the outside toilet, of course, the rooms were draughty and the lighting restricted to a gas mantle. The house was damp and the backyard overrun with vermin but they had a separate room in which to sleep. They recovered the furniture from under the sacks and joyously spread it out over their two rooms. Mrs. Waites allowed them to keep the single bed Ernie had got used to and Edith felt, for the first time, that she was at last a full-time housewife and mother.

She also began to enjoy the pleasure of being able to invite Sarah to their home and while young Charlie played with Ernie's toys they would sit at the fireside chatting and knitting. Knitting was an essential part of life for no one could afford manufactured woollens. Worn out jerseys and cardigans would be washed and the re-usable wool rewound into balls to be made up into socks, gloves, balaclavas and jumpers. There was no sense of injustice, no feeling of deprivation, for never having had the luxuries of life they never really missed them.

Most of the ordinary needs of life were met by traders who came from door to door selling their wares. First to arrive each morning was the milkman who carried his milk in a large brass churn and would ladle it into the customer's jug or bowl. Then would come the breadman with either a handcart or a horse drawn van, the smell of his freshly baked bread preceding him down the street and setting everyone's appetite on edge. The other tradesmen, such as a hot chestnut seller, pie and peas man and the fishmonger would visit daily and, for any other necessities, no one needed to go further than Addisons, the little shop tucked between the houses.

Bath night was a carefully planned occasion. The large zinc bath would be dragged in from the backyard and placed in front of the hearth with the fire well stoked up, not only for immediate warmth but in order to keep a constant supply of hot water available in the boiler by the side of the fireplace ready to top up the bath for each successive member of the family. The water was not changed, merely added to. Ernie would be the first to go in and, once he was wrapped in a towel, Edith would follow. Bert was always last for he was invariably the dirtiest. When his weekly ablutions were finished, water would be taken out of the bath by the bucketful and emptied down the sink until the bath was light enough for Bert to move it. He would then drag it outside, pour the water down the drain and hang the bath back on its hook on the outside wall.

Neighbourliness was an essential part of life and every street had its midwife or self-appointed expert who knew all the traditional cures so the very health of the community was in the hands of the local chemist and the next door neighbour. If real disaster should strike a household, the rest of the street would come to the immediate rescue; children would be looked after and help given in any possible form. Naturally, everybody in the street knew everyone else's business, but such was a small price to pay for the support which resulted.

In poverty, sickness and adversity they stuck together in order to survive, thereby creating their own welfare state with only the hope that things must improve to sustain them.

Cooks Row was within a stone's throw of Bert's mother and so there was no need for Ernie to change schools. He was happy about this as he had now made young friends there and when the new term began he found himself in the "proper school", he was no longer in nursery class. No longer would a spoonful of Virol be thrust down his throat every afternoon and no longer would he have to wear the brown pinafore in which each member of the reception class was wrapped immediately on arrival each morning. Instead his school dress would now be the uniform of privation - patched trousers, darned jersey and well worn boots with one of his socks wrinkled and fallen-down, which all boys seemed to find unavoidable.

His new classroom was different. The children now sat in rows, two to a desk with seats that folded back to gain access. The classroom was tiled in dark green to dado height and the upper walls were plain distempered brick. The floor was bare boards and at the front of the room a small cast iron fireplace occupied one corner and a blackboard and easel the other. In between was the teacher's desk, a tall wooden structure at which the teacher could stand comfortably with her arms resting on the fold-down lid. A tall stool was available behind it but was rarely used. A large notice board almost filled the inside wall on which were pinned maps of the British Empire and curling posters of wildlife while on the opposite wall, on the window ledge, stood the obligatory milk bottles containing wilting wildflowers brought in by enthusiastic pupils.

He was thankful he still got his mid-morning bottle of milk and looked forward to pushing the perforated centre from the cardboard top and slurping the contents up through a straw. He had grown used to it by now and no longer had the unbelievable pleasant sensation his very first bottle had given him; that first bottle, on his first day at school, had been the first time he had tasted fresh milk. Milk was a rare treat at home, and then only used when funds allowed to replace the thick condensed milk from the tin. More importantly, possibly due to favourable reports from Miss Ford, his new teacher made him "Milk Monitor". This meant that it was he who had to carry the milk crate to the classroom and he who had to wait on the other children, distribute the bottles, collect the empties and then tote the crate back into the corridor. The children did not see his role as serfdom but as superiority and he revelled in his first taste of responsibility.

They wrote on slates, trying to copy the immaculate copper-plate writing of the teacher; they sat, arms folded and resting on the desk top, reciting multiplication tables; they listened to the teacher in complete silence as she told them stories of history and read them extracts from classical books for children .... and they learned.

Christmas 1933 was a memorable one. Ever since they were married the festivities had taken place at Sarah's, this year, to Edith's delight, it was held at Cook's Row. Bert upstaged Charlie that year. To take the place of Charlie's gramophone, Bert had obtained a wireless set. It was a magnificent piece of equipment - a rectangular wooden box festooned with knobs and dials on the front and by its side was a large battery and an 'accumulator'. On the top was a horn loudspeaker. It all stood on a shelf Bert had erected across an alcove on one side of the fireplace and after dinner they all sat round the fire wearing their paper hats listening in wonder. Bert proudly switched it on and from the loudspeaker there came a loud undulating whistle as he turned the knobs to find a station. Eventually the pitch of the whistle fell lower and lower and then, magically, music filled the room. It was the sound of a "Palm Court" quintet playing Strauss waltzes and tunes from popular operettas. Ernie's reaction caused Edith the one moment of unhappiness to mar a wonderful day; when she looked at him she immediately thought of Amy and what she had told her about the band in the park. While little Charlie, oblivious to the modern miracle that was taking place, continued to play with his wooden toy soldiers, Ernie was sitting perfectly still with his eyes staring straight ahead, fixed on nothing. It was inexplicable and uncanny, as if he could hear something that she couldn't, and all the time his foot was following the rhythm impeccably. For the first and only time in his life Bert had deliberately gone into debt to buy that wireless, he had committed himself to paying a shilling a week for it but when he saw the family's, particularly Ernie's, reaction he begrudged not a penny.

They had an extra guest during the evening, Edith had invited Ted Stockell in for a Christmas drink. Ted lived next door at number 21, he was a 43 year old bachelor who had been gassed as well as badly injured at the Battle of Loos in 1915, he was able to do light work only and this he was able to find only in summer when Gala Land, an underground amusement park, was open. Ted had had his Christmas dinner with another neighbour and was obviously grateful for the Waites' hospitality at night.

Ernie's intriguing reaction to the music locked in Edith's mind and she realised that there was something in him that demanded some sort of satisfaction, something which if encouraged could give him immense pleasure. Week by week she managed to save a few coppers which she hoarded in a tin on the mantelpiece to buy something musical for his birthday present - an extravagance, she realised, but one she felt to be justified. She would have loved to have got a piano but, apart from lack of space, the prices were, of course, well beyond her means. Instead, she settled for a second-hand gramophone, an out-of-date model, it is true, with a large metal horn similar to Charlie's and Ernie treasured it. He had not been allowed to use the wireless but now he had his own music machine, complete with little tin of "Songster" needles. There was enough money left for him to purchase one record and she took him to Woolworth's where, purely at random, he chose "The Stein Song". That record became the bane of Bert's life, it was played over and over again and Ernie, with his gramophone, was banished to the bedroom with the door shut so his parents could listen to the wireless in peace.

On occasions Edith wished he would have stayed there longer. After school, and at weekends, he would often go out with his friends playing "alleys" with glass marbles in the gutter, kicking a ball in the road and breaking the occasional window which an apologetic Bert was forced to replace and indulging in the many self-invented games of the season. Some of these saw him travelling further afield to the consternation of his mother. The jetty at Sandside was edged by a heavy wooden beam which stretched from one end of the harbour to the other, it held various fixings to which boats could be moored and half-way down the sea wall was a similar beam for use at lower tides. The beams were a natural challenge to small boys who would attempt to travel along them, arms outstretched, like a tightrope walker. Beginners in the art would use the upper beam but the more experienced, and foolhardy, would attempt the lower one where the sea wall added a challenging obstacle. Ernie's first illicit visit there was made with Albert Mennell and two other friends. Albert was nine months older than Ernie and led the way, Ernie, not to be outdone, set off and followed him. He had almost caught up and was no more than a foot or so behind when he caught his foot on one of the moorings and promptly disappeared over the edge, dragging Albert with him. The tide was out so they landed in two feet of slimy and smelly mud. He looked up at the sea wall for assistance but the others were nowhere to be seen - they had decided that personal survival outweighed loyalty and were running hell for leather to vacate the forbidden area as soon as possible. Such is friendship. After slithering around for some minutes they were dragged out by two local fishermen and dumped unceremoniously on top of the wall. Their appearance was awesome and the aroma that emanated from them was nauseous. Albert ran off leaving a trail of muddy footsteps but Ernie spotted a nearby horsetrough for the use of horses belonging to the local cabbies. Here was his salvation - he climbed in and tried to remove the mud by walking in the trough. He had only made one traverse of the water when he was seized by the scruff of the neck by an irate cabby who saw his horse's drinking water being polluted and was promptly lifted out, given a cuff round the ear and sent on his squelching way home.

His reception at home was unsympathetic. After an initial recoil of horror Edith demanded to know how he had got himself in such a mess and he explained in great detail how Albert had persuaded him to undertake the exploit, much against his own wishes. She was outraged and, grabbing him by his collar, trundled him off in the direction of the Mennell's home ......only to be met by an outraged Mrs. Mennell propelling and equally protesting obnoxious Albert in her direction.

Albert was the self-appointed leader of the gang and he also specialised in beach combing. When the tide was out he would lead them to the beach and pontificate on the merits and value of their discoveries. This caused great disappointment at times because he would always denigrate the findings they made, particularly Ernie's. Ernie's treasure would be casually dismissed as "just a bit of wood" whereas his rusty Rowntrees Cocoa tin definitely came from a wrecked pirate ship. In his position as milk monitor all this was rather unbecoming and Ernie decided that he should be master of a new treasure trove. A derelict house off Castlegate was being demolished and, in it, he found untold bounty which he proudly exhibited one Friday playtime. He had a green glass bottle (which had once held a genie), a handle from a bucket (which was part of a witch's cauldron) and even some straw from the witch's broom, but, what made the collection even more unique, was that he had got them in spite of the house being haunted. Albert was dethroned. The milk monitor had justified his status. The problem came the next day - when they arrived for work on the Saturday, the men pulling the house down were horrified to find it overrun with half Friarage Infants' School and their leader was obvious. Ernie received his customary clip round the ear and, as the mob ran off in all directions, he was unfortunate enough to slide down a plank that had a nail in it and arrived home with his trousers split from top to bottom. Edith declared it was close season for treasure hunting in no uncertain way.

Autumn was the start of the conker season and he spent many hours throwing sticks at horse chestnut trees to dislodge the conkers, though he was baffled why his were ordinary conkers but Albert's were always "three-ers" or even "sixers". Nevertheless the falling leaves always heralded a time of great competition and bruised fingers.

He was so occupied with all the activities of a six year old that he never realised that his father was now not taking him out on the cart at weekends and that another man was cleaning out the stable and looking after the horse.

Bert had contracted tuberculosis. His chest had been troubling him for over a year but he put it down to the coal dust - until it deteriorated so much as to warrant a visit to the doctor. The prognosis was bad and Bert was sent to Aysgarth Sanatorium. His mother sold the coal business, for what it was worth, and moved to 89 Hampton Road, a better area but near the old tram yard, now redundant as the trams had ceased to run in 1932 and used as a general storage area by the local authority.

Edith was now reduced to relying on neighbours, friends, family and Parish Relief to eke out a living for herself and Ernie who was blissfully unaware of the latest tragedy she was facing. At first Bert was allowed to come home for weekends and as each week-end came it was clear he was a very sick man, and getting worse. When 1935 came in, his visits became more and more infrequent until, in March, he was unable to walk. He did make sporadic appearances, however, being pushed by Edith in a bath chair. The bath chair was Ernie's delight. It was basically a three-wheeled wicker basket with wheels at the back on each side of the seat and a smaller wheel at the front which could be steered by the occupant using a long tiller that was attached to it. The whole contraption was the shape of a greatly elongated pear and there was plenty of room at the front for a little boy, and one little boy grabbed the opportunity to use his imagination. The chair became Ernie's "motor car" and he would sit in the front making suitable engine noises as his mother sadly pushed it along the Foreshore Road.

Ernie got a new record for his birthday on May 4th, and "The Stein Song" was given a well earned rest, its place being taken by "Red Sails in the Sunset". It appeared that everyone was celebrating his birthday that year for preparations were going ahead for a street party. May 6th saw countless back streets and alleys laid out with tables laid out along the centres of the roads laden with cakes, sandwiches and jellies miraculously produced by mothers from their sparse larders. The children sat down to a feast under home-made flags and banners proclaiming "Silver Jubilee". But while Ernie joined in the communal gluttony Edith was sitting indoors, for once unable to disguise her distress and anxiety for the future.

Herbert Waites had died. Ernie was not made aware of his father's death, neither was he made aware of his funeral. The burial took place while the boy was at school and all he recalls, even to this day, is that the day was a memorable one .... when he got home from school there was corned beef for dinner!

Edith spent the next few days in lonely contemplation and was grateful when Sarah arrived one afternoon with a bunch of flowers and a paper bag of basic groceries,

"I guessed you'd have had no time to shop," she said diplomatically, "so I picked you a few things up on the way over."

Edith had no inclination to indulge in smalltalk and within minutes was unloading her concern on her friend.

"......so what can I do? Which way do I turn? It's obvious I've got to get back to work quickly, I'd go mad sitting here and, in any case, I can't live on charity for the rest of my life .... but what of Ernie? What's going to happen to the mite? I'll have to go back to waiting-on and that means mid-day and nights .... I've taken it for granted that you'd fix him up for his lunch, but what of the evenings? If it's anything like last time I'll be getting home approaching midnight!"

"What about a day job?" Sarah suggested.

"I've no chance, have I? You'd be the same, all we've ever done is hotel work - and even that's scarce these days. I hate myself for it but the only answer I can see is to put him in an orphanage."

"Oh, God, no!"

"What else is there, Sarah? Don't you realise I've been tearing my heart out over it?"

"Don't do anything hasty," Sarah advised, "something may turn up."

"Now you sound like Bert, I've been waiting for something to turn up for years .... all that's turned up for me is trouble."

But this time something did turn up. That week end she went to see Herbert's mother and the two women consoled each other over their loss. Ernie was happily playing in the back yard bouncing a ball against the wall and Edith explained her reasons for placing him in an orphanage.

"It might only be for a little while," Edith said, "as soon as I can find a day job I can have him back.'"

"It could be months, even years, and by that time you'll have lost him. He's not going to a orphanage if I can help it .... I'll have him."

"You can't afford to keep him."

"I won't keep him, you will. We can come to some arrangement, can't we?"

Ernie's immediate future was decided. It was finally agreed that Ernie should move to Hampton Road and that Edith would pay seven shillings and sixpence a week for his keep. This was exactly half of the wage she eventually got as a waitress.

So it was "goodbye" to the two rooms at 21A Cooks Row with its memories of outside toilet, whitewashed walls in the backyard, tin bath hanging on a nail and water heated in a brick boiler in the kitchen and "hello" to a new and strange environment which was to turn out to be a most unhappy time for the young lodger.

CHAPTER FIVE

Ernie was taken to his grandmother's the following Sunday and it was a bemused and tearful little boy who was left at Hampton Road after an emotional parting from his mother. He could not understand why his life had been uprooted, neither did he connect the occasion with the tears streaming down his mother's face. Charlie Reynolds helped with the move, carrying the battered suitcase containing his clothes and petty belongings. The one small compensation was that he was allowed to take his beloved gramophone which Charlie brought to him on a second trip. His bedroom was at the back, overlooking the derelict tram yard, a dismal sight for anyone even in the best of spirits, all it served to do was to heighten his sense of total abandonment and complete misery. That first afternoon he spent standing at the window, barely able to see over the sill, looking at the piles of bricks, rusting vans and broken crates wondering what was happening to him. A few days ago he had been driving on dad's car, choosing his new record at Woolworth's and gorging at the street party; now, suddenly, he was alone in a strange house with no mother, no affection and the prospect of a new school. He indulged in a consolatory bout of crying until his grandmother led him downstairs for a glass of milk and homemade scones. She tried to explain the situation; how his father had had to go away, how mam must go to work at the time she should be looking after him and how Grandma was going to take her place for just a little while, but it all fell on unreceptive ears and she, too, became depressed to hear his sobbing as he lay in bed at night.

On Monday morning grandma took him to his new school. Falsgrave Junior was noticeable for its clock tower, which still exists today, it was smaller than Friarage but the new boy was filled with apprehension as he waited while the formalities of his admission were concluded. He was then led to a classroom and, under the inquisitive eyes of the thirty or so other pupils, given his slate, pencil and a place at a vacant desk. He looked round disconsolately, hoping that by some miracle Albert Mennell might also be there, but he was disappointed. That morning, at break time, when the milk monitor placed a bottle in front of him his lower status was confirmed and a very miserable little boy followed the others to the playground. He stood alone with his back against the outside toilets, hands in pockets with one foot against the wall, while the mass of strangers yelled, skipped and ran round the school yard. After lunch at grandma's he was very reluctant to return to school and Mrs. Waites suffered more distress when she had forcibly to take him back.

Little boys, however, are resilient creatures and within a few days he was joining in the playtime games and he became a reasonably happy pupil. His application to school work, instilled by Miss Ford, stood him in good stead and he was soon fully occupied with lessons. In fact his time at school were the best times - the lonely evenings at grandma's were the worst, relieved only by the week-end visits to Cooks Row which, in turn, led to tearful farewells again each Sunday night as he returned to the cheerless bedroom overlooking the tramyard.

It was during this time that he became aware of his capacity to hear full orchestral sounds in his head. Not for him was the normal ability of remembering the tune of a song, he could imagine the counter-melodies and accompaniments that went with it. He would lie in his bed at night with his head under the blanket and conjure up the full sound of the Henry Hall Orchestra ... "Little man you've had a busy day" .... "The music goes round and around" .... and many others, until he fell asleep. Little did he know it but this gift was to stand him in good stead in later years.

His best times, though, were Saturdays when he would be re-united with Albert and the gang for a few fleeting hours and they would resume their treasure hunting, adventuring and "mischief nights". They were great exponents of "mischief nights" when the early darkness allowed them to pursue the hobby with little fear of discovery. They had several specialities. Ernie upgraded "Knock-a-door-run" to a fine art: The equipment was simple; a large button was tied to a short length of cotton and pinned (with a drawing pin borrowed from the school notice board) to a convenient window so that the button was against the glass. Another length of cotton, also tied to the button and long enough to reach across the road was then taken to the opposite pavement. To a passer by, innocent little boys were sitting against the wall, talking - but a discrete twitch of the cotton caused a "tap-tap" on the window across the street. They would sit nonchalantly as the unfortunate victim opened his front door and looked up and down the road. Finding no-one there he would return indoors to be met with the "tap-tap" again. The astuteness of the device was that it was re-usable and, should it ever be discovered, the culprits had the width of the road as a start!

Another favourite was the "jumping" game. Here, two of them would sit on opposite sides of a pavement, one with his back to a house, another in the gutter, each holding an end of an imaginary piece of string. When a likely victim, preferably a lady, approached, the third conspirator would start running and jumping over the non-existent string. In semi-darkness everything appeared to be normal and harmless. As the prey approached them they would politely go through the motions of lowering the "string" to the ground with the plaintive advice "Mind the string missus!" and get great satisfaction in watching her hitch up her skirts and gingerly step over nothing. Long gone are such harmless demonstrations against adult society, alas.

As the year went on even Ernie began to notice that his week-end happy days were being spent more and more in Ted Stockell's house, his mother cooking meals there, and not in 21A. If dinner was in his old well-remembered home then Ted was more often or not present, and mam seemed to be happy again.

Half way through the winter term he caught ringworm. It started just as he had begun to settle at the school and be accepted by his new classmates. He had to have special treatment which necessitated Ultra-Violet radiation and, as a result, all his hair fell out. His scalp could then be treated but although he was cured bodily he was severely scarred mentally. Schoolchildren are cruel creatures to the weak and he became the butt of ridicule due to his baldness. He was allowed to wear a cap in class but his image was sadly dented for months to come.

Christmas 1935 was celebrated at the Reynolds' once more. Ted Stockell was there and Ernie noticed that he was now very friendly with Sarah and Charlie, in fact, it was very much like old times. Charlie now had a wireless, a new one in a case with a pretty fretwork front and the loudspeaker inside. He noticed it sounded better than the horn .... he could hear more "deep" notes, though none of the adults seemed to notice much difference.

When the time came to return to Grandma's he broke his heart. For a few fleeting days he had re-lived the past and he was getting old enough to dread the future - he saw nothing ahead but that dreadful room, renewed loneliness and the taunts of "baldy". Parting was a dreadful experience for both him and his mother.

1936 dragged in and dragged him reluctantly with it. His hair grew again but the stain on his memory remained, it would be a long time, if ever, that his "baldy" nickname would cease to be used at school, and for a seven year old that was hurtful. Easter meant a few more days at Cooks Row and he enjoyed every minute of them, except one. It was when he experienced his first taste of nostalgia - a new and sad experience for a little boy. Albert Mennell lived next door to the caretaker's house of Friarage School and, going to call for him on Easter Sunday he had to pass the stable on Longwestgate. The door was open so Ernie went in to pat the horse and say "Hello" to his old friend but, before he could reach it a strange man who was cleaning the cart chased him away. It seemed all his past was forbidden him.

Then, in May, just after his eighth birthday life made a complete turnabout, in a matter of days it turned from despondency to elation. Once again he was not forewarned, once again he was told only when everything was concluded. All he remembers is that one day his mother came to take him home! His bag was packed in minutes and, with Ted carrying his gramophone, he went back to Cooks Row - not to 21A but number 21. After having his tea, his mother sat him in a chair and started to explain. He had got a new dad. His name was still Ernie

Waites but her name had changed to Mrs. Stockell. Their home was now at number 21. He would have a room all to himself in the attic. Early next year he would have a new brother or sister. Did he understand? He didn't know if he did or not, all he knew was that he was back with mam again, and that was all that mattered. Plus, he reasoned, he would be returning to Friarage School! The miracle he had prayed for had happened! As one of his records said "Happy days are here again!"

And happy days they were. Ted Stockell, for the first time, enjoyed the affection of a married man's life, he took to Ernie and spent many hours introducing him to the magic world of literature through the numerous books in his library. They would go for walks together through Peasholme Park, necessarily short walks because Ted would be gasping trying to drag air into his damaged lungs, but he pointed out the many peculiarities of different shrubs and trees and explained the variations in plants and flowers. To Ernie a tree had always been a tree, now he began to see beauty for its own sake and take a real interest in nature. Ted found the enchantment of a son and Ernie, for the first time, found the security of a father.

That September he returned to Friarage School much to his own delight and that of Albert Mennell. The gang was complete again! No longer did the end of the school day mean the reluctant slow walk back to Grandma's, now it signalled the return of the spells of tomfoolery and irresponsibility that accompanied their journey home -leapfrogging over each other or convenient bollards, chasing one another along numerous detours and sliding down the steps of Church Stairs Street on a piece of wood which had been well lubricated by rubbing it with candlewax. Needless to say, they arrived home eventually in a far more dishevelled state than when they had left home in the morning and received the customary admonishment or, if in an extreme state, clip round the head, but, for Ernie, the good days had returned.

The winter was severe in 1936 and one day their homeward journey was very delayed due to their spending a lot of time gazing at the interior of Addison's shop. This was a view to be savoured. They had seen the inside of the shop before, but never from this aspect - during a gale that afternoon the side of the shop had blown down. Workmen were everywhere, salvaging what they could and shoring up what was left of the premises. It was a distraction causing lateness that fully merited the "clip" and when he got home he got one!

That December also gave Ted his first taste of the dichotomy of fatherhood; whether to be the strict administrator of punishment or the provider of succour and comfort. One wintery Saturday afternoon they had made their way to the town centre to look at the new buildings, particularly the Odeon Cinema, when they came to the new Valley Bridge, and under the bridge was a duck pond. In the middle of the pond stood a structure that had always intrigued them - on a small rockery in the centre was a straw hut, a miniature version of the African huts they had seen in their geography books at school. They realised it was for the ducks but always wondered what was in it - and that day gave them the opportunity to assuage their curiosity, for the pond was frozen over. The pond was surrounded by iron railings to prevent access but that was of little hindrance to Ernie. He climbed over the gate and set off over the ice to investigate the hut, needless to say the ice was thin and he went straight into the pond. It was only a foot deep but he found himself in a re-run of the "horsetrough" adventure of two years previously - his friends ran off and he arrived home soaking wet and shivering with cold. Edith was out and Ted Stockell was at a complete loss as to how to deal with the situation. He dried him off, found him dry clothes and waited for his mother to return. Ernie waited too, knowing full well what his mother's reaction would be. To save her the trouble he went up to his room voluntarily and stayed there, playing his gramophone, until most of her wrath had subsided.

He was fortunate in that history intervened on his behalf. He was severely scolded and sent back to his room, Edith was pre-occupied with the wireless and the latest news about the abdication of the King.

His brother was born on February 9th, 1937 and he was christened Leslie Edward at St. Sepulchre's Church. The baby had been born at home. He immediately became the centre of attraction and Ernie, like all older children, at first had pangs of jealousy at the attention the newcomer was receiving. Ted was strutting around playing the part of father, a role he had thought he would never play and Edith, too, of course was enjoying the fact that she was a mother at last, though she was determined Ernie would never know the fact. Family life soon settled in to a normal routine and Ernie never realised the lengths Edith, particularly, was going to, to impress on him that he was not second best. He received the same full affection and attention she had always tried to give him, but still he was corrected promptly when he misbehaved, which was often! His primary misdemeanour was arriving home late from whatever he was doing, but there was so much to occupy an energetic young lad in Scarborough - a wonderful world of things to investigate, things like the Norman castle set on a hill with wooded valleys and paths which, at a flick of the imagination, could become a jungle or Indian trail fraught with unimaginable danger, or the Harbour with its romantic association with ships and adventure. In fact it would have been a strange child who could not have given free rein to his mental creativity and indulge in the perfect fantasy world he alone could create.

He was still closest to Albert Mennell and the two of them would walk for miles and miles around the area exploring places like Scalby Mills at the northern end of the North Bay and climbing to the top of Olivers Mount for the scenic view it provided. They had no thought for meals or concern for weather, everything was adventure, they were lost in their own concept of time, knocking on doors when hunger demanded, begging for food and drink.

If the weather was very bad they would join the mob of other youngsters at the Band of Hope on Saturday mornings in the room under St. Sepulchre's Church. These visits were innocent hypocrisy - they had to endure the short lectures on piety before they could enjoy the free film show which followed.

In fine weather the town, as a holiday resort, had a wealth of entertainment; the beach, amusement arcades stretching along the South Bay, more sand and rock pools in the North Bay, plus little haunts like Robin Hood's cave and Monkey Island. Everything contributed to a childish sense of well-being where time simply did not exist and it never occurred to Ernie that his parents might worry about where he was.

May always seemed to be a notable month in his life, apart from containing his birthday. In 1937 it saw the coronation of George VI and he, like every other child at school, received a free box of chocolates and a special beaker to commemorate the occasion. He was fervently selfish about that beaker, it was his and his alone, no one else was allowed to drink from it, and so it remained until many months later when he was making himself a drink of lemonade. "Lemonade powder"' was obtained from Addisons' where a halfpenny purchased a paper bagful of tartly flavoured yellow crystals which were usually consumed by dipping in a wet finger and then sucking it. This produced a characteristic feature of its consumers - dirty nails and grubby hands but the top half of the right index finger gleamingly clean! A spoonful of the stuff mixed with water made a palatable drink and Ernie was vigorously stirring such a brew when the mug slipped out of his hand and shattered on the floor. His second best personal belonging was gone, his possessiveness reverted solely to his gramophone.

That autumn a destroyer ran aground on the rocks and the wreck naturally became a great attraction for all the young boys, from nine to ninety, in the area. Ernie was inevitably drawn to the spot and his fascination earned him more chastisements for his consequent complete disregard for mealtimes.

When the baby was a few months old Edith allowed him to push the pram. In her presence he was diligent and careful, so much so that she gained false confidence and, on occasions, permitted him to take the baby out alone for a push round the park. She deluded herself. As soon as he was alone on the street the pram became a racing car and, oblivious to little Leslie's presence and accompanied by appropriate "Vroom-vroom" sound effects, he would make perilous circuits of the hairpin bends of the many paths in the park much to the danger of Leslie, himself and innocent park visitors. Luckily for all, St. Christopher must have worked overtime for the likely crash never occurred, but he got in customary trouble for being late home.

That year saw the first of an eagerly anticipated annual event - a long summer holiday with Granny and Grandad Robinson. Edith's father and stepmother lived in Annfield Plain, County Durham and it was at their suggestion that he spent a month there. This was the ultimate adventure, a long, long journey to unknown lands. Edith, carrying Leslie in her arms, while he carried his case, took him to the United Bus Station on Valley Bridge early in the morning and they boarded the bus to Middlesbrough. With a bag of sweets in his pocket he sat by a window taking in all the new and exciting places they passed; Whitby, Guisborough, and Stockton-on Tees, names he had only heard of in geography lessons. At Middlesbrough they changed to a bus to Durham, then Stanley and on to Annfield Plain, a place that was to provide a lifetime of happy memories. Edith would usually stay the night and return home the following day leaving him in the care of Granny and Grandad Robinson who became like a second mother and father to the young lad from Scarborough.

Like Scarborough, Annfield Plain was a wonderland for boys. It was in the country and offered farms, pitheads, railway crossings, walks across the "Bogs" and the little cinema on Saturdays. Aunt Ethel, Edith's sister, lived just up the road from Granny and regular visits were made to her house, with memorable meals in the little back kitchen and trips to Lanchester to see yet another auntie.

The only illumination for the houses was by paraffin lamps, each room having its own dim light but this did not distract in any way from the happiness in just being with such warm hearted people. He enjoyed the job of making the regular walk to the local store to get the accumulator charged so they could listen to the wireless and happy evenings were spent listening to music. In the back parlour Granny had a pedal harmonium with two keyboards and numerous 'stops'. Ernie was attracted to this wonderful instrument immediately and was enthralled by the strange noises coming from it as he ran his fingers over the keys pretending to be a great organist. On the music ledge were sheets of music; the mass of dots on lines meant nothing to him but he cast his eyes on the titles; "Red Sails in the Sunset", "My Prayer", "Underneath the Spreading Chestnut Tree" and, in his mind, could conjure up the sound of a full orchestra playing those current favourite tunes. He experimented with the keys and, after only a few minutes, Granny was astounded to hear a hesitant but recognisable melody coming from the parlour. That evening she asked him to show grandad what he could do and Ernie couldn't understand their amazement when he picked out "September in the Rain" - after all, it was quite simple, each key produced a note and all he was doing was pressing them in the right order, so what was all the fuss about? Anyway, he seemed to please them so he carried on. Towards the end of the month he was adding some low notes with his left hand and **that** pleased **him**!

Every Sunday they would all take a trip to Dipton where Grandad spent all morning playing bowls while Ernie sat watching, munching Grandma's homemade cakes. Grandma made all sorts of cakes and bread, nothing seemed to be bought ready-made from shops and every meal was accompanied by freshly picked vegetables and the bread spread thickly with real butter. Life was idyllic and simple, too simple for Ernie, and he began to introduce self-invented challenges. The milk had to be collected from the farm opposite the row of terraced pit cottages and this became his daily task. He complicated the job by trying to walk back from the farm each morning with the bottles held between his legs, to the amusement of Grandma and the few neighbours. Miraculously, he never broke one.

All too soon the holiday was over and he was back at home. His music lay dormant, frustratingly so after the pleasure he had found with Grandma's harmonium, until he returned to school for the winter term. He was now in the top junior class and for the first time had a male teacher, a Mr. Chapman, whom he had to call "Sir". Mr. Chapman played the piano in the hall and the class had regular periods set aside for 'singing', but the songs were old fashioned, "Greensleeves", "Will ye no come back again" and hymns. Mr. Chapman had been following this routine for years; the words were printed in very large type on sheets of well-worn paper that were draped over a blackboard on an easel, he sat at the piano and played and the children sang, it was all very straightforward .... until 1938. That September he played the tune slowly so the new children could learn it and, when he considered them ready, set them to sing in unison. As in every previous year, they did .... but something was wrong. As the keen choristers let forth with "Onward Christian Soldiers" he could swear that somewhere, one voice was singing a descant. This was impossible, of course, because he had never even told them what a descant was, let alone demonstrated one. He switched to "Away in a manger" .... and there it was again! He had chosen "Away in a manger" because the children knew it well and could sing it unaccompanied. He left the piano and signalled them to continue while he kept an alert ear. He found it.

"Waites!"

"Yes, sir?"

"Come here."

Ernie left his place and sheepishly went to the front
"What were you singing?"
"Away in a manger, sir"
"Who told you to sing it that way?"
"No one, sir."
"Then why did you sing differently from the others?"
" It sounded nice, sir."
"Who taught you to do it?"
The boy was puzzled, "No one, sir, I've always done it, in my head, to my gramophone and the wireless. "
"Wait behind afterwards, I want a word with you."

Ernie spent the rest of the singing lesson dry mouthed, he remembered Miss Ford .... what would a man teacher's wrath be like?

To his surprise Mr. Chapman was not annoyed at all. He asked him about music and Ernie told him all about his gramophone, Granny's harmonium and how he enjoyed pretending to be an orchestra in his head. Mr. Chapman suggested to him he should go along to one of the churches and join the choir.

And so it was that he started attending meetings at all the local churches and joining in their choir practices. He tried them all, not out of a search for theological enlightenment but because he preferred the type of hymns they were singing. He eventually gave most of his time to the Band of Hope and the Rechabites; they had temperance ideals and he had to sign a pledge against demon drink but that was not a hard decision to make when you were ten years old and they offered film shows on Saturday mornings and outings to the local countryside by train, plus sandwiches in the chapel after meetings.... but the main attraction was the music, even if it was limited to singing hymns.

His final year as a junior was a happy one. He sang with the choirs, he took Leslie out in his 'car', he had more adventures with Albert and Charlie; he could not understand why Mam, Dad, Uncle Charlie, Auntie Sarah and all the other grown ups seemed so bothered, they talked of "Munich", "Hitler" and all sorts of things that meant nothing to him but appeared to fill their lives. He had only one major mishap. In February, the school playground was a paradise for fun, the surface was frozen hard and loose snow covered the surrounding walls. They revelled in snowballing each other and people passing by outside, they rolled a ball of hard snow around until it was too big even to move and, best of all, they constructed a wonderful long icy slide that stretched from one side of the playground to the other. One by one they slid along it, arms flailing, going further and further as the surface iced up. Unfortunately, it was too good, and Ernie was the unlucky user when they found it so. He set off on his run, spread his feet and slid along the icy path - he couldn't stop, he crashed into the wall at the end and was out cold. Worried teachers carried him inside and when he regained consciousness tended to his wounded head. The caretaker was sent out with bags of salt and the slide disappeared.

Summer came in that year with a vengeance. It was very hot and Scarborough was full of sunseekers but the talk was of air raids, gas masks and, from the older generation, naval bombardment. Younger people listened to their elders' reminiscences of December 1914, when German battleships had shelled the town from the North Sea.

On the morning of September 3rd, Ernie had taken Leslie out in his "car" and as he passed St. Mary's Church he heard the congregation all talking about "getting home in time for Chamberlain". He didn't know what they meant but his curiosity forced him to run home too. He got home to find all the neighbours gathered on the pavement outside 21 Cooks Row listening to the wireless through the open front door. They were strangely silent. He arrived just in time to hear a solemn voice over the loudspeaker saying "....and consequently this country is at war with Germany."

He left them to it and set off on another circuit with his "car".

Top Left:
Waites' 1st Family Home, Market Street. (Today). (First floor, extreme right)
Top Right:
Edith Waites, 1956
Bottom Left:
Edith & Ernie, 1933
Bottom Right:
Ernie, aged 3

Top Left:
Herbert Waites' Stable, Longwestgate. (Today). (Grandma Waites lived next door)

Top Right:
Friarage School. The "stoned" windows

Centre Left:
The "Leeds Hotel" c1930
(Bottom left is corner of Princess Street)

Bottom Left:
Cousin Betty, Auntie Mary, Cousin Stuart, Ernie, Leslie Stockell 1940

Bottom Right:
Ernie in Peasholme Park. Aged 9

Top:
Sandside. The Harbour Wall c1930

Left:
Part of Cross Street c1928

Right:
Cooks Row c1930

Bottom:
Church Stairs Street c1930

Top Left:
Edith, Sarah Reynolds, Les Stockell, Mrs. C. Reynolds (Anice) c1954
Top Right:
Princess Street as it is today
Centre Left:
Ted Stockell & Edith 1958
Bottom Left:
Seamer Road Mission
Bottom Right:
St. Sepulchre Street, today.

CHAPTER SIX

The outbreak of war made little impact on Ernie's daily routine, he still went to school, he was still continually in trouble and he still looked upon punishment as a part of life. He was, as he well remembers, a "little horror".

It had been generally expected that the declaration of war would herald an immediate inferno of destruction and carnage and when nothing at all happened an air of complacency descended on the town. Within days "The Donkey Serenade" was blasting out from gramophones along the front again and one could be forgiven for thinking that everything was well with the world....except for the blackout. The blackout was the only burden that, at the time, the public had to bear. A hasty search was made for black cloth or material that could be dyed black to make up into curtains or blinds to cover all windows, and woe betide any careless householder who allowed even the tiniest chink of light to be seen from his home. Cries of "Put that light out!" echoed around the locality as zealous air raid wardens went about their nightly duties. Cars had to have their headlights dimmed to an absolute minimum and even the essential torch had tissue paper fixed over the bulb to reduce the light it emitted. Very soon, due to a spate of accidents, the car headlight rule was revoked in favour of a mask allowing a slit of light to emerge, but the absence of streetlamps and general darkness in the streets was an exciting environment and, as far as Ernie was concerned, a God-given cover for his natural mischievousness.

In common with all the neighbours Ted covered his windows with crosses of sticky paper tape to avoid them shattering in an air raid and a space was made under the staircase for shelter.

Edith and Ted had by now been married for three years and the initial romance had long worn off. They were struggling at a bare subsistence level with Ted unable to work through disability and Edith tied at home with the younger son. The added stress of possible air attack was most likely the catalyst that sparked off a spate of petty bickering that sometimes turned into arguments. Ernie's impishness compounded the delicacy of the situation and often set off disputes as to who was the cause of his misbehaviour, who should deal with him and how he should be corrected. Ernie was totally ignorant of the domestic strife that was developing and unknowingly continued to aggravate the problem.

They were all issued with gas masks, to be kept available at all times and carried around in a cardboard box with string for a shoulder strap. To Ted, of course, with his memories of the hell of Loos such a permanent reminder of the reason for his condition was agony and he would go into tirades of rage whenever he found that Ernie had gone out and left his mask in the house, which was often.

The first indication of the abnormal was the arrival in the district of evacuees from Hull. Dozens of children found themselves billeted in already overcrowded homes which, even before their appearance, had been below any level of acceptability. Most of the children had come from the dockland area of Hull so they saw little, if any, change from their own normal standards. With them came their teachers and, instead of integrating the two societies, probably due to numbers, Friarage School worked a half-time two-tier system, with the local children using the school in the mornings and the evacuees, with their own staff, being taught in the afternoons. This did not bode well for the general behaviour but was a heaven sent opportunity for Ernie and his ilk to indulge in more escapades! Stirrup pumps and buckets of sand had been placed at strategic positions in every street .... need any more be said?

The situation changed drastically early in 1940 when it was decided that the area around Cooks Row and Springfield had deteriorated into a complete slum and would be demolished. The residents were dispersed to outlying estates, thus terminating a society that had thrived on poverty and the tight little community disappeared virtually overnight. The Reynolds' were among the first to move, to number twelve Maple Drive, with young Charlie boasting to Ernie that their house must be the poshest in the row because it was the only one with a bay window. The Stockells found themselves in the southern area, at 146 Seamer Moor Road. Seamer Moor Road is not shown on any current map of Scarborough, it's name has since been changed and it appears as Newcoln Road.

The estate is built on a hill and the houses at varying levels. Ernie remembers about twenty steps from the road to the front door of the house and the front garden was just a steep slope of grass. At the rear a small back garden sloped just as steeply upwards, away from the house. But they were gardens, a luxury he had never before experienced. At the top of the back garden was a triple-barred wooden fence and beyond the fence nothing but moorland. The contrast to the surroundings of Cooks Row could not have been greater. Neither could the house. They had an indoor toilet and a bathroom with hot and cold running water.

The move, however, meant that Ernie had a new school, Gladstone Road Senior, and its distance from the home meant an hour's walk morning and night, for although buses were available money was not. With Albert still being at Friarage School the long walk, alone and, in winter, in the blackout, was a daunting experience. He would arrive home tired and, for a while, restrained.

One by one the manifestations of war made their grim appearance; an air raid shelter appeared in the middle of the road, a forbidding plain brick rectangle with a thick concrete roof, policemen wore "tin hats" in place of their traditional helmets and rationing was introduced. The advent of rationing, however, had an advantageous effect. With food becoming scarcer it was imperative that every scrap of rationed food was collected and very often these included nourishing items that some people had never been able to afford, small amounts, it is true, but for the ex-Cooks Row inhabitants their diet actually improved. Ted, like most others, took the opportunity to transform his precipitous garden into a vegetable plot, growing potatoes, onions and carrots so they had more fresh vegetables than they had enjoyed in time of peace.

Mobilisation caused the disappearance of the young men of the area as they were called up for the armed forces. Charlie Reynolds didn't wait for call-up, within weeks of the war starting, he volunteered, in common with many trawlermen, for the Royal Naval Patrol Service and joined the minesweepers at Lowestoft. Ted, together with the majority of 1914/1918 veterans, as well as many elder teenagers rushed to join the "L.D.V." as soon as Anthony Eden announced its formation over the wireless. The "Local Defence Volunteers" was the fore-runner of the Home Guard and their uniform was an armband. Ted became a "Parashot" which meant that should a German airborne battalion try to land in Scarborough it would promptly be dispatched by Stockell senior with his World War One rifle with no bullets. (As Rob Wilton pointed out on the wireless .... not **just** Ted, there **were** several others!).

During 1940 Edith joined the congregation at Seamer Road Mission, a tiny chapel about a mile from their house and became an avid member. Three times each Sunday she would take Ernie, walking each time of course, for the morning, afternoon and evening services. He remembers a Miss Stericker there, a kindly old lady who acted as superintendant and who played the harmonium for the hymns. A harmonium! Memories of Grandma Robinson came back and soon he had cajoled the lady to let him play at it after the congregation had left. He is convinced that that is where his foundations for a future in music were firmly laid. He soon found himself, although still only twelve, an important member of the chapel community; he was in charge of the distribution and collection of hymn books, a member of the choir who went on to singing the solos and eventually, after his fourteenth birthday, actually taking some services and giving the sermon. He feels that this, too, gave him the confidence for public speaking in the future.

His newly discovered sanctity did not, however, impeach on his general devilish behaviour, which sometimes even took place on Sundays! Due to Edith's enthusiasm, Sarah decided that the Mission would be an ideal place for Charlie junior to attend also, so one Sunday he was duly delivered at the Stockells for his spiritual enlightenment. Ernie and Charlie were re-united and sent off to the chapel together. "Oh what fools we mortals are!". They never, of course, arrived. Instead they finished up in Valley Road, near the infamous duck pond, where one of the houses had a back garden that was virtually an orchard. They were over the fence in a flash and gorged themselves on apples. Late that evening, when Ernie was in bed, there was a knock on the door and a policeman had called to interview the apple collector. Still in his pyjamas, Ernie received a stern warning from the policeman and, after he had left, a good hiding from his mother. The lesson was not learnt either by the boys or their parents. Charlie and his mother were regular visitors to the Sunday tea-table at Seamer Moor Road so the episode was to be repeated on several occasions. They were invariably discovered for they were far better at getting caught than stealing apples!

The local landscape still offered much to the lads for Olivers Mount was only across the way, the Mere at the bottom of the road with its pleasure craft and secret islands, the gasworks and locomotive sheds were just up the road - all combining with the blackout to make golden opportunities for healthy lads to get up to mischief.

The evacuation of Dunkirk meant little to a lad of twelve and he never realised the turmoil of the adults as they tried to face the possibility, and probability, of invasion. The Battle of Britain which followed did, however, grab his attention but, like all the youngsters, more as a game than a momentous segment of history. They scanned the shrunken newspapers for the daily reports of plane losses, treating the figures not as lost lives but as a football score .... and we were winning! They cut out pictures of aircraft, both British and German, and could recognise their types even from silhouettes, and every playground game was an air battle with dozens of childish lips making "Rat-ta-ta-ta-" machine gun sounds. Scarborough avoided the mass terror bombing suffered by towns and cities further south and the children were spared the first-hand horror of the war.

They got their first experience of enemy action towards the end of the year. The shape of the Mere and Olivers Mount with the water glistening in the moonlight could possibly, when the visibility was not good, be mistaken from the air as Hull docks. This probably was so, for what other reason could there have been for repeated bomb attacks on the area? Several times it was the recipient of German bombs, one causing a huge crater in the moorland only a hundred yards or so behind their back garden. On other occasions German planes would drop parachute mines in the harbour, some of which missed and landed on buildings. Needless to say, such incidents demanded investigation and sight-seeing resulting in missed meals, lateness home and more punishment.

Ernie never resented his mother's discipline, she was always firm but fair. He did resent some of the canings he received at school. In senior school he was, of course, writing with pen and ink. The pens were small wooden affairs with cheap replaceable nibs that were dipped into inkwells let into the top of each desk. The nibs soon broke or crossed and the teachers were very reluctant to change them, not only due to shortage of supplies, but because when fitted with a flight made of folded paper they made excellent darts. They were therefore used to their limit and ink would just fall off them. Ernie found it almost impossible to go through a day without dropping one blob of ink on his work and one particular master decided that this was a major sin deserving of the cane. He suffered badly from that teacher who, at least, taught him the meaning of unfair treatment. Punishment for misdemeanours he could accept, realising he received his just desserts, but for accidentally dropping a blot .....?

Just before his thirteenth birthday he got a week-end job as an errand boy at Robinson's Grocery Store with a two-fold effect. The work kept him somewhat out of mischief and the small wage helped at home and allowed him the odd pennies to be able to go to school on the bus.

By December that year he was consequently beginning to mature and be more responsible, he was in his own small way contributing to the family, his time to leave school was approaching and at long last he began to consider his future. It therefore came as a devastating blow when an incident occurred that was to have a profound effect on his life and remain irrevocably locked in his mind for the rest of his days.

With Charlie Reynolds being away on a minesweeper it had become quite customary for Sarah and young Charlie to come to Seamer Moor Road for tea on Sundays. A week or two before Christmas they were all seated round the tea table and everything was quite normal. The adults were passing idle gossip about generalities and rationing but mainly the Japanese attack on Pearl Harbour and the American entry into the war. The two boys were talking about the coming holiday when Charlie said,

"I'm having a bike for Christmas."

Ernie was inwardly envious of his friend but didn't show it, all he could think to do on the spur of the moment was to try to equalise the situation,

"So am I."

"So are you what?" Ted Stockwell asked. Ernie looked embarrassed, he didn't realise anyone was listening to their conversation. He was cornered but thought it best to maintain the bluff,

"Charlie's having a bike for Christmas, I said I was, too."

To Ernie's, and everyone else's, complete amazement Ted went into a fierce rage. No one had ever seen him in such a frenzy before, it was quite out of character but he stood up and ranted on and on about expense, hardship and the hypocrisy of Christmas in general, then, red in the face, stabbing with his finger, stuttering over his words and with venom in his voice concluded with,

"........so you won't be getting any bloody bike, this Christmas or any other bloody Christmas - you don't even belong to us anyway, you're **not** our child and we are **not** your parents!"

A dreadful hush fell on the gathering, Ernie was dumbfounded. Sarah looked down at her empty plate. Edith sat transfixed, her eyes on Ted. Ted sat down, a deflated man, chin in his hand. Ernie looked at his mother and caught her eyes. No word was said, his eyes pleadingly asked a question, her eyes sorrowfully gave the answer. He got up from the table and fled the room, tears rolling down his cheeks. He understood his previous dad had died and that Ted was his stepfather but he had never dreamed that Edith was not his mother. His world of happiness and affection built up over the past few contented years suddenly collapsed around him and he was plunged into utter despair.

Lying face down on his bed, his whole body heaving with sobbing, he heard the hubbub start downstairs. Edith was shouting at Ted and threatening to leave him, Sarah was making flustered apologies. He heard her leave with Charlie and then his mother was holding him in her arms trying to comfort him.

After an hour he had calmed down enough for her to lead him downstairs again where Ted was sitting slumped in an arm chair, ashamed and broken. Edith took his hands in hers and tearfully explained: He **was** her son, it is true she had not actually borne him but she was his mother for all that, when he got older, old enough to understand, she would have told him, and she loved him. But the damage was done, things could never return to the way they had been just an hour ago; from that moment a gap had appeared between Ernie and Ted that could never be closed, a gap which from that day continued to widen, for a trust had been demolished.

Christmas 1941 was, of course, a disaster and one that will remain in his mind for the magnitude of the misery that accompanied it. He spent Christmas morning trying hard to join in the festive celebrations at the Mission and then went to Sarah's and spent the afternoon riding Charlie's new bike, not realising that Charlie, right out of character, was allowing him complete and unbridled use of it. He returned home in the early evening to an awkward and silent household.

In its nobbled way life carried on. He left school on reaching his fourteenth birthday and found work at Plaxton's Bus Factory, which was then making boxes to hold ammunition. He became a labourer and odd-job boy at a wage of fifteen shillings a week. He would hand his wage packet to his mother every Friday and would be given sixpence for himself, usually with an admonishment not to spend it all at once. He was happy working because he had found some sort of independence and his receptive mind allowed him to pick up all sorts of tips and basic skills of the many activities going on in the factory such as painting and general carpentry. At Christmas he made simple toys which, in those days when such things were scarce, he sold to the neighbours for pocket money. His natural exuberance, alas, had to have rein and he was often embroiled with his fellow labourers and apprentices in practical joking and tomfoolery. One day he produced a masterpiece: The latest recruit, a lad from the local High School who considered himself to be working below his station, had been promoted to the job of sprayer and, dressed in boiler suit and face mask, would insist that Ernie was not supplying him with boxes quickly enough. They were supposed to be a team - Ernie would lift an ammunition box on to a small turn-table and the lad would spray one side with green paint, spin it round and spray the other. He seemed to delight in completing the job before Ernie could have the next box ready. He was, in fact, becoming a pompous pest. His pride and joy was a flat cap that, somehow, he had managed to obtain in spite of a lack of clothing coupons. One day Ernie threw a box on to the turn-table, the lad hastily painted one side and, in one action, spun it round and sprayed the other - just too late to see that his beloved cap had been nailed to it! He was the only lad present not convulsed with laughter and, in fact in a fit of temper, grabbed the now green cap and threw it at Ernie. Ernie picked up the nearest thing to hand, a wooden mallet, and hurled that back. Unfortunately that was the very moment the foreman came into the workshop, the target ducked and the mallet hit the foreman. Ernie was dismissed immediately and had to go home and explain that he'd "got the sack".

His dismissal was a terrible blow to Edith as his wage was the only income she could rely on but with the armed forces denuding the labour market of young men it was not too long before he found another job. This time he found work at Quartons, a firm of fruiterers on Westborough. The job entailed carrying sacks of produce from the cellars to the shop and delivering orders round the town. This work became of great benefit to the family as, from time to time, he would arrive home with the odd supply of fruit and tomatoes which had been considered unfit to put on general sale. It was whilst making a delivery one Saturday morning that he had a first-hand experience of an air raid. He was passing the Odeon Cinema at the top of Westborough on his delivery bicycle when he looked up and saw what he assumed was a Beaufighter flying low overhead. Like all boys during the war he was a keen plane spotter and suddenly realised that the plane was not a Beaufighter at all but a Junkers 88 dive bomber, and it was so low he could see the black crosses on the wings. He leapt off the bike and dropped it, scattering his deliveries in the road, and dived under an ornamental tree outside the cinema. He watched in fear and fascination as two bombs fell from the plane and appeared to travel down the high street before dropping in the harbour. The sirens wailed their banshee warning as the Junkers fled homewards with a Spitfire, which had appeared from nowhere, close on its tail. He joined the small crowd which had now assembled, jumping up and down and waving his arms as the Spitfire caught its quarry and shot it down in the North Sea.

The Battle of Alamein at the end of 1942 invoked a wave of optimism throughout the country and engendered an even greater surge of patriotism among the youngsters. Up to then many young men, on call-up, with the Battle of Britain uppermost in their minds, opted for the Royal Air Force, while lads from maritime areas had been traditionally asking to serve in the Royal Navy, now, with Rommel's "invincible" panzers in retreat from Montgomery's Eighth Army, more and more regiments were being specifically requested. Ernie was inwardly willing the years to go by, but, at fourteen and a half, he had four years to wait for his mobilisation papers.

One day, when he came out of the shop after work, he found Edith waiting for him, a thing she had never done before.

"I wanted to catch you, son, before you came home." She set off walking along Westborough and Ernie fell in beside her. She obviously had something definite in mind as she gave him no opportunity to ask questions but kept up a continuous one-sided conversation, "I want you to meet someone. It's your Uncle, Uncle Bill." Ernie was baffled now as he had never heard of an Uncle Bill. "You don't know of him but I think it's time you did - he's your real mother's brother. He comes to Scarborough every so often when there's work here. When he does he lets me know how she's getting on and takes my news back - he never stays long and this is the first time he's been since Ted let the cat out of the bag. Well he called round this afternoon so I think it's only fair that, this time, you should see him yourself. He's staying in lodgings in Roscoe Street."

"So she didn't forget me?" Ernie asked.

"How could she?"

"Then why hasn't she written to me?"

"For your sake, Ernie, can't you see what a turmoil you would have been in? She wanted you to have one mother - me, not have you split down the middle. She must have gone through Hell itself - wondering how you were getting on and yet not being able to confide in anyone. Bill has been marvellous, keeping us in touch, no matter how infrequently, and at the same time not telling her husband or her family. You're old enough to understand now, I hope, so I told him to expect you this evening. Ted wouldn't understand, would he? That's why I thought I'd meet you after work."

They arrived at Roscoe Street and Ernie found himself in a bed-sitting room with a man who told him he was his uncle. He was a kind man, though obviously struggling to make ends meet. His hands were calloused and he explained that, with work being scarce in Ireland, he took every opportunity to find casual employment wherever it was available. His strong Irish accent was strange to Ernie's ears and he had some trouble at first making himself understood but, over a cup of tea, with Edith sitting mute in the background, he explained to Ernie what had occurred in the past. He told him of his sister's predicament when she found she was pregnant, he told him of their Auntie Frances who used to live in Princess Street and he told him about his mother, Kathleen. When she returned to Ireland in 1928 she had worked for a while in Portlaoise and had subsequently married and settled down there. He told Ernie he had half-brothers and sisters but that they knew nothing of him and Kathleen wanted it to remain that way - but, whenever he had been to Scarborough and they were alone, she always asked how "Edith Waites' boy" was getting along.

Ernie walked back home, with Edith, more confused than ever and realised that Mam had been right in not telling him of his origins when he was younger - even at fourteen it was difficult to comprehend. Bill O'Brien had given him a present when he left - a pen that had three separate nibs and would write in any of three colours. He also promised to see Ernie again when next he came to Yorkshire. That meeting was never to take place.

Conditions at home were getting worse. Ernie never did find out what made an ordinary man like Ted Stockell suddenly flip as he did on that fateful Sunday, he never discovered what tensions and frustrations caused the outburst but no apology was ever made and, surprisingly, the incident was never mentioned again. But the rift between him and his stepfather had widened considerably, no longer did they walk in the park, no longer did they share books and no longer did the four of them go out together as a family. Arguments, both petty and serious, between Edith and Ted were becoming an almost daily occurrence and this, coupled with his feeling of "not belonging" made Ernie long for the day when he could leave the home for ever.

The Scarborough recruiting office was situated in the old Liberal Club at the top of Westborough and one day, just after his fifteenth birthday, he called in there for no other reason than pure curiosity. He went up the steps and enquired about joining the armed forces and as he entered he saw a large photograph of the Royal Marine Band on parade. A band! The Royal Marines with their splendid uniform of blue and scarlet! Plus music! He stood transfixed ... it was everything he could ever wish for. His dream was soon shattered when he was told they had no vacancies at all.

His disappointment must have been obvious and the recruiting sergeant told him to sit down while he sifted through some files. Ernie sat at the bare wooden trestle table with his heart thumping. He had gone in with no hope of being able to do anything at his age, but there was an air about the sergeant that promised some possibility, why else was he still sitting there? After what seemed a lifetime the sergeant told him that there was a local regiment, the Green Howards - they had a regimental band .... and they enlisted a few lads of fifteen as band boys! He gave all his particulars, left the office in a state of elation and floated on air all the way home.

He said nothing to his mother at the time, deciding that there was no point in starting more possible trouble until he was sure he would be accepted. When the letter arrived telling him to report for a medical he had to tell her of his ambition and, when he went to bed that night, he left a very unhappy Edith downstairs. Ted had made no comment whatsoever. At the medical they tested his eyes, looked down his ears and his throat, sounded his chest, banged his knees and elbows with rubber hammers and told him to wait again. Then the doctor sent for him, he went into the office in eager anticipation,

"Well, young man, you are perfectly fit ...." his heart leapt again, ".....but you are underweight." his heart fell. He looked pleadingly at the doctor,

"So I can't join?" he asked sorrowfully, head bowed.

"Not at the moment ......but why not come and see me again in, say, six weeks - put on seven pounds and we'll accept you." Over the next month he ate everything and anything he could get his hands on and, exactly to the day, returned to the medical centre. They examined his records, nodded, and told him to step on the scales. He tried to press down, willing the metal arm to remain still as the doctor pushed the sliding weight along it. It finally tipped. The doctor looked at him, smiled and said,

"That's fine. You'll hear from us shortly."

On September 13th. 1943 he was sworn in as 440096 Bandboy Waites E.T. of the Regimental Band, 1st. Battalion, The Green Howards. (Alexandra's Princess of Wales Own Yorkshire Regiment). He was to report to the Regimental Depot in Richmond, Yorkshire.

Apart from his trips to Grandma Robinson in Durham, Ernie had never been further than eight or nine miles out of Scarborough so the trip to Richmond was an exciting prospect in itself. On the Monday morning, following tearful farewells from Edith, he left Central Station little realising what a fateful decision he had made and how his life was about to take off in a completely different but meaningful direction. The carriages were crowded with men and women from all the various services and when it reached York the throng grew even greater with everyone jostling on the platforms for a place on the train to Darlington. Ernie felt out of place in his civilian clothes but gloried in the fact that the next time he made the journey he, too, would be in uniform. At Darlington he was interested to see the old locomotive "Rocket" on display as he alighted. He crossed to another platform to complete his journey by way of Scorton, Moulton and Catterick Bridge. All along the route people had left the train and it seemed strange that when he arrived at Richmond there was only one other traveller with him in the compartment, the majority having left at Catterick. When he came out of the station he was alone, he had been relying on someone else going to the barracks to show him the way. He was forced to use his own initiative - the first, but by far the last time he would be obliged to do so as a soldier. He found the R.T.O. Office and went in,

"Excuse me," he said to a sergeant with an armband labelled "R.T.O.", indicating he was of the Railway Transport Office, "but can you tell me the way to the Green Howards Barracks?"

"Why?"

"I've got to report there."

"Bit young, aren't you?"

"I'm a bandboy." He said proudly.

"Got your papers?" Ernie produced his documents which the sergeant scrutinised

"Is this you? Waites?"

"Yes, sir."

"Sir? Sir? What do you think these are?" he said, pointing to his stripes, "Officers are 'sir' lad, you call me 'Sergeant' .....and you'd better get used to it, quick!"

"Yes .....sergeant." Ernie had made his first encounter with army discipline, and wondered what to do next.

"You want to know how to get to the Green Howards?"

"Yes."

"Yes, what!?"

"Yes, sergeant."

"That's better. Right, just go outside - you can't go wrong, they're at the top of the bloody great hill."

Ernie realised he was being dismissed and left the office more bewildered than when he went in. As he went through the door the sergeant smiled widely.

Ernie soon found out that the directions were actually quite sufficient, for the trip from Richmond Station to the barracks is indeed one of the natural marathons of this world, as he and every other Green Howard has discovered in his time. When finally he arrived at the guard room he was booked in and escorted to a long "Spider" hut at the back of the barracks, given a bunk, issued with a mattress and blankets, taken to the cookhouse for a meal and told where to report next morning to be issued with his uniform and kit. Everything had been done for him, he had had to make no decisions for himself. He realised that from that moment on the Army in general and the Regimental Band of the Green Howards in particular were to be his mother, father, mentor and guide.

That night he laid in his bunk excited at the thoughts of what the next day would bring; he would be in uniform, he would start to learn music, he would be in a band! He drifted into a sleep of pure contentment.

CHAPTER SEVEN

Realisation often makes a fool of expectation and Ernie discovered this on his first full day as a soldier. As he had anticipated he did get his uniform but that was the limit of his dreams, and even that had its drawbacks! He was issued with boots - "....and they've got to shine so I can see my face in'em!", he was issued with his uniform-"....I want creases pressed so as I can cut your throat on 'em and buttons wot shine!", and he was issued with kit-"....I want that webbin' blancoed so as it can be seen gleamin' proper!" - and that was only part if it. As far as the band was concerned, there wasn't one, not at Richmond anyway.

With the country being involved in all out war the allocation of manpower to regimental bands had very low priority and it was only due to the determination of Bandmaster "Chippy" Lester that one existed at all. He had managed to mould a band made up of time-expired veterans from the 2nd battalion which had returned after service on the North-West frontier and older reservists who had been recalled, augmented by newly recruited and hastily trained bandboys, but even that combination was away from barracks.

The Regimental Band, it transpired, was regularly sent off to play at official functions and was often away for weeks or even months on end, this was one of those periods and due to the absence of band personnel the bandboys were put into the custody of the infantry, so instead of sitting on a bandstand he found himself marching up and down the barrack square, turning right, turning left, coming to attention, standing at ease and learning how to be a "proper Soljer". Even had the band been in barracks he would still have had to undergo the usual six weeks "square bashing", but, somehow, with the band not being around everything seemed bizarre.

Within a very short time he had gained a pride in the regiment of which he was now part and he found another interest in learning its history. The regiment was formed in 1688. In the eighteenth century it was customary for a regiment to be named after its Colonel, who, in 1744 was Sir Charles Howard, it was therefore "Howard's Regiment", but there also happened to be another Colonel Howard in charge of a regiment - which caused great confusion. The problem was solved by colour - one regiment wore green facings to their uniform, the other buff, giving rise to the nickname "The Green Howards". In 1873 the Regimental Depot was built at Richmond, Yorkshire, and two years later the Princess of Wales, later to become Queen Alexandra, presented the regiment with new colours and it became known as "The Princess of Wales's Own". After many slight alterations of name over the ensuing years its modern title was finally adopted - "The Green Howards (Alexandra, Princess of Wales's Own

Yorkshire Regiment).

The Princess actually designed the cap badge herself: The Dannebrog (Cross of Denmark) interwoven with her initial "A", surrounded by a coronet. He soon became honoured to clean and polish that cap badge that now claimed his allegiance, for at last he had begun to feel he belonged - in the army he had found a surrogate family and a feeling of security that he had never known as an adolescent.

He also found a friend, Peter Parrish, another aspiring young musician whose background was uncannily similar to his own. Peter had, however, been reared in an orphanage in Hull, had a natural flair for all things musical and had joined the army as a bandboy in order to nurture it. Unknown to each other they must have "signed up" within hours of each other because, whereas Ernie's number was 440096, Peter's was 440097. The two of them gelled and "Ponky" was to become a very close companion. This friendship was to prove invaluable as time wore on. Leave was uncommon during those years but when it was given it was heart-rending for Ernie, and Peter, to see their colleagues eagerly preparing themselves to go home where, no doubt, they would parade proudly in their new uniform for the benefit of their families, while they had to make do with relying on the comradeship of others who would kindly offer them the hospitality of their homes when their parents permitted it but the feeling of a reliance on charity could not be avoided no matter how welcome their hosts made them.

At the end of six weeks of saluting, rifle drill and parades they would normally have started their musical training - but the band hadn't returned, so to prevent their getting bored the infantry N.C.O.'s found them something to occupy them. The next intake of raw recruits had arrived so they put them in with them to do it all over again!

Their second stint of basic training was, of course, far easier than the first, in fact they became the "stars" of the course and the counsellors of the "rookies", acting like veterans even though they had been in the army only a matter of weeks themselves! They grew over-confident and headed for the inevitable nasty fall. Part of the course was "map reading" where, after a few lessons on how to read a map the recruits were herded on to a canvas covered lorry and the back flaps closed. They would then be driven some five or six miles on to the Yorkshire moors, dropped off in pairs at different desolate spots, given a map and told to find their way home! On the first occasion this had proved a nightmare and, unable to differentiate between a stream and a footpath on the map, Ernie had wandered aimlessly and had finally arrived back at Richmond some six hours later, footsore and exhausted.

This time, however, they were "old hands". They managed to contrive themselves as a team and Ernie and Peter were duly dropped off in Swaledale. Dispensing with the map they looked around and spotted a farmhouse in the distance and made straight for it. They knocked on the door and woefully pleaded for help as they "were lost". The days had long passed when every stranger was treated as a likely enemy parachutist so they were taken in by a kindly sheepfarmer's wife and given tea and home-made scones. While they were enjoying their treat the door opened and a man said,

"He'll be all right now, but keep that paw bandaged if you can." It was the local veterinary surgeon and he, too, was offered scones and tea, which he accepted. The lady explained to him that the two young soldiers were lost and had to get back to Richmond.

"Richmond?" he said, "That's where I come from, I'll give you a lift."

So it was that the two orienteers found themselves back in Richmond within an hour of setting off! They had been the first pair dropped on the exercise and they realised it would look rather suspicious if they arrived back at barracks before the lorry that had taken them out had returned, so they decided to kill time by looking around the town. Unfortunately for them the Band Sergeant had chosen that same afternoon to go shopping and they all met on the High street. How are the mighty fallen! The "rookies" were most surprised, later, to see their guides and advisers doing fatigues .... painstakingly repairing damaged music with brown paper and paste.

Twelve weeks of basic military training did not, of course, go without any other hitches, three to be precise. The hyper-critical N.C.O.'s were ever watchful for breaches of their ultra-high standards and Ernie seemed to be unable to avoid getting grease marks on his uniform. On each occasion they were only the size of a piece of confetti but they were spotted by the eagle eyes of drill instructors, resulting in a severe "dressing down" and subsequent patient rubbing with a rag dipped in petrol.

Christmas came and went, and by March 1944 the band still had not returned. After six months of repeating a six week course the bandboys, as can well be imagined, had become experts so they were then used to help train the constant flow of "rookies" arriving at regular intervals. They helped to instruct foot drill, arms drill, early morning physical training in the gymnasium and assault courses, all of which were very distressing to the recruits but invigorating games to the, by then, fit and healthy youngsters.

The band finally returned for a reasonable stay and Ernie was summoned to the Bandmaster's office for his first interview. He was questioned by a small man who introduced himself as Bandmaster Lester A.R.C.M. He was told to place his hand flat on the table - he did so. He was then told to raise his fingers individually - he did so. That was the end of the examination, he was promptly told he was to play a clarinet. To this day Ernie has never fathomed out the reasoning behind the method of selection but in no way whatsoever does he disagree with its correctness. Peter was assigned to the trombone.

Ernie was issued with the only clarinet available, a sharp pitch Bb Simple System and, after being shown how to assemble it, he was bundled off back to the oblivion of the barrack room to practice! The band went off on its travels again leaving the little group of seven to their daily routine of fatigues, drill, "bull" and practice. "D.Day" came in June, flying bombs ravaged London in July and Paris was re-occupied in August - while Ernie practised, practised and practised. An N.C.O., Lance Corporal Beech, was eventually appointed to instruct the bandboys in army music but very little personal instruction was actually given and any real progress was made primarily by dint of personal enthusiasm and hard work - with which Ernie steadfastly persevered in spite of jibes and harassment from some who just wanted to waste time. Music, helped no doubt by discipline, had transformed the irresponsible boy into a dedicated and diligent young man.

Their time was not taken up solely with music as, apart from routine daily chores, the afternoons were spent with sergeant instructors from the Education Corps who gave them lessons in general subjects rather reminiscent of their schooldays, except that the history lessons were very biased towards military matters. Their overall education improved rapidly for now they paid strict attention and the damage caused by inattention and tomfoolery at school was quickly repaired.

After eighteen months Ernie became a very accomplished player and the clarinet was to prove to be the making of him, it enabled his natural musical talent to flourish and within a very short time he was where he had dreamed of being - on the bandstand playing 3rd clarinet, participating with the band on all their engagements. A springboard had been created for his future development.

He was still only seventeen when the European war ended but by then, apart from never-ending practice, he had played in the band all over the country, with activities stretching from military parades in all weathers to troop concerts, factory shows and retreat beatings. Venues ranged from village greens to city centres at concerts extolling the virtue of saving money for the war effort through mediums such as "Salute the Soldier", "Warships Week", "Wings for Victory" and "Holidays at Home", the list was endless. Transport was by way of army "three tonners", open top canvas covered lorries which belched fumes and in which they would crowd, huddled together in bad weather, gasping for a breath of fresh air. Very often they would arrive at a destination to find a complete lack of organisation, no beds, no food, no warmth and nothing to do except look forward to the next engagement. They accepted everything in good heart, however, fully realising that there were thousands of other troops actively fighting wars overseas who would gladly have changed places with them!

Ernie was so absorbed in his music that he never really noticed the passing of time and these formative years are but a fleeting moment in his memory. There had been little in the way of leave and the only time he saw his family during his elementary training years was when the band played at Whitby, just twenty-one miles from Scarborough. Mam and Leslie cycled over the moors to visit him and were forced to go to the unthought of expense of staying overnight at a guest house before the return trip the following day, but for Edith it was worth every penny she had sacrificed for the pleasure of seeing her Ernie play in public - assisted, she did acknowledge, by the Green Howards Regimental Band!

The dropping of the atomic bomb in 1945 brought the Second World War to an abrupt end and the slow process of demobilisation began as hundreds of thousands of men and women made the transition back to civilian life. Ernie, however, had signed on as a regular soldier and so, for him, there was no sudden change of routine. The "Save Money" campaigns came to a halt but the band was involved in countless celebratory parades all over the area and he now fully appreciated the reasons for his long wait for its return to Richmond in those early days.

Probably his proudest moment during those days was when the Green Howards were given the freedom of Scarborough in 1945. To show their appreciation of the service given by the regiment other Yorkshire towns had accorded it the honour of being Honorary Freemen and when he heard that Scarborough was to join the list he prayed he would be in the band selected to lead the march, with bayonets fixed, through his own home town. He was, though not on clarinet, he was asked to play the cymbals. As they marched through the familiar streets he scanned the crowds hoping to spot his mother but, if she was there, he did not see her. After the ceremony they were taken straight back to Richmond so the break with home continued.

Early in 1946 the band was ordered to join the 1st. Battalion of the Green Howards in Schonigen, near Helmstadt in Germany, on the border with the Russian zone. Ernie was, naturally, very excited at the idea of his first overseas posting, with the prospect of foreign travel and was consequently bitterly disappointed when it was realised that he was still under age to journey outside the United Kingdom under military regulations. He did not know how, and certainly didn't care, but somewhere, somehow, some juggling with rules must have been done, for the visit proceeded with one juvenile clarinetist seeing for the first time a conquered and devastated country with starvation, poverty and deprivation everywhere. The experience had a profound effect on his future outlook of life in general -if he sees need, if someone needs assistance, Ernie will always be found among the first to offer help.

The band was billeted in some of the houses in the village which were still habitable and from which the owners had been evicted. The furniture and fittings were as they had been left and the band savoured a standard of living many had never before experienced. As well as enjoying good accommodation and army rations they had all their chores such as laundry and household cleaning done by local German women who were grateful for payment, gifts of food or soap, and the even more welcome cigarettes - which had become the currency of the black market.

Ernie had had first hand experience of poverty and was still young enough to remember it clearly, but even he was distressed to see children queueing at army swill bins with broken pans, rusty tins and dented enamel bowls to scavenge in the left-overs for some scraps to eat. He found his thoughts inevitably reverting to his own childhood and was nauseated to make comparisons and so accept that even Cooks Row had been luxury when related to this. He understood, for the first time, the true horror of war and when he sadly observed its real victims he realised how fortunate we had been to be the victors.

When the continental tour ended in 1947 the band returned to England to resume its round of parades and concerts. In the summer they enjoyed welcome working holidays playing at some of the many seaside resorts where public entertainment had restarted. These included Weymouth and Bournemouth in the south and Morecambe and Scarborough in the north. Scarborough! He was home again and, in fulfilment of his childhood dream, actually playing on the floating bandstand in Peasholme Park!

The euphoria of the occasion was soon dispelled when he took advantage of the opportunity to pay a rare visit home. His relationship with the family, and Ted Stockell in particular, had deteriorated badly after the upset of that tragic teatime revelation in 1941. He had seen his mother only once since, when she had cycled to Whitby, but he thought that time may have had some healing effect and he decided to pay them a visit. There was another reason why he had to go - at the end of the war, service men received a gratuity based on their service, Ernie had been awarded eighty pounds which had been deposited in the Post Office Savings Bank by the army paymaster and the book sent to his home address - he took the opportunity to collect it.

He walked along Seamer Moor Road for the first time in uniform and he could not avoid glancing up at the windows to see if any of the neighbours may be looking out. He climbed the steps to 146 and knocked on the door. His mother opened it and clasped him in her arms, only to release him rapidly as a voice from inside asked,

"Who is it?"

"It's our Ernie! He's come home!"

"It's **your** Ernie ... and it's not his home." Ernie realised immediately that Ted Stockell had not mellowed and that he had probably made a mistake in coming, but he was now mature enough to persevere.

"Come in, son." Edith led him into the familiar house, very little had changed since he had left it. Ted Stockell was engrossed in a newspaper and did not even look up to acknowledge him. "Sit down, son," Edith said. "I'll make some tea."

Ernie was touched by the way she referred to him as "son". there was still a bond between them that nothing could destroy.

"I was hoping you'd call," she said, tipping water from the kettle into the teapot, "I saw in the paper that the band was in Peasholme, I would have come to see you, but..." she glanced fleetingly at the newspaper, ".... I couldn't get there."

She poured the tea and demanded to know all that had happened to him and what he had been doing.

"I saw you in the parade when the Green Howards got the freedom," she said, "I was on the Valley Bridge." He was pleased about that, he hadn't seen her but she had seen him, that's all that mattered.

"I've been to Germany," he said, "it was terrible there, mam. Not for us, I mean, but the German people. They're starving, and the kids ....."

"No more than they bloody well deserve." Ted Stockell interrupted. Ernie remembered Ted's injuries of the First World War and could understand his bitterness.

"The children don't, surely?" he asked.

"They started it again, it's their fault, not mine." Ted said from behind the paper, he still had not looked at Ernie. Ernie could sense that Ted was using the paper as a barrier and he wondered if the man really wanted to bridge the gap between them but was too proud to try. He changed the subject,

"How's Leslie?"

It didn't work. Ted did not attempt to answer and, after an embarrassing pause, Edith said,

"He's fine, he's out playing somewhere, probably up to mischief .... he's just like you used to be. You'll see him later .... how long can you stay son?"

"Not long, in fact I've sneaked off while they're packing up after the band concert - Peter's looking after my stuff. I shouldn't be here really, I've only got a few minutes."

"Well, when you get a proper leave you must come home, son, and tell us all you've been doing. You're always welcome, isn't he Ted?"

There was no reply, not even a grunt.

"Is there anything you need for when you go back, son?"

"No, nothing mam, I'm fine. But I would like my post office book, they would have sent it here. Did you get it?"

The paper dropped.

"So that's it! I thought he wouldn't come back unless he was after something. Yes, we've got the book, it's in that drawer, and that's where it's staying!"

"But it's mine."

"Yours? Yours? Of all the bloody cheek! For all those years we brought you up without getting a penny ... and now you've got the bloody nerve to come here demanding a measly eighty bloody quid! Eighty quid for years of food and lodging! You can bugger off! You're no child of ours and you bloody well know it .... it's us who deserve that money, not you, and you're not having it!"

Ernie was completely nonplussed. He could see Edith turning white with rage and he realised that he had damaged any relationship she may have established with Ted, but he was determined he would not be subjected to humiliation again. A fierce argument developed between him and Ted while Edith sat in a chair, crying,

"It's his, Ted." she said.

"Oh, so now we know whose side you're on!" Ted snapped, "He's brought nothing but bloody misery to this house."

"It **is** his!"

Ted Stockell rose from his chair, went to the sideboard and opened a drawer. He took out a post office book and hurled it at Ernie.

"Go on! Take your bloody money .... and get out of my house! Don't you ever have the bloody cheek to show your face anywhere near it again!"

Ernie picked up the book, placed it in his breast pocket and left the room.

"Bye, mam," he said, "God bless!"

Before he reached the front door, Edith had caught up with him and clasped him in her arms,

"Don't go, son! Please! Not this way!" her grasp grew stronger. He had to force her arms from round his chest. Tears filled his eyes. He took the book from his pocket.

"Mam, I want you to have this."

"Never, son, I've been looking after that for you, hoping you'd come for it one day. I never thought it would turn out like this." He put his arms round her and kissed her,

"Bye, mam," he repeated, and left the house. The walk back to Peasholme Park was made in utter misery. He left Scarborough with the band, a very unhappy man, not knowing if he would ever see his mother again.

In the life of a soldier, however, there was no time for self-pity or recrimination and the end of the year found the Regimental Band back in Germany, this time to Celle and its surrounding area, with the bonus of trips to Berlin. He was now eighteen, he was fully accepted as a member of the band but his appetite for music was far from satisfied. His one ambition was to become a solo clarinet player and to this end he spent every available hour practising. He managed to borrow the parts played by the soloist and could be found in odd corners, at any time, struggling to perfect them. It was through this that, one day in 1947, he lost all track of time and missed a band practice. Normally, practices were held every morning after breakfast but occasionally, usually prior to an engagement, the Band Sergeant would call an extra one in the afternoon. Ernie was engrossed in his own private rehearsal after lunch when he suddenly remembered that an extra practice had been called that day, for two o'clock. He had lost all track of time. He packed up his clarinet and ran, but as he approached the practice area he could hear the band had started. His choice was to face the wrath of the Bandmaster or sneak away and hope he wouldn't be missed. He chose the latter and, with no repercussion forthcoming, was relieved to have got away with it.

Two days later, however, as he was leaving after morning practice he heard a voice,

"Waites!" He turned,

"Yes, sergeant."

"Report to the Bandmaster, immediately!"

Within minutes a very worried Ernie knocked timidly on the great man's door. He inwardly cursed the band sergeant.. He had missed a practice, he realised that., but surely the sergeant could have reprimanded him himself and not reported him to the bandmaster. After all, he wasn't the first one to have done it, and in the past...

"Come in!" interrupted his thoughts. He nervously opened the door, entered, and stood smartly to attention.

"096 Waites, Sir."

The great man stared at him,

"I hear you missed a band practice the other day." There was no point in trying to deny it,

"Yes, Sir."

"Why?"

"I was doing solo practice, Sir, and lost track of time."

"You do a lot of solo practice, I hear."

"Yes, Sir".

"Good, and you're going to do a lot more. I've had the most favourable reports about you from the band sergeant. I'm recommending you for advanced training, to Kneller Hall."

Kneller Hall! Ernie felt himself swaying, he felt tears coming, he closed his eyes to steady himself.

"At ease, Waites! I've been keeping an eye on you myself, and I think both you and the band will benefit. You've done well, congratulations!"

In the corridor outside the office, Ernie had to compose himself. For the first time in his life someone had recognised his dedication. He was going to Kneller Hall! It was the greatest advance any bandsman could dream of -he, the little lad who had started on Grandma's harmonium, was going to the Royal Military School of Music!

He walked on a cloud back to his hut where he met a barrage of questions,

"Had a good rollocking, Ernie?"

"Thought you'd be in the glasshouse by now!"

"That'll teach you to swot!"

He waited for some form of silence,

"I'm going to Kneller Hall." he announced.

Now not all band members had Ernie's enthusiasm, in fact some of them were there only because they had found the band a good life, and intended to get the most out of it by doing the least. He was in a minority, and his euphoria was not universally shared.

"Are you going?"

"Of course."

"You must be bloody mad! I've heard the bullshit there is worse than the Guards! Poor bleeding sod!"

CHAPTER EIGHT

During the Crimea War, the Duke of Cambridge visited the war zone and on a notable occasion revued the troops there. The revue was a major one involving many regiments, each with its own regimental band. All went well while the bands played as individual units but then the bands were massed to play the National Anthem. The result was bedlam. It seemed that each band played the anthem in its own key and used its own arrangement and the resulting chaos was enough to make the Duke realise that there must be some sort of standardisation of military music to cope with such situations. It is not recorded what comments the Duke made but, when he arrived back in England, he founded The Royal Military School of Music. There was a grand house, in what then was the pleasant countryside well to the south of London, which had been built by Sir Geoffrey Kneller, the court painter, and it was there that the school was founded.

Since then, of course, London has expanded to devour the countryside and today Kneller Hall, has been swallowed up by the capital's southern suburbs. It is at Whitton, near Twickenham, merely a stone's throw from the famous rugby stadium. It is a stately mansion, built in a similar style to Hampton Court, flagpoles surmount imposing towers and great columns support the portico at its entrance. This was Ernie's destination as he walked from Whitton Station, kitbag over his shoulder, on a November day in 1947.

As he approached he could see nothing of the Hall for it is surrounded by a high brick wall but directly opposite a public house appropriately named "The Duke of Cambridge" he came to a pair of heavy gateposts and realised he had arrived. He was at the rear of a large mansion house and just inside the entrance was a guard room where he reported and was directed along a time-worn path. He was overawed by his surroundings, buildings he never even dared to dream he'd ever see. Kneller Hall was on his right, dominating his view, while on his left was a building he assumed to be a recreation area or, perhaps the NAAFI, he'd find out sooner or later. What was obvious was the huge concrete structure in front of him - the biggest bandstand he'd ever seen. He was now at the front of the main building and before it was a huge gravelled parade ground. Just beyond the bandstand were a collection of huts, laid out like the spokes of a wheel. One of these was to be his home for the next twelve months. There was some accommodation in the house itself, but nowhere near enough to house the 150 or so students and pupils who arrived each year from the bands of all regiments. Some student bandmasters lived in the house but the pupils were accommodated in the huts, each hut being named after a famous composer. Inside the Hall were the administration offices, a chapel and a warren of staircases and corridors composed of small box-like practice rooms. Ernie reached the hutted area and was pleasantly surprised to find he had been allocated to "Elgar" Squad. This seemed to be a good omen because, as his musical knowledge had developed over the years, Elgar had become his favourite composer.

"Elgar" hut was just one of a collection of wooden buildings of First World War vintage, noteworthy only for the sparseness of furnishings. It held twenty-five iron framed beds and by each bed was a tall wooden locker. Heating was achieved by a circular cast iron stove standing on a concrete slab in the centre of the hut with a stove-pipe that penetrated the ceiling above. The brown lino on the floor glistened from years of daily buffing, sometimes done using the standard long handled "buffer" but more often by the unauthorised, but far quicker, method of laying a blanket on the floor and placing on it a folded mattress on which one man would sit, to add weight, while others, holding two corners of the blanket, dragged him up and down the hut.

Ernie soon settled in to the strict regime and quickly found out that if any student had assumed that Kneller Hall was to be a "working holiday" he was soon disenchanted, for in spite of a full time study of music they were still subjected to the rigid military routines of drill parades, room inspections, cross country runs, cookhouse fatigues and the hundred and one other complications that the army considered essential to normal daily life, but in spite of them all, his determination never wavered. Not all the intake agreed with his outlook however, because over twenty-five per cent of them were "R.T.U'd" (Returned to Unit) within two months, and many more were to follow as the training progressed.

He was fortunate to find a fellow devotee in Ray Pinkney, an Eb Bass player from the Kings Own Yorkshire Light Infantry. Ray was as obsessed with music as Ernie and they quickly became inseparable, going to any lengths to indulge in their common passion for anything musical. This helped them face each day stoically.

A typical day started with Reveille at 6.30, followed by "Hut Cleaning" which meant buffing floors to a sheen, laying out kit and preparing lockers and ablutions for daily inspection. Breakfast would be at 7.30, hut inspection at 8.15 and drill parade at 8.30. At 9.00 everyone would assemble on the massive concrete bandstand in the grounds and a band of over two hundred, including students, would attack the music selected to be played at the summer concerts which were given from June to September. This gigantic band rehearsal would be constantly interrupted as pupils left to attend individual lessons given by visiting professors on their various instruments. This bandstand practice, taken with all musicians standing, would last until 10.00 when it was time for the welcome NAAFI break, then it was back on the concrete box for another hour and a half. Even the climate could cause no break to the routine - if the weather was very bad everything transferred to the gymnasium!

Dinner was therefore very welcome at 12.30 and at 1.30 everyone would go to the huge sports field and line up in rows, suitably spaced apart, each with his own music stand. There they would do "Individual Practice" - probably the most disliked part of the day for there was no way one could escape the torment and cacophony of hundreds of wailing instruments each doing its own thing! There would be a short break at 3.00 after which the bedlam would resume until 4.00, when silence mercifully descended for tea. After tea there would be "Extra Practice" for those who had been discovered transgressing in any way throughout the day, then normal harmony and theory lessons until 7.30 p.m. The rest of the evening was their own and pupils had their individual ways of relaxing - Ernie and Ray would grab their instruments and make their way to the rehearsal rooms behind the NAAFI and practise anything from Bach Fugues to Overtures until they were forcibly evicted at 9.00!

Before any of this life became routine, however, Ernie was to suffer the biggest psychological setback of his nineteen years, and that occurred on his very first day at Kneller Hall. The morning had been spent on formalities of billeting, time-tables and allocation to tutors and in the afternoon he reported to a student bandmaster with his clarinet. He had no qualms about this whatsoever, he could play and play well, so well, he admits, he was getting rather cocky about his ability. How are the mighty fallen! He was, of course, still playing the instrument given to him in those early days as a bandboy; it was the only one available at the time, a sharp pitched Bb Simple system. The bandmaster took one look at it, "Good God!" he said, "You can take that outside right away, throw it in the dustbin, and then report to the instrument store."

Ernie was completely flabbergasted but did as he was told. At the instrument store they gave him a new clarinet-a Boehme system. It seemed the army had standardised their clarinet fingering systems and hence this issue of the Boehme. But the Boehme fingering system was completely different from the Bb simple ....he couldn't play it. He was back to square one! He tried but found it more difficult than when he couldn't play at all, for then it was just a matter of learning something new, now he found that while his brain was reading the music his fingers were still following the fingering on which he had learned to play, and had been playing for years. It was a crushing blow to his aspirations. The setback only made him more determined to succeed, but first he had to re-learn everything he knew. He practised, practised, practised, and soon, helped by Ray and their private practice sessions, he regained his old proficiency.

He was greatly assisted in this by his tutor. Ernie was fortunate to be assigned to George Garside, a Professor of the Clarinet who had recently retired from the London Symphony Orchestra where he had been 1st Clarinet for a long and distinguished career both as an orchestral player and soloist. Ernie accepts that the value of George Garside's instruction and encouragement can never be overestimated, for he brought all his experience to bear on a pupil who literally devoured everything he had to offer. George Garside, on the other hand, must have taken a great interest in his student for he would invite him to his flat in Twickenham on Sunday afternoons where Ernie would play for him, accompanied on the piano by Mrs. Garside - lessons that were given absolutely free of charge and which largely contributed to the attainment of the extremely high standard he eventually achieved. The relationship between Ernie and George Garside would appear to have grown closer than the normal pupil/teacher association, as Ernie always speaks of him as he would a dear friend.

For their individual lessons the pupils would report to one of the tiny brick and concrete tutor rooms where the only furnishing would be two chairs and a music stand. The professor would sit on one chair and the pupil on the other, with the music stand. Ernie described one such session:

"I walked in with my clarinet and music book, and there was this chap, looking rather like a younger Einstein, he pointed to the music stand and said "Come in boy! Sit down! Page Seven! Play!" Then he had me playing scales and exercises, non-stop. After my allotted time there was a knock at the door when the next pupil arrived. Some of the pupils just wanted to skive, and George knew it. He said to the newcomer,'Right, boy, what do you want to do, play cards, smoke or play the clarinet ?... I don't care what you do but don't waste my time!' The lad was honest and actually said 'Smoke'. It didn't bother him at all, he just said, "Right, you smoke, I'll give my time to someone who wants to play' ... and I'd get an extra lesson! This happened on several occasions."

George Garside had very poor eyesight, in fact it would seem he must have been almost blind at the time Ernie was at Kneller Hall, but he would never admit to it, although it was obvious to everyone. For example, he would take out his hunter watch and apparently look at it. He!'d then hold it for Ernie to see and say, "What time do you make it?" Ernie would look and say "Half past two, sir." (or whatever time it was) whereupon George would say "Yes, so do I" and put the watch back in his pocket.

In the NAAFI was a large low fireplace above which was a wide mantelshelf. George would, at times, feel his way into the NAAFI and lean on the mantelshelf, thinking it was the bar, and wait to be served. This caused great amusement to some pupils, which greatly upset Ernie, who would lead him to the bar or sit him down and fetch his tea.

At the Sunday practices in George's home he would talk at great lengths about his life of music and Ernie would sit listening, absorbed. Life is full of co-incidences and Ernie was pleasantly surprised one day when George told him that, some ten years before, he had played for a while with a resident orchestra on a bandstand in a Yorkshire resort called Scarborough. Ernie was pleased to be able to tell him he remembered it well, although he was only an entranced little boy at the time! George also warned Ernie not to emulate some of his own shortcomings as a young musician. He told him to concentrate on his score and not, as he had been prone to do, to sit admiring the legs of pretty young ladies sitting in the front row! It seems that, on more than one occasion when playing with the London Symphony Orchestra as a young man he would be so taken with such admiration that he would look away from his music and miss his entry.

Such a relationship between pupil and teacher must have been of enormous advantage to Ernie, and he had the sense to take full advantage of it.

In addition to all the work and training during the week, Ray and Ernie would attend Twickenham Parish Church on Sundays to sing in the choir, thus helping them develop both a musical ear and voice production which were to serve them well in the future - as did their regular sessions of a game they invented, a game that was quite simple in concept but extremely difficult in practice. They had formed a small "band" and each member would have a copy of "Hymns Ancient and Modern" from which one of them would choose a hymn. They would all start to play but at the end of each verse they would swop instruments, transposing at the same time! After a few weeks of this they found they could play each other's instruments quite passably, and in some cases, quite well, and consequently found themselves not limited just to the one. Ernie today is an accomplished player of the clarinet and saxophone, but can also play most wind instruments at a high standard. All this, of course, was to prove invaluable when, later in life, he began composing and arranging, as he understands the technical difficulties each player experiences. It was also through these "play" sessions that Ernie wrote his very first arrangement - a Bach fugue, arranged for Tuba and Clarinet! (himself and Ray, of course.)

Two episodes of life in Kneller Hall are imprinted on Ernie!'s memory. On November 20th, 1947 the whole school was gathered in the large practice room to listen to the broadcast of the wedding of Princess Elizabeth to Prince Philip, Duke of Edinburgh. The big attraction was that the Kneller Hall trumpeters played the fanfares - fanfares of which they had all grown thoroughly sick, having spent weeks overhearing the endless rehearsals!

The other was a mysterious succession of events one afternoon while they were lined up on the playing field for their usual cacophonous "individual practice". Ernie was practising and, despite the noise of dozens of different instruments playing as many different melodies all at once, he detected an alien sound. He looked round and there was a film cameraman fluttering about through the rows. Later on he was surprised to see the same character appear when they were on the bandstand. It transpired that someone was making a film about Kneller Hall and as a reward for the "extras", namely the whole intake, they were taken in groups for a night out in London . . . to the Windmill Theatre and its famous nude showgirls!

At the end of their training some pupils were selected to take part in a competition which included all aspects of music, theory, and instrumentation as well as competence in playing their instrument, the entrants being nominated by the professors and then gradually eliminated, until eighty names remained. These were then subjected to a searching examination which commenced at 8.00 a.m. when they all assembled to draw from a hat the order in which they would face the gruelling practical tests. Ernie drew number 47 and finally entered the examination room at 3.30 in the afternoon, where he found himself facing three examiners, all either Bandmasters or senior Directors of Music. The examination was daunting by any standards. First he had to play all scales and chords in both major and minor keys, then tested on Dominant and Diminished chords. This was followed by the playing of a test piece and a melody, selected by the examiners, of which he had no foreknowledge and which he had to sight-read. In his case it was a selection from Rigoletto, chosen, he found out later, by George Garside. He was then given music which he had to transpose on sight into both higher and lower keys before being allowed to demonstrate his ability by playing something he had chosen himself. Ernie chose "Annie Laurie" which he had to play in every conceivable key, both major and minor. As if this was not enough he was then obliged to face a barrage of oral questions fired at him by all three examiners.

The endless practice to which Ernie and Ray had subjected themselves paid off handsomely, for they had been rehearsing the known parts of the tests for most of their spare time and this, coupled with the fact that Ray could play the Eb Bass with the agility of a clarinet player meant that it came as no surprise to anybody that Ray was awarded the First Prize. Ernie finished a breathless fifth out of eighty contestants, which was in itself an achievement considering that, from his first day at Kneller Hall he had played an instrument that had been, at first, completely foreign to him.

At the end of the course Ernie was presented with the runner-up parchment for "Exceptional proficiency on clarinet" with the recommendation that he should return to Kneller Hall at a later date for training as a Bandmaster.

And so his year of intensive training ended, by which time Ernie had become an acknowledged accomplished musician. We cannot, however, leave Kneller Hall without recording an incident in his latter days there which made Ernie recall his mischievous boyhood. He was certainly not the culprit on this occasion but his own early expertise made him, in some way, admire the still unknown perpetrators!

The bandstand was a huge concrete structure composed of concentric semi-circular steps, each rising higher than the one on front and on it would stand the masses of instrumentalists. Every week a major concert would be given, the grassed area in front being filled with heavy folding chairs which the band itself had to set out ready for the invited audience. Each item on the programme would be conducted by a different student bandmaster but the final piece would usually be conducted by the Director of Music himself and this finale would, of course, be a spectacular, such as the "1812 Overture". On this particular occasion the Director of Music had chosen "The Battle of Waterloo" and to perform it the 200 or so musicians had been divided into five units. Four of these were marching bands, each representing a country, and they would march off and on the bandstand playing the music of the nation they represented as it occurred in the composition. The fifth group remained on the bandstand throughout while the remainder of the pupils who were not playing were given the job of providing sound effects from behind. Some of these had bass drums, cymbals and anything else that could be banged to create battle effects while the rest were given fireworks and smoke bombs to set-off at pre-arranged times.

The spectacular piece was going well and the atmosphere building to its climax. The Director of Music was sweating under the strain of controlling such a mammoth event and the bandsmen were getting breathless both through blowing and intense concentration. No one ever found out how, and no one ever confessed why, but suddenly, at an exhilarating stage of the battle sequence, a smoke bomb came flying over the back of the bandstand and landed in the middle of the musicians.

Thick pungent smoke enveloped the band in seconds, no one could see their music, let alone read it, and Ernie remembers gasping for air while trying to follow the Director's flailing arms through the fog, not knowing whether he was trying to keep tempo or waft the smoke from his face!

The audience was very impressed by the reality of the interpretation but, needless to say, the "effects" were never repeated!

At the end of their course in November 1948 the pupils returned to their various units. Ernie arrived back at Richmond Barracks carrying his newest prized possession, a Boehme clarinet. He had, of course, had to return the one he had used during the course to the music store, but he had been fortunate to find a fellow pupil who had one which he wanted to sell. The price was reasonable and Ernie bought it - the first musical instrument he had ever owned.

To his disappointment he was not welcomed by the band, they were away in Khartoum. He was sent to a transit camp at Strensall, near York, where he understood the next step was to be a transfer to the 1st Battalion, but then news arrived that the regiment was to move to the Canal Zone. So it was that he found himself a member of an advance party going to Suez to prepare for its arrival and in December he embarked on the troopship "Dunera" for Port Said, realising he would thus spend Christmas Day in the Mediterranian Sea.

It all seemed a gloomy prospect until, walking on deck as the ship headed towards Biscay he was delighted to see a familiar figure - Ray Pinkney! What followed was inevitable.

All gloom disappeared and as the ship ploughed the Mediterranean the tribulations of ship's food, crowded mess decks and sardine-like sleeping arrangements in hammocks strung from the ceiling, were forgotten as their hastily formed band found any available space to entertain their fellow passengers. Even Christmas Day was a happy one because they were together again, doing what they enjoyed most - making music. Instead of dragging, the days flew by until they reached Port Said. This was Ernie's destination and the two friends exchanged sorrowful "Goodbye's" as he disembarked, leaving Ray to continue on the long journey to re-join his regiment in Malaya.

CHAPTER NINE

When he left the troopship Ernie, now dressed in tropical uniform of khaki shorts, shirt and webbing, was directed to an enormous camp of canvas tents sited just outside Port Said. Here hundreds of men going to, and coming from, their various units were housed temporarily while their travel arrangements were finalised. He was a lonely young man sharing a tent with three complete strangers who were as "brassed off" as he was. There was nothing to do except wait, think, wait, speculate and wait. At each daily parade individuals and groups would be called for and dispatched on their way but it was a full week before he was called. He was told that the "'Advance Party" of the Green Howards had left Khartoum and he was to meet them at a desert camp to prepare for the arrival of the battalion. He was sent off with his kitbag, clarinet and travel documents to the railway station where he boarded a train heading down the track bordering the Canal, heading for Suez.

From his school books he had imagined the area would have been a sweaty desolate space of nothingness and was therefore surprised to find it was cold enough for him to need to wear a cardigan and that the landscape around the Canal was green with vegetation. After a few miles, however, the green disappeared suddenly and his imagined landscape took its place. Sitting in the crowded train on a seat made of wooden slats he could see nothing but sand and sand dunes, cut in two by the Canal on his left. School lessons also took life when he saw along the Canal bank, Egyptian peasants drawing water from the canal with their nodding shadufs.

After passing the Bitter Lakes, the landscape became even more desolate and all he could see from the right hand window was sand stretching to a horizon which was obscured by mountains in the far distance. His last overseas travel had been in Germany - this was a complete contrast and he began to wonder what was in store for him, he was soon to find out.

All along the Suez Canal were military camp sites dotted at some four mile intervals. These had been laid down for the defence of the Canal and it was to one of these that Ernie finally arrived, tired, hungry and dirty from the smoke of the engine. The "Advance Party" had got there the day before and preparations for making camp were well under way. His being a bandsman meant nothing to the working group - he was pitched into the basic hard work of the pioneerng soldier.

The camp was about a thousand yards square, its perimeter being marked by coils of barbed wire. In one corner there were some permanent flat roofed buildings which housed the cookhouse, officers' mess, sergeants' mess, administration and showers but all amenities were at a bare minimum level - the "showers", for example, consisted of an open pipe which dropped water on to a concrete slab below. In the centre of this huge square rows of tents were being erected and Ernie found himself a member of a squad where, armed with a wooden mallet, he assisted in rigging the hundreds of tents which the regiment would occupy. Each tent housed four men and they were laid out in straight lines, lines would eventually be allocated to the different companies which made up the battalion. When the band arrived it would be housed in "H.Q" line but, during this construction time, the twenty or so members of the party lived together in a few tents. The only means of illumination was a hurricane lamp and the sand was so infested with various bugs, lizards, scorpions and other creepy crawlies that they had to stand the legs of their beds in discarded tin cans filled with creosote to deter any unwelcome nocturnal visitors. Toilet facilities were non-existent, consisting merely of large trenches dug in the sand and covered with a wooden boards. Ernie recalls one of his greatest fears when using them was the thought of an adventurous beetle jumping up from the depths! As time went on and a latrine became insanitary the trench would be covered with quicklime and filled in and a new one excavated.

On the third night Ernie took his turn of guard duty and spent the time marching round the camp armed with an unloaded rifle and a pickaxe handle, listening to the cheeps and chirps of insects and trying to prevent his imagination from running riot. He heard nothing untoward as his tour of duty expired, neither did his fellow guards, but when dawn broke they were astounded to see an empty space which, the previous evening, had been filled by a tent! Naturally, the guards received a blasting from the officer in charge but it was clearly not the first occasion such a thing had occurred and with so few men trying to watch a two-mile stretch of wire against expert thieves the episode was accepted as part of desert life. In fact they were all going to discover that the "locals" were accomplished pilferers of anything left unattended for more than seconds!

These were hard days for Ernie, made worse by the fact that, in the quiet of the evening, he could hear music in the distance - the Royal Marines were encamped about three miles away and the sound of their bugles spanned the gap between them. It was a happy day when, some ten days later, the camp was suddenly full of army lorries, two of which were carrying the band. He rushed to greet them and to his delight one of the first to leap over the tail-board was Peter Parrish.

"Ponky!"
"Ernie!" They said in unison.
"How was Kneller Hall?" Peter asked.

"Great!" Ernie replied, "How's the band been?"

"Spot on," Peter said, "in fact, it was when you'd gone that we found out what had been wrong with the clarinets!"

He dodged the playfully flung fist and the two friends helped to unload the band "gharrie". The amount of luggage carried by a military band is almost unbelievable, for, apart from cases containing all the instruments and music stands there are boxes of music holding the band library.

That evening, ensconced in their allotted tent, they began a long dialogue exchanging adventures, Ernie telling the story of Kneller Hall and Peter the travels, and trials, of the band.

The band, it appeared, was sadly depleted. With the end of the war many members had been demobilised and reservists had returned to civilian life. Only half of the band Ernie had left still remained, mainly those who, like Peter and Ernie, had signed on for nine years' service.

"Hey! But we've got one new addition! Wait 'til you meet her!"

"Her?" Ernie asked, furrowing his brow, "Her?"

"Aye, Salome."

"Come off it, Ponky!"

"It's right, Juddy Judson found her in Khartoum."

"I'm not having that! Reg Lester wouldn't stand for a woman around, let alone an Egyptian bint."

"Oh, it's not a bint, it's a bloody monkey! - and I hate the bloody sight of it - and it hates me too. I'm sure of that! Anyway, you'll meet it tomorrow . . and that's another thing .. .. Reg Lester's gone."

"Gone? Where?"

"Don't know, retired I think, we've got a new Bandmaster, Jerry Jarrett.

"What's he like?"

"Seems a good bloke, nowhere near as military minded as Reg - throws much more responsibility on to us. I think you'll get on well with him .... you know, seeing as you're part of the bleedin' elite - Kneller Hall trained!"

He fell back on his bed as Ernie pushed him over. They extinguished the hurricane lamp and slept.

The next morning, after parade, the band sergeant told Ernie to report to the Bandmaster and with great curiosity he met Jerry Jarrett for the first time. As Peter had told him, he found the new bandmaster to be very approachable and was pleased he had taken the interest and trouble to send for him so quickly to congratulate him on his course results. He explained a new infrastructure that was being introduced; bandsmen were going to be graded on a "star" system, one to five, and Ernie was, as of then, of "Five Star" status. He then told him he was to report to the Commanding Officer to receive the certificates awarded by Kneller Hall.

"Thank you, sir." Ernie said, turned about smartly and went to march from the room. As he reached the door he heard

"Waites!"

He turned again, "Sir?"

" ...and from now on, you are solo clarinet. Congratulations."

Ernie left the office and marched to meet the Commanding Officer feeling ten feet tall. He'd done it! His ambition was fulfilled. He was Solo Clarinet in the Green Howards Regimental Band. The chrysalis had at last metamorphosised into a butterfly.

From then on even the desert seemed to lose some of its repugnance. He became acclimatised to the boredom of daily life and spent his abundance of spare time practising even more. The one thing he never overcame was the revulsion of the flies. They were everywhere, big buzzing insects that seemed to pervade everything. Around the camp perimeter dozens of cages of raw meat had been hung in an attempt to attract them away from the cookhouse and living areas, but to little avail, and the sight, on entering the mess, of thirty or so trestle tables completely covered with a living black tablecloth was enough to defy even the sturdiest of stomachs to accept food. They would be swept aside only to fill the air for a few seconds and then return almost immediately .

For security reasons a room in the permanent buildings had been made available as a band store and it was there that Ernie went as soon as it was possible to borrow music to practise. The storeman was Juddy Judson, who had made it his own living quarters. Ernie went in,

" Morning Juddy!" he said, "Can I have the solo clarinet for La Traviata?"

"Hang on a minute."

Ernie waited while Judson began sifting through files of music stacked in boxes against the far wall and marvelled how quickly Juddy had organised the place. It had been swept and the instrument cases were all stowed methodically. Automatically his eyes wandered over the variously shaped cases, the drums, the basses, the trombones .... suddenly he froze, momentarily stunned, something small was definitely about to crawl up his leg, he could feel a slight weight on his foot. It moved. "Keep still!", he told himself, "don't move." Was it a scorpion? No, too heavy. A snake? He began to sweat. It was now at the top of his boot. He forced himself to turn his head, very slowly, and glance downwards. To his surprise he saw the green and white regimental colours!

"Oh, there you are!" Judson said, "Come here, you little bugger!"

He dived at Ernie's boot and snatched the culprit .

"You've not met yet, have you?" he asked, "Ernie - this is Salome, Salome - meet Ernie!"

The monkey looked ridiculous. It was a small grass monkey dressed in an old football sock which Judson had adapted as a jersey. It leaped out of his hands and landed on Ernie's shoulder, where it promptly urinated. Ernie stood astounded as the liquid ran down his shirt.

"Oh, don't let that bother you," Judson said, "she does that to everybody. Here's your music."

Ernie removed his shirt, wiped himself with it and returned to his tent. Peter was there,

"Ah! I see you've met Salome!"

"She pissed on me!"

"She would, she's a good judge of clarinet players!"

Life in the Canal zone was very monotonous as the only area available for any sort of recreation was within the camp perimeter and, apart from infrequent visits to Port Suez or the local open-air army cinema, time hung heavily on everyone's hands. Consequently the Regimental Band was constantly called upon to entertain and to do so in addition to normal parades and general military duties. The camp was in the desert about ten miles from Suez and, at weekends, occasionally one could get a lift into the port on a visiting lorry or, if so inclined, could take the local ramshackle native bus that ran on the road parallel to the Canal. The army cinema, the "Britannia", was a collection of wooden benches set up in the open air a mile or so down this road towards Port Tewfik but, obviously, could operate only after darkness had fallen. This was a permanently built facility which also provided a NAAFI canteen but, once again, a visit there was made easier with some form of transport, an advantage that was an instinctive challenge to Bill Fraser.

Bill was an enigma to Ernie. He must have been the perfect soldier in the eyes of the parade N.C.O.'s, always immaculate in his dress; buttons polished and boots gleaming, for he was ever cleaning his uniform and his kit. He was also a brilliant musician, an accomplished player of euphonium and bass instruments, a skill he had learned before he joined the regiment when he played in Salvation Army bands. To all intents he had everything needed for rapid advancement but he had an Achilles heel - a fetish for wheels and anything that ran on them. He must have been a very contented baby, being pushed in a pram but had matured into a Jekyll and Hyde - a military paragon that could transform into thief at the sight of a wheel! If the Post Corporal's bike suddenly went missing everyone knew exactly where to look for it; if a motor bike disappeared from the Motor Transport Pool, a visit to Bill Fraser's alter-ego would locate its whereabouts.

Bill was therefore probably the most avid cinema-goer in the band and reprimands, admonishments and punishments did not seem to deter his obsession.

They had been at the camp for about a month when Ernie and Peter decided to take the opportunity to visit Port Suez. The cinema had shown "Casablanca" the week before and their curiosity had been aroused to see how Suez compared. When a lorry was bound for the port that Saturday they were among the first to leap aboard for a lift. By the time it left camp it was full of passengers and among them was Bill Fraser. When the lorry dropped them off to go about its official business they found themselves in a square in the bazaar area and were immediately besieged by Arabs persistently trying to sell them anything from magic potions to live snakes. They made their way up a narrow alley bordered by open-fronted shops stacked with merchandise; hammered metalwork, fabrics and fly-ridden food all in a grand mish-mash of eternal haggling of raucous voices. The shopkeepers, dressed in long jubbahs, ridiculously contrasted with the names above the shops; "P. O'Mulligan", "S. Doherty", "J. McTavish"! Ernie decided that there must have been a recent immigration of Irish and Scots who were dark skinned with a liking for long shirts and fezzes!

Bill joined the hagglers and eventually came away with a butterfly brooch, allegedly made of filigree silver.

"I'll send this home," he said, ". . . to my mother."

Ernie and Peter just glanced at each other and Bill never realised how such an innocent remark could hurt.

After an hour of shop gazing and mingling with a crowd in cosmopolitan dress ranging from western fashion to women in purdah they found themselves back in the square where, incongruously, amongst the carts and battered bicycles, stood a military jeep and an American car. They could only assume that its owner had come sightseeing from the town area or its owner had brought a visitor to savour the "Casbah". Whatever the reason, Bill Fraser was drawn to the car like a magnet.

There was no sign of any of the occupants and Bill started peering in the open window of the Buick,

"Hell! Just look at this!"

"Come on Bill," Peter said, "let's see what's up there."

Bill was not for moving, he was walking round the car covetously, relishing every piece of gleaming metal and admiring the white walled tyres.

"I don't like the look of this," Ernie said, "let's go." The two of them hastily retreated down another market alley leaving Bill to his inevitable fate. They stopped to watch a "gilly-gilly" man extracting money from gullible members of his small crowd who were betting on which of three shells the pea would be under when Ernie looked back.

"Bloody Hell, Ponky, look!"

The car had gone and two military police were gazing round the square, then they boarded the jeep and drove off at high speed, scattering chickens from a kerbside vendor's cane cage.

"What's the stupid sod done this time?" Peter asked,

"I know what I'm doing," Ernie replied, "I'm getting as far away as I can!"

They pushed their way as best they could through the shoppers but had gone only a hundred yards or so when a breathless voice behind them said,

"What's the rush? Why didn't you wait for me? I only went in that shop to get some figs for Salome, and when I came out, you'd gone!"

"See, Ponky," Ernie said, "....give a dog a bad name.."

"What are you on about?" Fraser asked.

Peter shrugged his shoulders and laughed, "Nothing, Bill," he said, "....Nothing.

Juddy Judson was delighted when Fraser gave him the bag of figs,

"Hey, she'll love these, nice of you to think of her, lads"

"I wasn't thinking of her," Fraser replied, "I thought if she had a go at those she'd leave my bloody sweets alone!"

Salome was a simian jackdaw, she would steal anything and then jump up to a place where she was just out of reach and apparently taunt the owner. Nothing was safe from her pilfering; watches, lighters, cigarettes - and Peter Parish swore that she kept a special look-out for when his back was turned. Her main love, however, was sweets which she would grab and then leap with her prize to the top of a locker where she would disdainfully unwrap them and throw the paper to the floor. It was through this routine that Ernie became her mortal enemy. One day, when she was around, he deliberately left a pretty blue "sweet" on a table by his side. She was on to it instantly and took it up to her "perch" where she opened it and thrust it in her mouth. It was the blue screw of salt from a packet of crisps. Her little face screwed up and she went into a paroxysm of teeth baring and spitting.

At band rehearsals she was a complete pest. She would pass from bandsman to bandsman, sit on their shoulders, probe in their ears, climb up their legs, tear the music, swing on a trombone slide, and even try to prise their fingers from the instruments .... all while they were trying to play! Ernie recalls these rehearsals as being similar to "aerial dogfights", with each bandsman glancing nervously over his shoulders wondering where she was going to land next !

The only time Salome really behaved herself was when, every evening, Judson would fill a bowl with warm water and give her her daily bath. She would sit in the water quite contentedly and Ernie swears there was a smile on her face as Juddy scrubbed her back with an old bootbrush. As soon as she was dry, and with her "Green Howards jersey" back on, she would throw herself into mischief-making again.

Life in the desert for Ernie was a succession of differing emotions: Boredom during the day, exhilaration during concerts, humour at rehearsal (especially when Salome took part) and misery at post-call. The band mail would be delivered by the Post Corporal and then distributed by the Band Sergeant. Ernie and Peter would stand there listening to the sergeant handing out the letters from home which were eagerly taken away to be read over and over again. They would hear the names being called: "Judson - three for you.", "Clancy - blimey! Five for you!", "Fraser - two for you, and a parcel." . . . and so it would go on, until the last letter was gone. They would not say a word but always walk away disconsolately empty handed. After a while they found it less harrowing not to attend mail distribution.

They lived for the band concerts, especially those out of camp. The band would be invited to play at many functions and these relieved the monotony of life. Within the band a new group had been formed, a far from military Dance Band, in which Ernie played clarinet and saxophone . This became a very popular "swing band" which played in the Officers' Mess, Sergeants' Mess and at venues in Port Suez. Within Port Suez a British society had evolved, composed of Civil Servants and civilians who were resident there and the dance band, particularly, was in great demand. The band enjoyed these civilian, functions as they were made very welcome and, above all, paid for their services Ernie remembers getting something like ten shillings for an evening's playing, which was a fair addition to his army pay!

It was the day after one of these lucrative engagements and they were sitting in their tent when they heard the cry,

"Mail up!" The mail had arrived. Ernie said to Peter,

"I think I'll go to see what's come."

Peter said, "What the hell for? Even if there's ten lorry loads, there won't be one for us." He laid back on his bed. Ernie said,

"I'll go, anyway, you never know."

He was back twenty minutes later.

"Well?" Peter asked.

"Nowt."

"You knew that before you went, don't know why you wasted your time."

That evening Ernie said,

"Fancy a trip to the "Britannia?" ... and the NAAFI?"

"Why?"

"It'll make the day different, come on, I'll spend my ten bob!"

"Bloody hell, Ernie, what's up with you? You've been like a bloody zombie all day, and now you want to rush out."

Ernie sat on the bed beside him, "Sorry, Ponky, but I wanted something to remember today by. I was hoping for a card ... I'm twenty-one today."

Peter got up, picked up his beret., and said,

"Right, pal, let's go ... I wonder if Fraser can lay on some transport?"

Ernie spent his twenty-first birthday in the NAAFI with the one man he called a real friend.

The military band was by those days getting seriously depleted. Its numbers had been sorely reduced when it arrived in the Canal Zone and, even during the eight months it had been there, numbers were still falling. It was clear to everyone that some drastic measures would have to be taken, sooner or later, to recruit new members, and the only place that could be done was back in England. Orders had been received that the regiment was to be posted to Malaya which was becoming a hotbed of anarchy and rebellion. The final orders were for the regiment to proceed straight to Malaya but the band was to return home to recruit and reform before following it.

During the period before the departure, however, an important engagement had to be fulfilled, so arrangements were made to use "massed bands" and the Green Howards were augmented with two other regimental bands. It was a grand occasion attended by the Commanding Officers, civilian dignitaries and a large invited audience. The programme was a long and ambitious one, selected specially for the occasion and, amongst many other items, Ernie was to play solo clarinet in "La Traviata". He was supremely confident, he'd been practising it for weeks, and looked forward to his first major role.

The concert went well and, at the interval, they received standing applause. The "V.J.P.'s adjourned to the Officers' Mess for coffee, or perhaps something stronger, while an appreciative buzz filled the audience who remained. "'La Traviata" was the opening item after the interval and Ernie relaxed over a cup of tea and steeled himself for his big occasion, enjoying every minute.

The audience re-assembled and settled themselves for the second half of the show. The bandmaster called the band to order and the strains of the famous music filled the air. Ernie was in his element as he fingered the clarinet, the audience forgotten - he was playing for himself and for George Garside, who had told him of moments such as this. He reached the beautiful well-known slow passage of the work, his favourite part, he had no need to read the music, he knew the notes as if he had written them himself, he closed his eyes and began to lose himself in the beauty he was creating......"BOING! BUING! BAING!" He flew out of his reverie."BAING! BUING! BOING!" - there it was again, but backwards! Had the tympani player gone mad? He could sense trauma behind him. "CRASH!" - a music stand had fallen over. He had a horrible thought. He glanced behind him. His nightmare was true. He saw a glimpse of green and white streak across the trumpet section. A trumpet player flashed out an arm and, in doing so, knocked his own music over. The music stand fell on to the clarinets in front causing a domino effect. More fell. Ernie steadfastly continued. Salome was in full flight by now. She leapt on to the bandmaster's shoulder. He flashed at her with his baton. She bounced into one of the other bands who were wondering where this gigantic green and white hornet had come from. they were ducking and weaving to avoid her. Judson left his trombone to try to catch her. He tripped over the euphonium player's foot on his way. Salome avoided him by jumping across the tympani again. "BOING! BUING! BAING!" The tympanist tried to catch her, missed, and added another "BOING!" to the pandemonium. The bandmaster signalled the band to stop.

At this time there was a comedy band in England that called itself "Syd Millward and the Nitwits" but none of their carefully rehearsed mayhem ever reached the standard of hilarity that the audience enjoyed that night in the desert, mis-produced, mis-directed and generally mis-arranged by a tiny grass monkey. Ernie's great moment collapsed into utter farce - Salome had wreaked her revenge for the packet of salt!

A few weeks later the band played its last engagement in Suez. As a troopship left the port with the regiment aboard the Regimental Band was crowded on landing craft circling the ship, playing the Regimental march, bidding their comrades farewell. Within a few days they themselves would be at sea, returning to England, Richmond and home.

Salome, of course, had to be left behind. She was adopted by another regiment as band mascot....some folk will never learn!

Left:
Bandboy Waites 1943

Right:
Band Master Reg Lester, A.R.C.M.

Centre:
Green Howards in Scarborough 1945 (Ernie 4th in line nearest camera, on the left of Band Master Reg Lester)

Bottom:
Green Howards Band 1946

Right:
Ernie at Kneller Hall 1947

Centre:
Elgar Squad, Kneller Hall 1947
(Ray Pinkney 3rd, Ernie 7th, back row from left)

Bottom:
Kneller Hall Professors 1947
(George Garside back row 2nd from left)

Top Left:
Ernie & friend. Malaya 1951

Top Right:
Proud Green Howard! Malaya

Bottom Left:
Band Sergeant Waites 1952

Bottom Right:
Corporal Waites, Malaya 1951

Top:
Massed Bands - Schonbrunn Gardens, Vienna 1953
(Green Howards, Cameroons, Middlesex Regts.)

Bottom Left:
Peter Parrish 1951

Bottom Centre:
Band Master Jerry Jarrett 1948

Bottom Right:
Brian Clancy 1951

CHAPTER TEN

The band arrived back in England in September 1949 and "Jerry" Jarrett began the task of rebuilding it to its former strength. This was no simple task for musician recruits were not numerous and the position of "bandsman" not one that was sought after. All regimental bands were suffering in a similar manner and the reason, partly, was the lack of the prospects of promotion. A band of thirty-five, for example, would have only three N.C.O.'s, one sergeant, one corporal and one lance corporal. As most bandsmen were regular soldiers, serving an average of nine years, it virtually meant waiting for someone to die before promotion became a possibility. As some of the N.C.O.'s had signed on for twenty-one years, promotion was practically out of the question, regardless of ability.

Army bands, consequently, were not attracting new blood, and in an attempt to alleviate the problem the War Office allowed regiments to increase the establishment to three sergeants, three corporals and three lance corporals. As a result of this Ernie was promoted to Lance Corporal immediately they reported back to the Regimental Depot at Richmond.

This was the time of National Service which gave the recruiting officers some slight advantage. A prospective bandsman reporting for two years' service could now be shown promotional chances and many would sign on for five years as a musician rather than, in their eyes, waste two years as a conscript. The results were quite encouraging and very soon the band was up to strength in numbers if not in quality. The high standard of the band could only be achieved by hard work and from late 1949 until early 1951 every effort was aimed at this goal, giving Ernie his chance to use his talents as an instructor, training the new members. This training was, of course, not solely musical. They had to be taught military discipline, how to play on the march and the many parade drills. Ernie proved to be an able instructor and after a year was promoted to Corporal.

By March 1951 the band was back to its normal strength and efficiency and the end of the month saw them on board the "Empire Trooper", bound for Singapore. The troopship was an ex-German vessel and conditions on board were familiar to those experienced by the hundreds of thousands of men who have travelled on troopships. Ernie, Peter and the rest of the band were on a low deck, just above the waterline. Long tables and benches were fixed to the deck, each table with a raised lip to prevent plates sliding off when the ship rolled. They slept in hammocks above the tables, hammocks which had to be rolled in the approved manner each morning and stacked in a large bay. After everybody had crowded into the ablution area, fruitlessly trying to get any lather from the "salt water soap", the duty team for the day would then go to the galley and bring back the dixies of food for breakfast. If the weather was at all rough the amount would be sadly diminished by the time it arrived at the table ! Then would begin another day of boredom.

They travelled through the "Med" and the Suez canal. As the ship approached Suez, Ernie looked out over the desert and wondered if, somewhere in the sand, Salome was still making life amusingly hellish for some unfortunate band ! They crossed the Red Sea and, now kitted out in tropical gear, headed for the Indian Ocean. The temperature was now almost unbearable below decks and, apart from a welcome breeze from the ship's movement, almost as bad on top.

Some of the newcomers, for whom this was the first sea voyage, under the misguided opinion that they were inventive, tried to do their laundry by tying the dirty clothing to a rope and throwing it through a porthole, thus, they imagined, giving it a thorough washing as it dragged through the water. The old hands, of course, knew just what would happen and gained great amusement from the faces of the "laundrymen" as they recovered the tattered remnants of their shirts, coated white with salt and looking like battle-torn standards from the Crimean War!

In the Indian Ocean they encountered the worst weather that could be imagined. The ship rolled and pitched in huge waves and, if anyone had a stomach of cast iron, second and third helpings were available at every meal due to the numbers of men who couldn't eat, due to sea sickness, yet throughout the six weeks at sea the band provided the only organised entertainment on board, playing on deck every day and in the canteen every evening, whether they had managed to eat or not! They arrived at Singapore on May 14th.

Any romantic illusions they may have had about exotic life in the Orient were dispelled immediately. A veteran of obvious experience gave them a lecture about the habitat they would encounter and the reality of their future existence. Malaria was rife, snakes and mosquitoes a permanent hazard and no mercy would be forthcoming should they fall into the hands of the rebels. The rebels took no prisoners, it seemed, they dealt with any captive by prompt beheading. None of this did anything to cause great enthusiasm among the new arrivals! They were issued with mosquito nets and Paladin tablets to combat Malaria and a short-barrelled Lee Enfield rifle, equipped with a flash eliminator, and fifty rounds of ammunition to avoid decapitation! They were then packed aboard a train with wooden seats and no windows which was to take them to rejoin the regiment.

The vegetation on each side of the track was lush and green, the climate was hot and humid making conditions in the carriages almost unbearable to a group of musicians who had suddenly found themselves playing the part of real fighting men, it was all so foreign to them and each and every one was surreptitiously guarding his rifle. They knew exactly how to use a rifle, it had been part of their basic training, they could dismantle it, clean it, and re-assemble it, blindfold. They could load it, point it at a target and fire it, that, too, they had learned on the range at Richmond, but here things were different; this was not a range, this was not Richmond and they would not be firing at a target. This was terrifyingly real - and the "target" would fire back, or, more likely, first! Each one of them became apprehensive and, at the same time, each was determined not to show his apprehension to the rest. They settled down ostensibly to reading, playing cards or, like Ernie and Peter, just talking .

With a squeal of brakes the train came to a sudden stop, hurling them forward. A hubbub broke out in the corridors, doors were slamming and everywhere was the sound of running feet.

"What are you doing in there?" someone yelled, "Get out!"

They grabbed their rifles and opened the door. All along the train men were jumping down to the track and throwing themselves to the ground. They followed suit and Ernie found himself with a group of obviously hardened veterans.

"What's up? " he asked.

"Ambush!"

"Christ!" Peter said, What do we do now?"

"Keep your bloody head down!"

The tension lasted an eternity for Ernie until a distant voice called,

"False alarm! Back on the train!"

It was a very relieved band that reassembled in the carriages but also a very anxious one. Their anxiety was not appeased when the same routine was repeated within an hour.

They were to be uprooted four times on their journey, causing Peter to say,

"Ernie, just imagine, we could be enjoying the flies and the shit at Port Tewfik!"

"Aye," Ernie replied, "and we thought that was rough! I wonder what Salome would have made of this bloody life?

Eventually, and with great relief, they arrived at Tampin, a small village in the state of Negri Sembilan, where the battalion was stationed and, thankfully, found themselves with the Green Howards again. They began to regain a feeling of security. Accommodation was in large "bashas", huts about sixty feet long and built of wood and straw on a thick concrete base. The bashas were divided into rooms and Ernie and Peter found themselves sharing a room with, among others, Brian Clancy. Brian played the french horn and was the Jeremiah of the band, forever bemoaning his fate and ostensibly dissatisfied with life in general. As they erected their mosquito nets over their beds he maintained a diatribe on the latest conditions,

What a bloody dump! .... "I can never sleep under these things .... it's too bloody hot ...."

"Belt up, Clancy," someone said, "save your griping for when you really suffer .... wait 'til you go out to the detachments!"

The lay-out of the battalion was similar to a wheel where they were stationed at the centre, which housed the headquarters. From the centre imaginary spokes protruded into the jungle and, at the end of each spoke, was a company. There was no easy way through to these detachments and they were supplied by air drops until their tour of duty ended when they would be relieved and make their difficult way back through the jungle.

The work of the band would be to visit each of these outposts in turn, give two or three concerts and then return for a two day break. During these two days they would go through the old routine of rehearsal and band practice.

They had visited only one company and were on their first "break" when Ernie woke one morning, washed, shaved and returned to find Peter still in bed,

"Come on Ponky, you lazy bugger," he said, "get up!"

Peter sat up in bed,

"Ernie, I feel rough."

"What's up?"

"I don't know, I feel terrible - and my head's splitting."

Ernie looked at him and realised this was no act of skiving. Peter was grey.

"Come on, Ponky," he said, "let's get you down to the sick bay."

Peter got out of bed but immediately fell back again, it was clear he couldn't attend sick parade.

"You stay there, I'll send for the M.O."

Ernie reported to the Band Sergeant who returned with the sick bay attendant. He could do nothing, went away and returned with the Medical Officer, who began his examination.

"It's all right, Waites," he said, "leave him to us now, get your breakfast."

By the time Ernie returned from breakfast, Peter was on his way to hospital. When the band gathered for its routine practice Ponky's sickness was the main subject of conjecture. The Band Sergeant arrived and their rehearsal began. They had been practising for about an hour and were playing the Florentiner March by Fucik when they were surprised to see the Bandmaster himself appear. He spoke to the sergeant who signalled for them to stop. There was an expectant hush, broken by the Bandmaster who said quietly,

"I'm afraid I have some very bad news. Bandsman Parrish died on his way to hospital this morning."

No one spoke. An eerie silence ensued. The bandsmen merely looked at each other with unbelieving stares.

The Bandmaster was clearly finding it difficult to maintain his decorum, he was swallowing deeply and blinking repeatedly. "The funeral will take place this afternoon," he continued, "....at the military cemetery in Kuala Lumpur. I would like you to perform the military honours."

The news had not really sunk in. Everyone was engrossed in his own thoughts. In a tightly closed community like the band the impact was exactly like losing a member of the family. As only Ernie knew, the band **was** Peter's family, the only family he had ever known, and Ernie had been the nearest he had ever had to a brother.

The silence became even more pronounced. The Bandmaster realised that, for their own good, they must not stand around morosely. He pulled himself to attention,

"I'll give you all details later. Meanwhile, Sergeant, please continue from where I interrupted." He marched away.

The sergeant raised his baton. "Right! Florentiner March!" he said, and the band continued. It was indeed unfortunate that that particular piece should be the one they were playing at that moment, for it has a heart-rending melody and to finish it, many with unashamed tears, must surely have been the most difficult task the band ever accomplished.

The funeral was at four o'clock. The band members went, not as a band but as mourners, on a three ton lorry to Kuala Lumpur where they collected the coffin from the mortuary where the air was permeated with a sickly perfume and took it to the cemetery. Ernie and five other bandsmen carried the coffin up a hillside along a narrow road bordered by smart lawns with neat rows of headstones to an open grave. They gathered round informally as the Padre conducted the funeral service and then the band solo trumpeter had the most harrowing task of all - to play the Last Post and Reveille. This he did immaculately, even though tears were streaming down his face.

He was not the only one - they were all in tears and, most affected of all, as the final notes of the Last Post echoed over the cemetery, Ernie broke down and had to be assisted away, back to the lorry. Everything was so unreal-even to the fact that as the trumpet sounded Reveille a freak thunderstorm crashed over the area. On the way back Ernie tried to rationalise his emotions but failed - at half-past eight that morning he had been talking to his closest friend, now he was alone again. He tried to adopt a nonchalant attitude but it took months for the immediate effect of Peter's death to diminish and, indeed, it is clear, when he talks of those days, that a scar remains that will never be completely healed. He has made hundreds of arrangements for many military bands and hundreds more for the Ashton-on-Mersey Showband of today but he is determined he will never arrange, or play, the Florentiner March. "Even if I did," he says, "I don't think I could go through with the performance."

The trips to the outlying detachments became routine but the whole way of life seemed somewhat incongruous. Armed patrols he could understand, the need for armoured raids into rebel territory he could accept, but it did seem rather ludicrous for men to go out into the jungle, armed to the teeth in lorries bristling with Bren guns, to perform a band concert! Yet, after the performance, and remembering the delight on the faces of thirty or so men squatting in a clearing listening to familiar melodies, everything seemed thoroughly worth-while.

They were returning from one such foray in a convoy of six trucks, four full of veterans returning to headquarters followed by the two band lorries when they heard gunfire. They had been trained to deal with attacks from bandits and knew that the usual site for an ambush would be at a bend in a road. That afternoon as the leading truck rounded a bend the band heard the shots. The lorries stopped and everyone followed the drill of diving into a roadside ditch and forming a defensive position. For some unknown reason one of the band fired his rifle. The reply was instantaneous and bullets whistled over their heads. This was their first taste of action and some measure of panic must have prevailed for all the band started firing. The exchange continued intermittently for about half an hour until, during one lull, they heard an authoritative sergeant-major type voice shout,

"Will you lot soddin' well stop firing!"

There was silence. One intrepid member climbed out of the ditch to investigate and came back to report. The leading lorries were out of view, round the bend in the road. It seemed that the front one had let off a volley at a suspicious shadow in the verge and the rest had been pure panic - they had all been firing at each other! Amazingly, there had been no casualties because everybody had been well out of the line of fire in deep ditches.

Some excursions could have been even more dangerous for the band. One day they were invited to the Tiger Brewery, a local establishment where they were made over-welcome and, after sampling every product made there, had to be assisted back to the lorries! A load of trigger-happy drunks, each carrying a rifle and fifty rounds of ammunition, is not conducive to strict safety, especially when one or another has a long-standing grudge about a particular N.C.O.!

While the band had been reforming in England, Ernie had been developing his ability to make musical arrangements for various combinations of wind instruments and had written numerous works, all of which were being used regularly by the new band. With this new-found skill he was able to shape its repertoire by arranging popular pieces which were not obtainable through publishers, he had also started serious composing.

The morale of the band had been sinking due to the lack of popularity with the troops of the stereo-typed music then available, and the attitude of some of the senior N.C.O.'s which seemed to be to do the minimum amount of work in order to spend more time in the Sergeants' Mess. The band felt that no one cared whether they played or not. Ernie set about trying to remedy this lethargy. He gathered the rest of the band together and started his own rehearsals in the evenings using his own arrangements of popular songs and melodies that he felt would appeal to the listener with a view to playing concerts in the canteen. The improvement was almost instantaneous; the concerts were a great success, the morale of the band rose and a new spirit started to emerge. Soon the band, on its trips into the jungle, was playing the music the audiences wanted to hear.

Like most of the men overseas Ernie was periodically homesick, a condition that was not alleviated in his case by the eagerly awaited letters from home. He decided to write to the Scarborough Evening News and wrote a long letter telling what life was like in the tropics and asking if they would send him some photographs of his home town. He now enjoyed the anticipation of a letter back from England, even if it was only an impersonal acknowledgement from a newspaper.

The most enjoyable periods for them in Malaya were the occasions when they were seconded to Singapore for six weeks as "Duty Band". For these they were kitted out in a special uniform of white drill and stationed at Tanglin Barracks. They played at all official functions, such as receptions at the High Commissioner's residence and also at many informal venues, either as the full band or the subsidiary dance band. They enjoyed every performance in Singapore; at the top hotels, Singapore Race Course, and the Airport. Ernie has a treasured photograph of the latter event which was attended by H.R.H. The Duchess of Kent with her sixteen year old son, the present Duke of Kent. The highlight of the tour for Ernie, however, was one performance they gave at the famous Raffles Hotel where, for the first time, the band played his own composition "Clarinet Concertino".

Another of Ernie's works, however, brought him nothing but embarrassment. He wrote a march which he entitled Tampin after the village where they were stationed. Without his realising it at the time the middle section started with the same notes as "I do like to be beside the seaside." Within the march itself the notes of the famous ditty did not stand out, but taken out of context the tune was plainly recognisable. The band latched on to it and when they played it they would follow the bandleader impeccably until the middle section was reached. They would then all stop simultaneously and burst into song - Oh, I do like to be beside the seaside!" The march became unplayable because of the spontaneous laughter as the passage was reached. Ernie's pride took a good-humoured battering.

At the end of the six weeks the band returned to its normal duties and jungle excursions. Later in the year for some unknown reason it was decided the ceremony of Beating the Retreat should be performed in Tampin and the band assembled on the "padang", a large open space, near the village. As evening approached the ceremony started but within minutes the heavens opened as the monsoon began. The villagers scattered as the torrential rain flooded the area but the band was determined not to lose face and, as a matter of pride, continued and actually finished the performance. Their way back to camp was marked by trails of runny white blanco and they were literally soaked through. Noel Coward would probably have marked the occasion with a song "Mad dogs and Englishmen beat retreat in the monsoon rain"!

Then the day came when Ernie got a letter. The bandsmen present gave a good-natured cheer when his name was called. He was surprised that the newspaper had hand-written the envelope. When he opened the letter he realised it was not from the newspaper.....

"My Dear Ernie,

I saw your letter that was published in the local paper and ..." It was from Edith. The flame was rekindled and the contact with home re-established. It was a reconciliation that Edith had desperately needed and, as she re-affirmed in her letter, she wanted her first born son back. She explained that her disagreements with Ted were mainly through her defending Ernie against Ted's criticism, and begged him to try to understand. She told him they had moved. They were now living at 18 Maple Drive and beseeched him to maintain contact. From that day on Ernie wrote regularly to his mother and he, in turn, became a frequent collector of mail.

Easter 1952 saw the band back in Singapore, but not without an hilarious beginning to their tour. This time they arrived at two o'clock in the morning to find no transport waiting to take them to Tanglin Barracks. They sat on the railway station surrounded by their instruments and music boxes. Someone started to sing. Now the band had, by now, also developed an efficient male-voice choir and the ad hoc singing changed into a full choral ensemble. They went through the choir's repertoire which lasted for a full three-quarters of an hour. When they finished they were astounded to hear loud clapping. They looked up and all around the station the lights were on in the windows of houses and flats and people were leaning out applauding. They promptly gave an encore and were still singing when the lorries turned up.

"About bloody time!" Bill Fraser said.

"Shut your mouth, corporal!" There was a sergeant major with the transport.

"What took you so long?" the Bandmaster enquired.

"We were delayed at barracks .. but then we've had a mass of irate phone calls telling us to remove a load of noisy bloody soldiers from the station!"

They never found out how the complaints belied the applause but the episode resulted in their making a series of broadcasts on Radio Malaya: "The Choir that sang on the station"!

The Fiji Regiment joined the British forces in Malaya and their newly promoted Band Sergeant came to stay with the Green Howards to train. He was followed by his band and a close friendship developed between them. The Fijis invited the band to their "Ceremony of the Cava". Cava is a drink they make out of powdered roots and Ernie's description of it is simple - "One drink of it and you're flat on your back!". The ceremony was performed with everyone sitting in circles on their haunches. Afterwards the band reciprocated by inviting the Fijis to go with them for a drink and they took them to Bugis Street. Bugis Street was notorious in Singapore, being the centre of the low life of the city with sleazy bars, dives, down-and-outs and everything evil. Needless to say, with a few drinks added to the Cava, they soon degenerated into a crowd of drunks. They reformed their "cava" circles in the middle of Bugis Street and the normal nefarious activities came to a halt as the combined British/Fiji choirs gave a non-stop impromptu performance well into the night.

Ernie had been to Bugis Street once before on their previous tour. He went there with Brian Clancy out of curiosity, having heard of its reputation. Their stay there lasted but minutes. Not knowing the way they hailed a taxi outside the barracks and said "Bugis Street". It was dark when the arrived. The taxi stopped. opened his door and stepped out. .. into a three-foot deep ditch of fetid muddy water!

Bill Fraser, too, was a victim of Bugis Street . He decided to visit the den of iniquity and, as was his wont, looked for a suitable transport to "borrow". A three ton truck was backed up to the band building and he considered that a golden opportunity. He got in, started it and let out the clutch, not realising the truck was in reverse gear. He went straight into the band building, backwards, and the truck was buried in a pile of bricks and mortar. Fraser was escorted to the guardroom by two lance corporals and was subsequently court-martialled. He was sentenced to twenty-eight days in the "glass house" and stripped of his corporals' stripes.

Ernie recalls a humorous coda to Fraser's story: He was in military prison but whenever there was a dance in the Officers' Mess he would be brought out to play the Euphonium and then promptly locked up again! When he was eventually released he seemed a changed man and his wheel-thieving days temporarily came to an end.

The regiment left Malaya after a tour which had lasted eighteen months and they returned home glad to be rid of life in the jungle with its clammy atmosphere, mosquito nets and discomfort. They arrived back in the middle of November and were sent to a moorland camp outside Barnard Castle. Within days, many were wishing they could be back in a warm climate!

Ernie took the first opportunity to get a week-end leave and eagerly rushed to Scarborough for the re-union with his mother. When he arrived at the house Edith crushed him in her arms but his relationship with Ted Stockell was still distant. They tolerated each other's presence but, unfortunately, there was no sense of affinity.

CHAPTER ELEVEN

The thing that sticks in Ernie's mind about the camp at Barnard Castle in the winter of 1952 was the cold. They were housed in the traditional army units, brick built with corrugated roofs and the usual cast iron stoves for heating, but fuel was in short supply. Most of the time they wore their outdoor clothing inside, in a futile attempt to keep warm. The daily round was back to the boring routine of parades, drill and band practice. These conditions allowed Brian Clancy to give full rein to his catalogue of woe:
"I wish we were back in Tampin."
"You moaned all the time we were there," Ernie said.
"At least it was warm."
"Warm? It was bloody hot!"
"Now I'm bloody cold." Brian bewailed, "Put some more wood on that stove."
"We've run out of wood, it doesn't grow on trees, you know."
The remark fell on stony ground, Clancy was blowing into his cupped hands, "There's only one thing for it, Ernie, - it's down to the Black Lion again."
Since Peter Parrish's death Brian and Ernie had become good friends, initiated by Ernie's constant rejoinders to Brian's incessant griping and a happy bond of repartee formed between them.
"This must be the worst band in the army." Brian would pronounce.
"No wonder," Ernie would say, "you're part of it!"
They set off on their nightly visit to the public houses in Barnard Castle, a pretty town in the south of Durham, about four miles from the camp. In the pubs they would usually find other band members where they would sit in the warm, drinking pints of draught Bass. At closing time they would call for fish and chips at the nearby shop and eat them out of newspaper as they made their way to the bus stop. They usually managed to catch the last bus but, on occasions, missed it and were faced with the long walk back to camp; which gave Brian ample time to give full vent to his opinions of the Yorkshire Dales, the band and the army in general.

Early in December Ernie took advantage of a forty-eight hours' pass to visit Scarborough where he spent an uncomfortable leave at Maple Drive because of the on-going coolness of Ted Stockell. It was with real regret that he had to refuse the invitation of his mother to spend Christmas with her. That terrible Christmas all those years ago was still in his mind, and he knew it would be in Ted's also, so he considered it more prudent to go with Brian, who had suggested that he should go to his home for the holiday. He consequently spent his Christmas leave in Huddersfield with Mr. and Mrs. Clancy who made him extremely welcome and gave him a memorable Christmas but the time was occupied mainly by a series of conducted tours round the public houses! For some reason three melodies stuck in his mind during the holiday; "Limelight", Al Martino's "Here in my Heart" and Eddie Fisher's Lady of Spain". He was so taken by "Lady of Spain" that he made a special arrangement of it for use by the band.

Early in the New Year the regiment was sent to Hawick in Scotland for training and the band soon followed to spend a short period with them to entertain. It was soon after Hogmanay and, one evening, the band decided to join in the Scottish spirit both figuratively and literally. It was the home of "the malt" and they indulged too well and, long after midnight, there was so much noise and revelry coming from the band quarters that the Regimental Police thought they had a riot on their hands and sent for reinforcements before entering the hut.

A very subdued band went to bed that night, the slightly less inebriated, who could still reason, were fully convinced that they were all due to follow Bill Fraser's pioneering visit to the glass-house.... a thought brought to mind because Bill Fraser was missing. He had last been seen reeling out of the door an hour earlier to fetch another bottle from his own hut.

They only found out afterwards what transpired after the police had left.. The Bandmaster had been called to the Commanding Officer to discuss what action should be taken and, luckily for them all, he had persuaded the C.O. to allow him to deal with the matter. They knew nothing of this, of course, until the following dawn.

More accurately, it was long before dawn! At five o'clock in the morning they were all harshly roused from their drunken stupor by the Bandmaster, immaculately dressed as if he was going on an Aldershot parade, shouting

"OUT! The lot of you! Outside! In five minutes! With your instruments!" With aching heads full of steam hammers, bleary eyed and parched mouthed, they dressed, grabbed their instruments and went outside into what remained of the freezing cold night..

"Fall in! Right Turn! Quick March!"

They marched out of camp, desperately trying to focus on the man in front. Once clear of the camp he started them playing a march ... and they marched, and marched and marched. As soon as one march was finished he would shout "Carry on!" and they would start another, and another ... and still they marched, out into the wilds of Scotland. They were falling asleep as they marched, bumping into each other; the bass player fell over and dented his bass, the trombones were hitting the men in front in the back of the neck with their slides and the bass drummer, and anyone anywhere near him, was wincing in agony every time he hit the drum. And still they marched. They had no chance to talk, they were gasping for breath from the endless blowing and Ernie thanked God they were not in Malaya with loaded rifles - the Bandmaster would not have lasted long! They had been marching for over two hours and were thankfully on their way back to camp when, as they rounded a bend, they saw a motor bike lying by the roadside and, beside it, a very woe-begone figure sitting on the verge with his head in his hands. It was Bill Fraser. He had obviously reverted to his old habits and had been sitting there all night.

"Frazer! Fall in!"

Without the band stopping Fraser joined the motley phalanx and, asleep on his feet, marched with them back to camp.

As they reached the guardroom the Bandmaster gave the command, "Halt!"

Two grinning N.C.O.'s came out. The bandmaster went to them and Ernie saw them nodding in agreement with what was being said. The Bandmaster returned to his squad. They had obviously evaded charge proceedings and would hear no more of their escapade. He was tired, but relieved.

"Oh, and by the way, sergeant," the bandmaster called, "you'd better send someone out from the M.T. section, I've no idea how it got there but there's one of their motor bikes in the verge about two miles up the road." He re-took his place at the head of the column.

"Quick March!"

They arrived back at their huts, footsore, exhausted and hardly able to stand.

"Get your breakfast. Band practice in an hour! Dismiss!"

They fell out and staggered into their huts. Brian Clancy said,

"He's all right, is that Jarrett."

"Coming from you," Ernie said, "that makes him a saint!" and he fell on his bed having decided that half an hour's rest was preferable to breakfast!

It is said that good, and bad, things come in threes and this was certainly true for Ernie that Easter. First, he was promoted to Sergeant, then the regiment got orders to go to Austria and finally, on a short leave before going overseas again a rapport developed with Ted Stockell. He went home merely to say "Goodbye" to his mother but to his pleasant surprise Ted was most affable and they spent many hours talking about the First World War and Scarborough. Ernie decided to spend the rest of his leave at Maple Drive and, by the end of it, a form of friendship had developed between them. Hearing first hand of Ted's torment in the trenches Ernie, in some way, began to comprehend the man's tortured mind and felt that perhaps his own unhappiness over the Christmas incident was small when compared to what he could now recognise - the unhappiness of the marriage. Age had matured Ernie and he could clearly see that Ted was suffering mental scars as well as physical ones and that his mother must have found the relationship extremely distressing. He began to see Ted's view of the situation, he could not forgive him but at least he was able to accept that the unfortunate outburst could have been the culmination of personal difficulties of which he was too young at the time to be aware. He actually enjoyed his leave.

The regiment arrived in Austria in April, and were stationed at Graz, a picture-postcard garden city in the province of Steirmark. The city is built around a large hill on top of which stands a castle with a majestic clock tower. It is an ancient town abounding in outward signs of culture; an opera house, museums and a university. They were stationed in what had been a German army barracks and they were amazed at the comparative luxury it afforded them; three-storey concrete-faced blocks with central heating and excellent facilities. There were six such blocks, plus all the expected military accoutrements, parade square, motor transport yard, guard houses etc. The barracks was some four miles from the city.

The band was soon in great demand, playing for the local populace and spending weeks at a time away touring nearby towns and villages. Ernie once more saw a limitation in the band's repertoire - the lack of music suitable for the country and he re-started his evening practice sessions with any bandsmen who were interested, which was most of them. Soon the sounds of Lehar and Strauss were echoing from the band rehearsal room above the garrison church. When he considered that the standard was high enough he approached the bandmaster and suggested that the band should play music more appropriate for an Austrian audience.

"That's a great idea, sergeant," Jerry Jarrett said, "get them practising immediately."

"There's no need, sir" Ernie replied, "they're ready!"

They went off on another trip, this time playing waltzes, Viennese music and, most popular of all the "Radetsky March." As the applause resounded, night after night, the morale of the band rose to new heights and even Brian Clancy said,

"Do you know, Ernie, we've got the best band in the British Army." For the first time in his life Ernie could find no riposte.

The NAAFI canteen in Graz was sited in a pre-war hotel and was, of course, a very popular meeting place for the local military personnel. It had an English manager but was staffed by Austrians, most of whom were female. The work was of great advantage to them because, apart from being able to eat there, they could also take food home to their families. From his very first visit Ernie found himself attracted to a pretty young lady behind the counter, which was a completely new experience for him. Throughout his army life music had taken preference to female company but in this girl he saw something that actually seemed more interesting than crochets and quavers! On his third or fourth visit he plucked up the courage to suggest a date. She looked at him blankly - she could speak no English! Ernie, of course, could speak no German, so he found himself at an impasse. Love conquers all things, however, and he sought out another girl who could understand.

"Would you please ask your friend if she would like to go out with me one evening."

"Which one?"

Ernie pointed, "Her, over there."

The girl happened to look over just as Ernie was pointing at her and she looked puzzled. The second girl smiled at Ernie and went over to the first. Ernie saw them in giggling conversation. The second girl returned,

"She say No."

Ernie took his tea and bun and rejoined Brian at their table.

"What are you up to?" Brian asked.

"I was trying to get a date with that fraulein."

"Stick to your clarinet, pal, at least you know how to cope with that!"

The following evening the band was engaged in "Beating the Retreat" outside the Opera House and all the important personalities of Graz were in the audience. They received their now customary tumultuous applause, and at the end of the performance the bandmaster signalled for the National Anthems to be played. The band had formed up before the dignitaries in its usual finale position with the brass at the front and the woodwind behind them. Ernie was consequently about half way back. He was so familiar with the music played on these occasions that, like many others, did not bother to take music cards on parade but played from memory. Whether it was the lack of the cards, which would have been in playing order, or whether his mind was on the NAAFI fraulein we shall never know; what we do know is that as the brass section played "God Save the Queen" Ernie blasted out with the Austrian National Anthem! The woodwinds all followed Ernie, the brass carried on with "The Queen" and a running musical battle ensued where neither section seemed prepared to surrender. Both anthems were therefore played simultaneously! Amazingly no comment was made after the performance, the audience probably assuming the whole farce had been a clever and diplomatic arrangement! The following morning, however, Ernie was called in front of the bandmaster, who made it abundantly clear that he, at least, was not at all impressed!

After band practice the next day Brian said,

"Where are we going tonight, Ernie? How about "Mama's?"

"Mama's" was a local "gasthaus" where the band members had found themselves very popular due to their choral ability. They would sit at tables, singing all the Lehar melodies, and be on the receiving end of an apparently endless supply of free beer as the steins lined up in front of them.

"I don't think so, Brian," Ernie replied, "how about the NAAFI?"

"The NAAFI! We have to pay for everything there!"

"It's comfortable."

"It's also got a certain Austrian fraulein ... O.K. I'll play gooseberry."

Ernie had by now invested in a german phrasebook, but unfortunately it did not contain all the phrases he needed. That evening Brian found a place at a table while Ernie made straight for the counter where the girl was serving,

"Zwei tasse tee, bitte." He said proudly.

She fetched the teas.

"Ich bin Ernie," he continued, "Wie heissen sie?"

"Frieda." She said, and waited for his next question. Ernie hadn't rehearsed any further than that so he handed over his money and waited for his change. She handed him some coins but did not go away. He felt he was making progress. He beckoned the second girl over,

"Would you ask Frieda if she would go out with me?"

The girl rattled off in German at great length, Ernie began to wonder what she was saying to make such a long speech from a simple question. Frieda joined what had now become a conversation. The second girl walked away, indicating that Frieda should answer for herself. She did. She turned to Ernie, who was still counting his change, and said, quite sweetly,

"Nein, bitte."

Ernie took the teas over to Brian and said,

"Drink that quick - let's go to Mama's."

For the next week their time was taken up with rehearsal, both alone and with the bands of other regiments. June 2nd. 1953 was to be Coronation Day and the massed bands were to play at the Schonbrunn Palace in Vienna. It was therefore a fortnight before Ernie turned up again at the NAAFI. He was alone this time and as he entered he was disappointed to see no sign of Frieda. He began to regret he'd not gone with Brian to Mama's. The manager was behind the counter and while he waited for his tea Ernie beckoned him over,

"Frieda not in tonight?" he asked conspiratorially.

"She's around somewhere," the manager replied, "why?"

"Oh, nothing. Er.." he paused as a woman gave him a cup of tea, took his money and left, ".. you wouldn't know if she's got a boyfriend, would you?"

The manager laughed, "So that's it! You're the one! The girls here are pulling her leg something rotten over you, I tell you! You picked a wrong'n for an interpreter, you did, pal!"

"Why?"

"She's the NAAFI gestapo is Irma, she's already told everyone here about Frieda's secret admirer. If she fixed you up with Frieda it would be all over Graz, and Frieda knows it - she dare not accept!"

"What if whatsaname. Irma, didn't know?"

"I think you might stand a chance, mate. Ask her when Irma's not around."

"I can't. I can't speak German, and she doesn't speak English." Ernie paused for a while and then added, "Any chance of you asking her for me?"

The manager smiled, looked around and said,

"Hang on here, she's round the back, I always fancied myself as Cupid."

Ernie sat at a table close to the counter and started studying his phrase-book as he sipped his tea. The manager came from behind the counter and sat next to Ernie,

"Well, you're fixed up. I've had a word with her and she'll see you on Saturday - that's her night off. She says she'll be outside the station at seven."

"Come down to Mama's tomorrow night," Ernie said, "I owe you a pint or two!"

As he got up from the table he saw Frieda standing behind the counter, she gave him a coy smile and waved her fingers surreptitiously. He set off to join the band in Mama's with his feet hardly touching the ground.

On the Friday he was called into the Bandmaster's office. Jerry Jarrett was informal:

"Sergeant," he said, "I thought I'd have a quiet word with you about your behaviour."

"Sir?" Ernie was perplexed, he could not recall having done anything untoward.

"There's some uncomfortable talk going round the Sergeants' Mess. We've got to maintain discipline, you realise that?"

"Yes, sir."

"... and that can't be done if the senior N.C.O.'s are too familiar with the lower ranks."

"I don't follow you, sir."

"You have taken to going to a gasthaus with bandsmen and indulging in raucous behaviour, or so I'm told."

Ernie began to understand. "Hardly raucous, sir, it's my choir and we entertain."

"The members of the mess don't see it that way... I strongly suggest you think twice before going again. And I hear you spend most of your spare time in the company of a bandsman."

Ernie could feel his hackles rising, but controlled himself. "The band have been my friends for years, sir, I can hardly cut them off just because I've been promoted. I find, actually, that my rapport with the band has improved its performance - they give a lot of their own time to my extra rehearsals. And as for Clancy, sir, he's been my close friend ever since Peter Parrish died. As you know, I was close to Peter and Brian helped me a lot. I'm afraid I cannot cast him aside for the sake of an extra stripe."

Jarrett thought for a short while. "Well, it's up to you, Sergeant, but I wouldn't be doing you any favours by not telling you of the feelings in the mess."

Ernie left the office bristling with anger. He had grown to love the army but this snobbery was anathema to him. He now realised why most men changed units on promotion but he was one of "the band", he could see no way of reconciling his way of life to the strict code of rank distinction his "friends" in the sergeants' mess demanded. He pondered on the problem all day and decided that if it came to it, he'd prefer to revert to corporal again rather than abandon his true friends in the band. By Saturday evening he had put it out of his mind. After all, if things went right for him with Frieda, he hoped he wouldn't be spending night after night at Mama's!

He was outside the station promptly at seven but there was no sign of her. By ten-past he had started to wonder whether she had changed her mind or whether women were the same all over Europe - claiming their prerogative of being late! Then he saw her approaching. It was a warm summer's evening and she was dressed in a worn but smartly kept two-piece.

"Hello!", he said, "thanks for coming." She didn't know what he had said but smiled. They stood looking at each other embarrassingly until Frieda said,

"Wollen wir zum gasthaus gehan?"

It was Ernie's turn to look vacant. He realised this was going to be difficult. His phrase book helped him ask questions within limits but it was useless when trying to find answers! She took his arm and led him to a cafe. In the cafe he sat her at a table and went to the counter.

"Zwei tasse tee, bitte." It was all he was able to order but it was at least a start. Perhaps, later in the evening, he would be able to make himself understood and then she could order a meal somewhere. He paid for the teas and took them to the table. This gave him an idea and they soon discovered a way of making conversation, he pointed to the table,

"Wie heisst das?"

"Tisch." she replied.
"We call it a table ... table."
"Table." She repeated.
"Wie heisst das?"
"Stuhl."
"Chair."
"Wei heisst das? We say window."

"Fenster." She said, and so it went on with the two of them happily giving language lessons. They left the cafe and wandered round the streets, looking in shop windows and, all the time, exchanging words. They laughed, they giggled, they acted like any young couple enjoying themselves. They were sitting on a bench in the park when Ernie consulted his pocket dictionary and said,

"Ich bin . .. in a gruppe." She started. She looked at him inquisitively,
"Nein!"

He realised he'd got something wrong and took another look at his dictionary. There it was: "Band = Gruppe". He read on and truth dawned - below it, was "Band = Kapelle". Apparently he'd just told her he was a gangster! He pointed hastily to the badge above his stripes,

"Nein, nein," he said, "Kapelle!" She laughed,
"Ach! Musiker!"
"Ja," he said, miming, "clarinet. Wei heisst clarinet?"
"Klarinette." She said. He'd learned another word!

Ernie spent one of the happiest evenings he could remember in her company, she was charming and vivacious. He walked back with her, to her home in Bienengasse and soon learned that this meant, literally, Bee Street. This information was got across with much miming, buzzing and giggling. They stood talking in the street for nearly half an hour, until Ernie, fumbling with his phrase book, found something apt,

"Wann schen wir uns weider?" he spluttered slowly, reading each word as best as he could. She understood,

"Samstag?" she suggested.

Saturday! Ernie knew that much. A full week to wait, but he grinned joyously,

"Samstag," he said, "bitte. The week can't go quick enough!"

She looked at him, shrugged her shoulders, smiled, gave him a quick peck on the cheek and opened the door.

"Auf weidersehn!"

The door closed behind her and Ernie set off back to the barracks, his boots echoing across the Lendplatz. He didn't think Jerry Jarrett would have any more complaints about him spending all his time with lower ranks ... he'd found a far better way to fill his off-duty hours!

The band spent many summer evenings playing concerts in the parks, playing a large number of the Viennese items that Ernie had prepared for the band. The local people appreciated both the standard of their performance and the altruism of their giving them their own popular music.

During these concerts in the parks, Ernie developed a new act - playing xylophone duets with a bandsman named Hughie Mett. They called themselves "The Two Imps" and would stand side by side banging away at the wooden keys producing passable melodies. Ernie recalls those episodes with great amusement, admitting they played many, many wrong notes but, to use his own words, "They all sound the same on the xylophone anyway!"

As the friendship with Frieda developed so did Ernie's German and Frieda's English and soon they were chatting away quite fluently in a mixture of pidgeon English and pidgeon German which became a language all of their own. Frieda, however, was becoming more and more embarrassed by Irma's constant interrogation about her relationship with Ernie, so much so that she decided to leave the NAAFI. She found work at first as a saleslady in a shop but did not enjoy it and left after a week or so. Eventually she found work as manageress of a newsagents cum tobacconists and it was there that Ernie would wait for her to finish work for what had become nightly meetings. They spent their evenings walking, dining out or, occasionally, at her room. She lived in one room on the upper floor of a large house with a harridan of a landlady. Ernie remembers the house as like something out of a war-time film melodrama and recalls the eerie feeling of hidden eyes watching every movement. At the slightest creak of a stair a downstairs door would open and a head come out to investigate. If Frieda had been caught taking Ernie upstairs she would have been evicted immediately!

Ernie was granted leave and they spent it at Frieda's family home in Spital am Semmering. The house was built on a mountain crag in a landscape that was a picture postcard. Josef Lutz, Frieda's father, a caricature of an Austrian, with a feathered alpine hat and toothbrush moustache, had been a railway fireman before his retirement and had chosen this home which was adjacent to the main railway line to Vienna. The view was breath-takingly magnificent but conditions were primitive. The floors were bare boards, white from regular scrubbing, water was obtained by a hand pump in the yard and toilet facilities, although indoors, consisted of just a hole with a septic tank below it. The rooms were cramped, so much so that Ernie and Frieda slept together in a double bed alongside another occupied by her father and his third wife! The line to Vienna was up a very steep gradient at this point, so steep that a second locomotive was hitched to any train to enable it to climb the mountain, so every hour or so their sleep would be interrupted by the hissing, groaning and clunking of engines dragging their loads towards the capital. This hardly affected Ernie as he didn't get much sleep anyway - on the bedroom wall was a large wooden cased pendulum clock which chimed every fifteen minutes throughout the night!

He was made very welcome in the Lutz household, enjoying Austrian food that was basic but excellent. Frieda's family was pleased that Ernie could make himself understood in German and regaled him with their own stories of the war. The eldest son, also Josef, had spent most of the war helping the Yugoslavian partisans and, inevitably, the Gestapo had discovered his activities. They were taking him to Germany when he escaped by jumping from the train window and had spent the rest of the war hiding under the floorboards of that very house. When the Russian Army overran the area his story was confirmed and the Russian authorities subsequently made him Town Clerk.

Ernie was to spend two more leaves in the picturesque village and it was during the last of these, after they had been going out together for nine months, that he proposed marriage. Frieda had some reservations at first mainly at the idea of living in England but her family's enthusiasm overcame any doubts and she accepted. Preparations were started immediately for the wedding to take place in Austria.

Ernie returned from leave to break his joyous news to Brian and the rest of the band but his elation was short lived. When he arrived back in Graz he was told the regiment had been posted and was being moved to Minden in West Germany.

CHAPTER TWELVE

The move to Minden was the only posting in the whole of his army life that caused Ernie any anguish. Up to then every move, whether it had been to the Middle East, the Far East or back to England had been an adventure and every journey had been one of interesting anticipation, but this one, after twelve months in the comforts of Graz, most of them with Frieda, was traumatic. For the first time he suffered the wrench of leaving loved ones, for the first time he shared the heartache he had seen the married men endure, but had never really understood. He also discovered the emotion of parting and realised what had been missing from his life since childhood. He boarded the train with a heavy heart, urging Frieda to keep in close contact and to make what preparations she could regarding the marriage.

The regiment was stationed at Queen Elizabeth Barracks, another ex-German military base built on very similar lines to the one that they had left. The buildings were once more three storey blocks, the only difference to Graz was that here the parade ground was in the centre of the complex, a concrete square surrounded by buildings. The tone, however, was in complete contrast. Minden was a garrison town, part of the Army of the Rhine, and they had to re-adjust to a life of strict discipline and rigid formality, but the band soon re-adapted and returned to the old procedure of practice, performances and parades.

As soon as he could he began the arduous task of making arrangements for his marriage. He discovered nothing but obstacles wherever he enquired and soon found it was not a straightforward procedure for a member of the British Army to marry a girl from an occupied country. Document after document was demanded, always in triplicate. He wrote to Edith asking her to send his birth certificate and adoption papers.

Ernie's friendship with Brian Clancy seemed to grow stronger over the first few weeks at Minden. The band was suffering from another haemorrhage of its life blood as older members reached the end of their service and hasty reformations were made. Brian was promoted to Lance Corporal to Ernie's pleasure and surprise - he always said that the only cure for Brian's "bolshie" attitude was for him to accept responsibility, the surprise was that Brian accepted it! He had little to occupy his lonely evenings as he could find no enthusiasm for the functions in the Sergeants' Mess, which comprised mainly of evenings round the bar, Ladies' Nights and other activities which never seemed to include music. He consequently spent more and more of his time with Brian and the band, practising and talking "shop". The social life of the band also diminished, even the choir disbanded as old faces returned to civilian life.

He realised that, very soon, the time would come for him to make the big decision about the army and his future part in it. He had signed on for nine years' duty and as this period was calculated from the time he was seventeen and a half (time spent as a bandboy did not count) he would be eligible to leave the army in November. He had only a matter of months to decide whether to leave or sign on for a further period. The decision was almost taken out of his hands when, one morning in June, he was summoned to the Bandmaster's office. When he entered he saw a distinguished looking man in civilian clothes sitting with Jerry Jarrett,

"Sergeant," Jarrett said, "This is Lieutenant Colonel McBane, he wants a word with you."

Lieutenant Colonel! Ernie wondered what such a high ranking officer would want with a mere sergeant. McBane studied some papers on the desk at some length and then said,

"Do you know who I am, Sergeant?"

"I'm afraid not, sir."

"I'm the Director of Music, Kneller Hall. I'm very impressed with your record here, and the comments made to me by your Bandmaster. I would like to ask you a few questions myself."

He interviewed Ernie at some length and then said,

"I'm completely satisfied, Sergeant. You are no doubt wondering what this is all about. I've come to offer you a place at Kneller Hall for further training to become a bandmaster."

Ernie was stunned, this was the last thing he had anticipated as he had entered the office yet it was what he had been waiting for - a chance to further his army career with the real possibility of being commissioned and the attainment of high rank.

"Well, Sergeant, what do you say?"

"I'm overwhelmed, sir."

"It's no more than you deserve. So you accept the place?"

"Yes, sir, and thank you."

"Right, I'll see you at Kneller Hall next year. Congratulations."

Ernie left the office a very confident man, it would appear that his married life, when it began, would have a firm foundation. A few days later the mail brought the official papers from Edith, and Ernie had copies made to send to the various authorities, only to find that these would be needed in German as well as English .. and, of course, in triplicate! He began the long task of getting the translations made and the copying done. He was grateful to a German secretary in the barracks who was kind enough to help him. He then heard from Frieda that she, too, was encountering hurdles in Graz where the British authorities were asking for police certificates stating her lack of criminal records, proof of her having no Nazi tendencies and official certification that she had never been involved in prostitution or the organised black market.

Meanwhile the routine work with the band had to continue, playing for Company parades every morning and concerts on many evening. Ernie had now started singing solos with the dance band and clearly remembers the first number he ever sang at a public performance. It was "Cara Mia Mine", a popular tune recorded at the time by David Whitfield and, to his great personal gratification, the audience seemed to like his presentation of it.

One morning, just before a Company parade, Jerry Jarrett called him over to the edge of the parade ground.

"Sergeant.," he said, "I've been thinking. Seeing that you're going to be a bandmaster, you ought to get in a bit of practice. Do you agree?"

"Yes sir." Ernie said.

"Right .... get going, take the parade."

"What! Now?"

"Why not? Good luck!" Jerry Jarrett walked off the parade ground and left Ernie standing there open mouthed. He'd attended parades every day - but never led one. It was simple enough to be at the back, listening for orders and making rude remarks or carping criticism about the bandmaster, but to be out at the front giving the orders was an entirely different kettle of fish! He marched to the front, praying he'd remember what to do and terrified of making a complete fool of himself.

"Marker!" he yelled. "Band! Fall in!" Miraculously, he managed it. He took the full parade and after he had dismissed the band he marched off the parade ground - to see Jerry Jarratt standing in one corner with a demoniac grin on his face. That night was one of the rare occasions when he stayed in the Sergeants' Mess after the evening meal. He was having a drink at the bar, when the Regimental Sergeant Major approached him,

"Don't often see you here, Sergeant."

"No Sir."

"You have better things to do, I suppose. doesn't our company suit you?"

"Oh, yes, sir, but I like to get out of barracks now and then"

"Where?"

"All over, walking round town, sometimes I go for a drink somewhere."

"With the band members?"

"Sometimes."

"So I've heard. I can't understand you. Why do you want to mix with the lower ranks? This is just a friendly word, Sergeant, nothing official, but watch yourself. Your place is here. You'll be heading for trouble if you don't remember that - especially if the C.O. gets to hear of it."

Since becoming a sergeant Ernie had discovered something about the army he had never seen in all the eleven years he had been in uniform and which was disconcerting to him - the elitist attitude of some senior N.C.O.'s. He had tried to justify his third stripe by gaining the respect of the bandsmen through his leadership and musical ability. In this he felt he had succeeded and saw no reason to stand apart from them in his private life. This was the one sphere where he realised his disposition was at odds with the military mind and it caused him great apprehension about the future.

The weeks went by and the correspondence regarding his marriage piled up. It had became manifest that trying to clarify all the complications and to satisfy all the requirements of the authorities solely by correspondence was clearly a non-starter, so he applied for a short leave in order to tackle the problems in person. When this was eventually granted, he went back to Graz armed with a thick file of papers.

The first interview with the Austrian Registrar proved that his decision to deal with the matter personally was correct. It proved to be a difficult enough matter even when talking over a table - to have attempted to explain by post would surely have been a complete impossibility. In some way he understood and had to accept that the problems were not all due to sheer authoritarian rigidity - his situation was bad enough to explain in English - in German it bordered on farce! Part of just one such interview would appear like a comedy sketch at a seaside revue:-

Registrar: "Your birth certificate, please."
   (Ernie hands it over. Registrar writes)
      "Ernest Terence O'Brien" ?
Ernie: "No, Waites."
   (Registrar looks up at Ernie, then back to certificate)
      "I was adopted at birth"
   (Ernie hands over adoption papers. Registrar erases "O'Brien" and writes in "Waites")
Registrar: (Writing) "Adoptive mother Edith Waites"
Ernie: " No, Edith Stockell."
   (Ernie hands over marriage certificate,
   Registrar erases "Waites", substitutes "Stockell")
Registrar: (Writing) "Adoptive father Edward Stockell"
Ernie: "No, Herbert Waites"

(Ernie hands over death certificate, registrar reaches for his rubber again.)

And so it would go on, the same confusing routine in office after office. Papers piled up, British documents with Austrian copies for Ernie, Austrian records with British translations for Frieda, British authorisations for Frieda, Austrian confirmations for Ernie. Then came the additional complication of the Church, it would be a mixed marriage as Frieda was Roman Catholic - the R.C. padre wanted to see him to explain his religious commitments. He began to despair of ever getting married.

He endured another sorrowful parting from Frieda and returned to Minden once more to await developments. Very soon after arriving back he was summoned to the Commanding Officer himself. He assumed some progress had at last been made regarding his marriage and marched to the Headquarters block with light steps. He entered the office, saluted, and waited for the good news. The Commanding Officer glared at him with a stern face,

"Sergeant. I've had some very disturbing reports" about your behaviour. I hear from the Sergeants' Mess that you are most reluctant to join in mess activities and are more interested in fraternising with the lower ranks. I consulted your bandmaster for confirmation and he informs me that he has already had occasion to mention this to you himself. The Regimental Sergeant Major is most concerned about maintaining military discipline and feels that you are undermining him."

"But, sir.. "

"Don't interrupt me, Sergeant! I am surprised and disappointed in you. A man with a fine record of musical achievement such as yours, a man who has been selected for training as a bandmaster, should reconsider his attitude!..."

Ernie didn't hear much more, his head was buzzing with conflicting emotions. How could his so-called friends in the Mess do such a thing? Why? In his mind he began to list his alternatives. If he accepted the Kneller Hall course would he be condemned to this pettiness for the rest of his life? If he refused it he would have no option but to leave the army to a future offering nothing but insecurity. On the other hand, if he stayed in, there would be no risks and the possibility of rapid promotion through commissioned ranks, but could he reconcile this with his general attitude to life? It had taken the bigotry of a few N.C.O.'s to make him recognise that he was not really suited to a role as a military authoritarian. But he also had Frieda to consider. He forced his brain to listen to the words that were still issuing forth in the background.

The voice came back into focus.

".....so I hope you have fully understood what I have said, Sergeant, and that you will decide to act in a different manner in the future. Now, what have you got to say?"

"There is not much I can say, sir, except that the Mess will not have cause for complaint for much longer. I intend to take my discharge when my time expires in November."

That was it.. His mind was made up. He had lost the will to fight the system and it was time for him to plan the rest of his life in a new direction.

The following day he began writing letters to major companies in England who had bands attached to their works. Letter after letter went out to firms such as Fords, Jaguar and Fodens. Then, purely by coincidence he received a letter from an ex-bandsman who had left some weeks previously extolling the virtues of the Royal Canadian Air Force Band. It appeared he had applied to them and they had accepted him with open arms, and they had more vacancies. Another letter went out from Minden.

The result of this was an invitation, complete with travel warrants, to go to R.A.F. Uxbridge for an interview and audition with a bandmaster of the Royal Canadian Air Force. He was subsequently offered a place in the service as Band Sergeant.

He then resumed his solitary life in the Mess and, not knowing which members he could talk to in confidence, felt more secure keeping his own company. Eventually, after six months of travel, correspondence, interviews and setbacks the formalities of authorisation were finalised and the organisation of the marriage could go ahead. The ceremony was to take place in Graz but Ernie, being so far away, could do little to make the necessary arrangements so he left everything in the hands of Sepp Pucher, Frieda's brother-in-law, who was also to be his Best Man. The date was fixed for November 13th, and, having obtained leave, Ernie went back to Graz on the 11th, where he booked into a small hotel.

Sepp had everything well in hand, even to having made an appointment for Ernie to receive priority treatment at a local gents' outfitters to obtain the traditional Austrian wedding outfit. This was a black hat, suit and silver tie with a white shirt, all covered by a long black overcoat. Ernie looks back at his image - "The overcoat was very long and, coupled with the rimless spectacles I wore at the time, made me look just like a conventional wartime Gestapo agent!" He remembers wearing that suit, minus the overcoat of course, as an evening dress on stage for many years after!

They were married at the Kalvarienburg Church in Gosting, a suburb of Graz, with most of Frieda's family present. The ceremony was the Roman Catholic rite, without Nuptual Mass, which made it very short, and was conducted in German. All Ernie had to do was say "Ja" whenever he was prompted. Frieda wore a long dress of pink with a matching headdress and carried a posy of flowers. As she walked down the aisle on her brother's arm Sepp disconcerted Ernie somewhat by whispering out of the side of his mouth "I hope you know what you are doing!"

The reception was held at the Hotel Strasse and was attended by ten of Frieda's family and her landlady. Frau Brunner may have had suspicions of what might, or might not, have been going on in her lodging house - she was probably relieved to witness her lodger being made into an honest woman! The celebrations lasted from twelve noon until midnight, accompanied by a blind pianist who, during the party, pleased Frieda by making a point of playing her favourite melody - the waltz from "The Gypsy Princess" by Emerich Kalman. Ernie's diary shows that the whole affair cost him fifty-three pounds eighteen shillings, which included all clothing, wedding rings and train fares to Minden! They spent their honeymoon at the family home in the mountains near Spital.

They had not finished with bureaucracy and officialdom, however. Ernie and his bride then had to travel to Dusseldorf to get Frieda registered as an army wife. They spent a whole day there going from office to office, producing documents and signing forms. It was frustratingly tiring but worthwhile for at the end of the day, Frieda was officially a British citizen with her own passport.

As soon as he returned to the barracks at Minden, Ernie applied for Married Quarters but was informed, to his immense dismay, none were available. This made him realise that, once again, he was in the military machine where his own initiative could not assist. He became pessimistic about whether the military life would be any different in Canada and, deciding it would probably not be, wrote to the R.C.A.F. refusing the place he had been offered.

He was spending his third night in the Sergeant's Mess as a married man alone, sadly propping up the bar, when he felt an arm round his shoulder,

"Well, how does married life treat you, old son?" It was Les Garforth. Les was a Colour Sergeant in the Green Howards and was one of the few members of the Mess with whom Ernie could find any affinity as he, too, had an Austrian wife.

"Very rarely," Ernie said, "there's no room in Married Quarter's, so I'm here while Frieda's stuck in Austria."

"Cheer up, Ernie, I know just how you feel, it happened to me, too."

He was comforted by the fact that he was now almost eligible to leave the army, his nine years being nearly completed, but he did not look forward to the financial difficulty of getting Frieda back to England with all her personal belongings. Then, to his relief and pleasure he discovered that the rigid army regulations could actually work in his favour. At the time Ernie originally signed on, the minimum entry age as an adult had been eighteen, the reduction to seventeen and a half had been made towards the end of the war. Consequently, if he so wished, he could request that his service should be counted from his eighteenth birthday and, as the band was due for repatriation early in 1955, he grabbed the opportunity of serving the extra six months. This not only gave him more time to find a civilian occupation but meant that Frieda could accompany the band back to England as an army wife, all expenses paid.

The following night he got another encouragement when Les Garforth came to him and said,

"Ernie, I've had a word with Brigitte - we've got a large spare room in our married quarters and she's quite happy to have you and Frieda stay with us, if you're interested."

Interested! He jumped at the opportunity and sent word to Frieda to come to Minden immediately. The arrangement had a two-fold advantage; they could begin their married life and Frieda would have the companionship of a fellow Austrian-born army wife to help her acclimatise to her new lifestyle.

Frieda and Brigitte became friends, the sharing of married quarters caused no difficulties and Ernie was quite prepared to serve out his few remaining months as a soldier in the manner the authorities demanded. This was not difficult as he no longer had any great desire to go off to the beer cellers of Minden and he spent his evenings at home or with Frieda in the Sergeants' Mess.

To his great relief replies had come plentifully from his letters regarding civilian work, most offering him token work in the factories by day and playing with the Works Band in the evenings and for engagements. It seemed he would be spoilt for choice when he returned home!

The band left Germany in February 1955, and returned to Richmond. Frieda was growing more and more excited about her new nationality and haughtily produced her British passport when demanded at Harwich. They were given a short disembarkation leave and Ernie took Frieda to Scarborough to introduce his bride to his mother. Edith was pleased with her daughter-in-law and made room for her to stay at Maple Drive. Ernie had had some trepidation as to how Ted would react to an Austrian girl in the house but to his relief he was most friendly to her and they spent many happy days visiting Ernie's old haunts while Frieda enjoyed the many sight-seeing trips he insisted on making on her behalf.

When he returned to Richmond he found the place deserted. The only occupants of the barracks, apart from the band, was a skeleton staff consisting of a mere handful of men. The band, too, was reduced in numbers as more men came to the end of their service. Many had had the same idea as Ernie and had gone to join works' bands up and down the country.

The lack of manpower in the barracks, however, meant that the band had to perform all duties and Ernie, as a senior N.C.O., found himself, at times, responsible for the guard. This was not an arduous task, as all it really meant was to ensure that the guardroom at the gate was manned, and that the standard was lowered at Sunset and raised again at Reveille. Ernie admits that on one occasion when he was in charge there was the rare instance when the flag was late coming down and equally late going up again! Army regulations are uncompromising, however, and although he had only a matter of days to serve, he still got a "rollicking"!

His last few days with the Green Howards were indeed happy ones. With so few members in the Sergeants' Mess he spent his time back with the band and, particularly, Brian Clancy. He was still debating in his mind which job to accept as he became a civilian when he received a telephone call from Geoff Eggington. Geoff had been a trumpet player who had left when the band was repatriated in February. He had gone to work at R.A. Lister & Co, a marine engineering company in Dursley, Gloucestershire. He told Ernie how he was enjoying the work there and this swayed him - if he worked at Lister's he would at least be with one of his old friends of the past. He arranged to start work in April.

Then came the day that he had both dreaded coming, and yet excitedly anticipated - the day of his discharge. He sorted out his music, giving some to friends who could use it. He handed in his kit at the Regimental Store, feeling a particularly poignant pang as he passed over his ceremonial uniform. He went to headquarters to collect his discharge papers. His final Certificate of Service says:

"Military Conduct - Exemplary.

Sgt. Waites has been employed in the band of the 1st Btn. of The Green Howards during his service in the army and has performed his duties with great credit. He is outstanding as a musician and instrumentalist. He is a keen and hard worker who is always prepared to put in extra time. Reliable, efficient and trustworthy. He is absolutely honest."

That was it, it was all over. He spent some time saying "Good-bye" to the friends he'd known, in both happy and tragic times, over so many years. He spent a long time with Brian Clancy, too long, because he then felt he could take no more. He had been allowed to keep his battle dress to travel home, it was to be posted back later. He hitched the haversack containing his few personal belongings on his back and walked out of Richmond Barracks, past the guardroom, for the last time.

He did not look back as he made his final journey down the so familiar hill. He paused when he reached the Green Howards War Memorial where the standards had flown so proudly every Sunday when he had been on parade there. He stood at the foot of the steps and thought of Kneller Hall, Minden, Graz, Tampin and Suez. He smiled as he remembered Salome, he shed an unashamed tear as he remembered Peter Parish. They had joined the army together, most probably they would have left together. He had an eerie feeling he was not alone. He stood erect, and lowered his head,

"Good-bye, Ponky," he said, "I'll never forget.."

He hurried down the cobbles of Frenchgate and almost ran to the station. He felt he had to get away as soon as possible .

CHAPTER THIRTEEN

Ernie had little trouble finding Geoff Eggington's home as Dursley turned out to be just a small village in the south of Gloucestershire. His journey from Scarborough had seemed to take an eternity as every mile took him further and further away from the one place where he felt secure. It had been a strange experience having to pay for his ticket at Scarborough Station, stressing on him that he was now a civilian. Gone were the days when travel meant merely being given a destination and collecting a travel warrant - now every train journey would mean spending money and that, at the time, was a scarce commodity! When he had arrived back at Maple Drive after leaving Richmond he had only his four-week leave pay which, after paying his final army dues, left him with eighteen pounds, ten shillings. Most of this he had left with Frieda for her upkeep so he was looking forward to starting work and drawing his first civilian pay packet.

He spent that Saturday evening chatting with Geoff, giving him the story of his last weeks with the band and answering his endless questions about mutual friends. After breakfast on Sunday he went out on the search for lodgings and was fortunate to find one room at a house occupied by an old lady at 38 Woodmancote. The rent would be three pounds a week and they would be allowed to share her parlour. He paid in advance and wrote a letter telling Frieda to come immediately. He returned to Geoff Eggington's, collected his few belongings and moved in.

On Monday morning he found his way to the diesel engine factory at R.A.Lister's. His hours there were to be from 8 a.m. to 5.30 p.m. and he would be working Monday to Friday, for a wage of £6.15.0 per week. It was going to be a completely novel way of life but he relished the thought of being completely free for week-ends - a luxury he'd never experienced before throughout his adult life.

He reported to the office, gave all the required personal details and was then taken to his place of work. He was numbed at his first sight of the factory floor. He looked across the area filled by rows and ranks of robot-like figures manipulating machinery, each to his own alloted task and, amidst the noise and bustle, subconsciously compared it to the open air of the parade ground and the precision formation of the band. He realised at once that he had made a great mistake and his heart sank at the thought of a lifetime in such an environment. He was put to work fixing tappets. He had no idea what a tappet was but was teamed up with two other men and told to do exactly what they were doing. He did, for two whole long boring days. It had been explained to him that the band met every Tuesday and Thursday. He couldn't wait for Tuesday evening to come.

Two days in the army would have flown by, the two days endlessly probing with feeler guages seemed like two years. On Tuesday evening he thankfully grabbed his clarinet and sought the band room. The band met in a permanent practice room within the factory and he rushed upstairs to find band members idly sitting around, reading papers or chatting while awaiting the arrival of the bandmaster. In an army band room they would have been playing - a cacophony, true, as each played his own personal whim of the moment, but there would have been an air of enthusiasm. Here he could detect only lethargy and an apparent complete lack of real interest. He felt insecure and vulnerable with the sensation of critical inquisitive eyes boring into him and felt that he had to justify his presence there. He no longer wore the three stripes showing his status as an instrumentalist so there was only one way to do it. He took his clarinet from its case, adjusted the mouthpiece and blew a few notes. He sat in a corner and ran his fingers over the keys playing scales and then, partly to prove his competence and partly to show off, he launched out into full gallop with one of his specialities. He finished.

"Hgh!" a disgruntled voice said, "I'll give you six weeks."

At least someone was talking to him, "Why, what's wrong?" he asked.

"Nothing's wrong, mate, that's just the point - you're too bloody good." A long pause then, "Yeah, six weeks - at the most!

Ernie was trying to glean the exact meaning of the comment when the bandmaster arrived and they all shuffled to their obviously customary places. The bandmaster saw Ernie and said,

"Oh, you're the new bloke ... sit there." and pointed to a vacant chair at the end of the third clarinet stands."

It was the lowliest place in the band but Ernie took his place and the rehearsal began. He was appalled and even more bored than he had been with his tappets! The music demanded his playing the simplest parts imaginable. They played "The Dam Busters March", a standard military band arrangement which gave him no satisfaction whatsoever. He had to force himself not to blast out with the version he had been used to playing and wondered what the reaction would have been had he done so. At the end of the session the bandmaster said to him,

"I was listening to you, lad - you can move up to second clarinet on Thursday."

He may have meant it as a compliment but Ernie felt angry. Then his anger turned to amusement. It was all rather pathetic, really - the ex-solo clarinettist of the Green Howards was, he gathered, supposed to be honoured by being allowed to play second clarinet in such an ensemble!

He was surprised at the mundane quality of the band and its choice of arrangements. Before the war many big factories had their own bands and that of R.A. Lister was renowned as among the best. It had been a competition band, winning many trophies and being in demand to play at numerous sea-side resorts. It had struggled to survive during the war and afterwards never re-established itself or regained its former excellence. Ernie felt very let down when he heard them that Tuesday.

Wednesday dragged by, Thursday reluctantly followed and with it the second band rehearsal. He was now playing second clarinet but the parts still demanded absolutely nothing from him. He felt he had returned to the dark ages of musicianship. He grew more and more miserable as he walked back to his lodgings but cheered up when he found Frieda had arrived. They spent the evening walking round the village, happy in each other's company, but Ernie was now convinced he could not stay there. He assessed the future to which he had condemned himself - boring repetitive work, undemanding music with the band, the company of the old lady indoors or a visit to the one small cinema in the evenings. He began to scan the "Vacancies" columns of "The Melody Maker".

There he saw it - an advertisement inviting applications for an alto-saxophone player to join a band for a summer season in Porthcawl. He found a telephone box and applied the same evening and was asked to go to Porthcawl for an auditon the following Saturday. He drained their dwindling resources, bought his ticket and travelled to South Wales. His audition consisted of sitting in with the band as it played at a regular concert. He'd never practised the items or met any of the other bandsmen - he just sight-read the parts and, in some way, enjoyed being in the midst of musicians again. There was no doubt about the outcome - at the end of the show the bandleader asked him to start as a permanent member as soon as possible. After explaining that he was obliged to work a further week at R.A. Lister's and promising to join the band the following week-end he returned to Dursley to break the good news to Frieda.

On the Monday morning he gave his notice went back to his tappets in good heart knowing he could now count the days left on the fingers of one hand. The bombshell fell on Thursday. He got a terse letter informing him that the man he was to replace in the band had decided not to leave after all and that therefore Ernie's services would no longer be required. The episode had cost him both time and train fare he could ill afford but it did give him his first lesson in the vagaries of show business.

Sheer panic now seized him. He was stuck, with his wife, in one room in an unfamiliar area, out of work and with no money. He searched the "Situations Vacant" column of the local newspapers and was forced to take the only job that was available at such short notice - shovelling coke into a boiler. The wage, however, was the highest he had earned to date - fourteen pounds a week! To earn it, though, he had to work for ten hours a day and would stagger home each evening completely worn out, fit only to grab a meal and crawl into bed. It was obvious he could not keep up such a way of life for long, both mentally and physically. He sent several letters replying to further advertisements in "The Melody Maker".

History seemed to repeat itself. He received a reply from an Eddie Shaw asking him to travel to Sale, a suburb of Manchester with a postal address in Cheshire, to attend an audition at the Locarno Ballroom. Once again he spent money on train fare to the north and on arriving at the ballroom, dressed in his Wedding suit", found a dance in full swing. As at Porthcawl, he was asked to "sit in with the band" and play.

After three of four sets of dances there was an interval when the stage revolved, carrying the band backstage and a trio into view of the dancers.

The bandleader turned to the alto-sax player and said,

"You can go home," then, to Ernie, "you - play for the rest of the night. I'll put you up, you can go back tomorrow." Ernie thoroughly enjoyed playing for the rest of the dance, it was obvious he now had a job. At the end of the evening he was taken to Eddie Shaw's bachelor flat to spend an hour or so talking about his army days. In the morning they were having breakfast of eggs and toast in the kitchen while reading the morning papers when Eddie said,

"Shove the kettle on again, we'll have another brew."

Ernie filled the old fashioned copper kettle, put it on the stove, lit the gas under it and returned to his boiled egg. "Wooosh!" there was a flash of flame - he'd left the newspaper on the stove and it was now blazing away fiercely. There was nothing he could do but prod the burning paper with a tablespoon to keep it on top of the hob until it was reduced to ashes.

"Bloody marvellous," Eddie said, "I give you a job and you try to set my flat on fire!"

That was the first time the job had been mentioned.

"So I've got it." Ernie said, cleaning up the mess with a dishcloth.

"Of course you've got it. Ten guineas. Seven nights a week, 7.30 to 11.30. O.K.? How soon can you start?"

Ernie remembered Porthcawl. "Is that it? Is there any form of contract?"

Eddie Shaw said nothing. He got up, opened a drawer, took out a piece of scrap paper and a pen and wrote, "I promise to employ E. Waites at the Locarno Ballroom at £10.10.0 per week." and signed it.

"Right," he said, "that's it."

That gesture, Ernie was to find, was typical of Eddie Shaw, a man of brusque manner who spoke with short sharp sentences - if he had to use sentences that is, as he never even used a sentence if one word would do. This was entirely different from his manner on stage where his verbosity could charm a hostile audience and persuade a crowd that even the most mundane performance was a gala occasion. He was a very stout man, always immaculate when on stage in smartly pressed evening dress with his hair brushed flat with haircream. He was the epitome of a showman and Ernie speaks of him as being in the same mould as Barnum, admitting that his time with Eddie Shaw was the finest tuition he had on how to manipulate an audience.

Ernie left the flat in a state of exhilaration. Ten guineas a week meant he could now afford to pay the rent, the hire purchase on his saxophone and still have enough to live on. He spent Monday morning looking round Sale, exploring his new environment and at the same time searching for somewhere to live. He found a bed-sitting room in Moorfield Grove at two pounds fifteen shillings a week and arranged to move in there the following week-end. He went back to Dursley, ended the coke-shovelling job and, with the remains of the money he had left, bought train tickets for himself and Frieda. They travelled to Manchester the following Saturday.

Playing every evening in a dance band was a far cry from the daily army routine of rehearsal and parades but he soon adapted. His days were his own and although he had once thought that having so much free time would be pleasant, he found that it also had its drawbacks. They lived in the one room, sharing a kitchen and its facilities when the landlady was not using it. Frieda had an obsession with cleanliness and would spend ages washing clothes the Austrian way - scrubbing away on a rubbing board and then giving the laundry uncountable rinses. The small garden had room for only a tiny washing line and friction developed with the landlady over its constant acquisition by her lodgers. He therefore found himself for ever acting as mediator and would escape by leaving the house and wandering round the town. He wished at such times that he could have attended a band rehearsal but, unlike the army, the dance band seemed to work on a code of "make it up as you go along".

He also discovered that his saxophone was of poor quality. He had bought it in a hurry when first he had been asked to "double up" with his clarinet. He bought what he could afford at the time and it was obvious to him, now that he had got used to it, that it was out of tune and would need to be replaced. He was paying for it on hire-purchase at two pounds ten shillings a week and when he went for a new one was offered very little in part-exchange. The outcome of the negotiations was that he had a brand new saxophone and a new agreement to pay five pounds a week! This took all the slack from their budget and Frieda had to find work. She became a cleaner at Sale Girls' Grammar School.

He went to work on a bicycle in those days and recalls the winter of 1955 as being one of many fogs and smogs. One foggy night in December he could see very little as he cycled home up Marsland Road with his saxophone strapped to the carrier. Bent down over the handlebars peering for the kerb he never noticed the traffic crawling behind him until he turned into the narrow cul-de-sac where the house was situated. When he got off the bike at the front door he was amazed to see a line of cars lined up behind him! One driver had been following his rear light through the fog and the other cars had tailed on, each seeking guidance from the one in front. Chaos ensued as they then all tried to back out again on to the main road!

New Year's Eve was, of course, a major event at the ballroom and it was in the early hours of 1956 that Ernie finally arrived home, exhausted, to be met in the hall by an irate landlady who had been waiting up for him. She wasted no time on preliminaries,

"OUT!", she yelled, "Tomorrow!"

Ernie turned on the charm he had learned from Eddie Shaw but to no avail. He gathered that the landlady and Frieda had had another of their disagreements about using the kitchen and washing line but this time it had blown up out of all proportion. The landlady was adamant, she turned them out of the room at a few hours' notice and he spent New Years' Day hunting for accommodation again. After searching fruitlessly all morning, following address after address in the local paper, he was fortunate to find somewhere to live late in the afternoon. He went back to collect Frieda and, with their cases balanced on his bike, they walked to the town centre and moved into 29 Sibson Road, a house owned by a kindly lady, Miss Harms. She allowed them to have the front bedroom but, on the same floor, they also had a small kitchen and a bathroom. This, to them, was luxury. It was to cost them three pounds a week. Frieda found a better paid job doing kitchen work at the "Coffee Pot" on Washway Road.

Business was beginning to fall at the Locarno as this was the start of the decline of popularity of ballroom dancing. Eddie Shaw tried all ways of keeping interest in the hall. One of his ideas was the introduction of an additional attraction - "The New Orleans All Stars", a Dixieland band which would play a special cabaret spot during the evening. For a while it did the trick and was a great success. What really happened was that when the stage revolved to bring on the trio during an interval, six members of the band, including Ernie, would hastily change into striped jackets and straw hats. Two of them would grab banjos and Ernie his clarinet. The stage would then revolve again to reveal the "special attraction". They would play for about twenty minutes and then go round again, change back into black and re-appear as the Eddie Shaw band! Ernie actually enjoyed those interludes, though, as it gave him the chance to shine on the clarinet again as a soloist. He became invaluable in the band.

In May, Eddie said to him, "How do you feel about doing a summer season?"

"Where?" Ernie asked.

"In Llandudno. Payne's Cafe. Six weeks. You're in charge. Six days and special Sunday Gala. Fifteen quid a week."

"Who's going?"

"You, a bass player, trumpet, pianist and drummer."

Ernie should have known better, but the money was attractive. "O.K.", he said.

Payne's Cafe was a very up-market establishment with a large banner outside extolling its latest attraction -"Eddie Shaw's Broadcasting Band". Ernie went inside to find opulent surroundings complete with host and hostess in full evening dress. In the afternoon Ernie assembled the musicians Eddie had sent him and, with the host and hostess watching critically, set the "Broadcasting Band" to play. They were terrible! The trumpeter could play, the bass could cope, the young drummer couldn't keep time and the pianist was diabolical - and they had no music! Ernie was in trouble! The room was full for a "Tea Dance" and all he could do was say "Try to follow me" and would blast out full power on his saxophone in an attempt to drown the noise coming from behind him. The host and hostess seemed to take it in turns angrily whispering "Too fast!" or "Too slow!" while keeping a gaping false smile on their faces for the benefit of the customers. It was a nightmare. The host would announce "Ladies and Gentlemen, take your partners for the Moonlight Saunter."

"Wot the 'ell's that?" said the drummer.

"What shall I play?" asked the pianist;

"Anything!" Ernie said, "they all sound the bloody same from you." He lifted his sax and blasted out something resembling a barn dance.

As the afternoon progressed the reaction of the host and hostess changed from disbelief to anger, reminding Ernie of the "double takes" so expertly done by Laurel and Hardy!

After a few days the boss called Ernie to his office,

"What the hell's going on?" he demanded, "that lot have never played on radio! I'm not standing for this!" He snatched the telephone and rang Eddie Shaw. As he talked on the 'phone Ernie was intrigued to see his anger subside and then change into geniality. As he rang off he was positively friendly.

"Right, Mr. Shaw," he said, "I'm looking forward to seeing you, and thanks very much." Ernie's opinion that Eddie Shaw was a genius when it came to public relations was enhanced once again!

The following day, during the interval, Eddie walked into the restaurant, beaming confidently. He saw Ernie,

"Hi! How's it going?"

"It's a disaster."

"Don't worry! I'll go see the boss."

"He's got a point you know," Ernie said, "they're bloody awful!"

"Leave it to me . ."

The band was playing again by the time Eddie came out of the office with the owner, laughing and joking as they shook hands. As Eddie passed Ernie he said,

"Bloody hell, you're right! I'll find you a new lot."

He arrived the next day with different musicians and took the others away in his car. The replacements were not much better but were good enough to be able to bluff it out. In any case, Ernie was beginning to acquire a very thick skin.

Then came Sunday and the "Gala Night" which was heralded by a poster outside listing the guest artists who would be appearing, but Ernie had seen nobody by the time the show started. Eddie Shaw was leading this one himself and he made his customary grand entrance, immaculate as usual. Ernie still had no idea at all as to what was going on. Eddie sat at the piano. "Ladies and Gentlemen," he announced, "A medley from Showboat!" There was complete silence. "Well, go on!" he whispered to Ernie.

"Go on, what?"

"Play something, for God's sake!"

"What?"

"Showboat, you silly bugger!"

Ernie launched into "Old Man River", busking, while Eddie played flourishes on the piano. At the end Ernie changed to "Make Believe". The trumpet player added a few notes, the drummer was banging away ad lib and the bass player was lost completely.

After half an hour of similar confusion, Eddie went to the microphone and announced a guest artist . ."That famous Welsh Tenor David Waites!" Ernie

looked round for a few seconds until the name registered,
"Go on!" Eddie said, "Sing!"

Ernie sang and brought the house down. Consequently David Waites, the celebrated Welsh tenor, sang at every Sunday Gala for six weeks. With no extra pay of course!

Later on in the show the trumpet player was astounded to hear Eddie announce that he was a noted member of the London Symphony Orchestra and found himself playing "Somewhere a Voice is Calling" with no shoes on. He'd removed them for comfort and hadn't had time to put them back on when he was suddenly promoted to soloist. .... and Ernie remembers his feet smelt awful!

Ernie fell for it again the following year, this time at Lewis' Stores in Manchester. Lewis's had a restaurant upstairs and Eddie was booked to provide a trio to play there.

"Lewis's," Ernie was told, "Ten 'til one, two-thirty 'til five. Extra ten quid a week. See you there ten o'clock Monday. Not sure if bass player can get there dead on ten but he'll be there as soon as poss. He's leaving his bass on the stage ready. I'm playing piano."

Ernie should have learned his lesson but he turned up dutifully on Monday morning. Ten o' clock came and went, with no sign of anybody else. The manager was glaring at him so he sat down at the piano and started to play waltzes. After a while the manager approached him,

"Where's Mr. Shaw?"

Ernie had to think quickly. "Delayed," he said, "he's been called to the phone," and continued with "The Merry Widow".

Half an hour later Eddie arrived, brashly nonchalant as always.

"O.K." he said, "I'll take over, you get on the bass."

"You what?!!!"

"Don't tell me you can't play the bass!"

"I can't. I can pick a few notes out, that's all."

"That's enough ... get on it!"

So Ernie made his debut as a double-bass player and played for an hour before the owner of the instrument appeared. Ernie thankfully unpacked his saxophone.

"What are we playing next?" Eddie asked.

"I don't know, you're in charge!"

"You suggest something. no I have to do everything?"

"What about Lisbon Story?" Ernie whispered.

"What's in that?"

"Pedro the Fisherman."

"That'll do. You start, I'll follow."

It was the same every day. Neither of the others ever turned up on time and Ernie learned how to sit at a piano, idly fingering the keys, and yet keep an audience amused

One afternoon the restaurant was suddenly filled by a huge crowd of members of the Salvation Army, there must have been over a hundred of them, all in uniform. Eddie summed up the situation and latched on in a flash.

"Quick!" he said to Ernie, "Nip downstairs and get some religious music!"

In those days Lewis' had a music counter. Ernie ran down and purchased "Bless this House" and "The Holy City". He returned, handed them to Eddie, who opened them in front of him at the piano.

"Off we go!" he said, "You sing."

"I don't know the words!"

"Sod it!" Eddie said, "Here!" He handed the sheet music to Ernie. "You sing - I'll busk it!"

Ernie sang. There was an uproar of applause. Eddie sat at the piano, beaming.

Eddie Shaw proved to Ernie that, at times in the music business, it **was** possible to get away with murder! During those years he served an apprenticeship in show business that no amount of money could buy.

CHAPTER FOURTEEN

It was early in 1957 that Ernie began to sum up his achievements and assess his progress and he was far from satisfied with what he saw. He had a regular wage coming in but he would often wallow in nostalgia and wonder where he would have been and what he might be doing if he had not so impulsively left the army. The sight, the sound, and the precision of a military band on the television in Miss Harm's lounge would, at times, create a longing to be back in uniform playing the challenging music on which he had been weaned. He had work, it was true, and he was grateful for it but he needed to give more than the plebeian entertainment it provided. He needed to be a leader again. He would dream of a band of which he was in sole charge, playing his own arrangements in the way he wanted them played. The dream would last for only a matter of minutes for he was worldly enough to see that the days of the "Big Band" were numbered. It had taken him years of training and experience to be able to fill a concert hall with sound -now, with the advent of electronics, raw youths with practically no musical knowledge or ability could create a similar effect merely by turning a switch. He had bouts of depression about where it would all lead.

Domestically, too, he saw nothing to cheer him. They were still living in a self-contained rented room in somebody else's home, his work, coupled with the shortage of money precluded holidays and Frieda was not finding it easy to adapt to life in England. Her knowledge of the language had improved amazingly but it was clear she suffered from a lack of family contact and, possibly due to shyness, was not making any close friends. She spent her daytime hours working on domestic chores in the manner she had been used to as a girl, steadfastly refusing to adopt any labour saving machinery. While others threw their dirty linen in a washing machine or took it to a laundrette, she would continue her self-imposed ritual of boiling, scrubbing and rinsing, innocently monopolising Miss Harm's kitchen. It was only after weeks of persuasion that Ernie cajoled her into using an electric iron. She was meticulous in all she did, so a job that other women would skimp over in minutes would take hours of her time. She was a born worker, and she worked.

With Ernie at the Locarno every evening their social life was therefore nil, and the happy carefree days of Graz could never be re-created. In turn, Ernie would envisage those happy days in the Austrian mountains and would despair at his inability to re-live them. The bouts of depression, luckily, did not last long, usually relieved by his music. He was also getting some satisfaction in seeing the progress of the few private pupils he had accepted. He now had four or five budding clarinet players and he would travel to give them tuition in their own homes.

The Locarno, and the band, got a valuable publicity boost when it was used by the B.B.C. as the venue for its programme "Come Dancing". For these shows Eddie Shaw would augment the band, bringing in some top-class instrumentalists to improve its quality. Most of these would be from the B.B.C. Northern Variety Orchestra and included such players as Johnny Roadhouse, Norman George and Fred Hefferen. Come Dancing was a regular broadcast and very soon Ernie had made friends with many members of the N.V.N. In turn, Ernie, found himself joining the B.B.C. band for regular broadcasts.

In those days of the mid-fifties the B.B.C. Northern studios, then housed on Piccadilly, were one of the major contributors to the national broadcasting network, particularly in the field of comedy, with acts such as Morecambe and Wise, Ken Dodd, Al Read, Ken Platt and Ted Lune, in shows with producers like Barney Colehan and Ronnie Taylor. One of the longest running of these, Ronnie Taylor's "Variety Fanfare", was recorded on Sunday evenings at the Hulme Hippodrome in Manchester and the orchestra would often gather with the cast and technicians at a couple of local public houses, "Kennetts" or the "Lord Raglan" which was managed by Ted Lune, before he joined "The Army Game". Ernie spent happy hours in their convivial company and at the same time set the foundations for his future role in the hectic world of radio and television.

With the Northern Variety Orchestra, which was later to be re-named the Northern Dance Orchestra, Ernie found the musical empathy he had been lacking ever since he had left the army for in their company he was once again among men who loved and lived music making and were experts at their calling. Some of them lived in Sale and nearby Altrincham and a close friendship developed with Ernie Watson, trumpet, Les Lovelady, baritone saxophone and Freddie Hefferen, alto saxophone. He also found a natural kinship with Johnny Roadhouse, a man whose playing he had admired for many years, having listened to him with esteem on the radio while in the heat of the Suez and the Far East. Johnny had a music shop in Manchester and Ernie would go there to buy spare reeds and then spend many happy hours comparing their very differing histories.

The publicity generated by "Come Dancing" helped the Locarno make a temporary revival and Ernie recalls the hall being crammed on Saturday and Wednesday nights with a thousand or so people, young and old, thoroughly enjoying themselves together, without an alcoholic drink in sight for there was no licensed bar in the ballroom. How soon things were to change!

On the domestic scene, however, things were not improving. The spectre of confrontation over washing lines and cooking facilities was rearing its head again and Ernie could sense the signs of displeasure in his landlady. Miss Harms was too polite to make a scene but the old adage of two women being unable to share one kitchen was undoubtedly true and Ernie was at a loss as to how it could be dealt with amicably. During an interval one evening he confided of his concern in Jimmy Brewer, the trombone player,

"It's unfortunate but it's just her way," he said, "she falls out with everybody over housework, of all things!"

"You need a place of your own then, its obvious, Jimmy said, "my flat's vacant."

"I didn't know you had one! Why didn't you mention it before?"

"You never asked me, you idiot. There's a complete flat, empty, at the back of the shop."

Jimmy owned a wallpaper shop on Northenden Road and, the next day, Ernie went to have a look at it. Behind the shop was an unfurnished flat. It was small but it had two rooms, bathroom, kitchen and at the back a small garden with plenty of room for a washing line. For the first time since his marriage Ernie saw the the opportunity of their having privacy and Frieda being mistress of her own domestic life. He accepted it on the spot, agreeing to pay a weekly rent of three pounds, fifteen shillings. The hire purchase payments on his saxophone conveniently concluded that month so he could now afford the extra outlay in rent... or so he thought! Parkinson's Law, "Expenditure will always rise to meet income!" applied itself - for now they were faced with the expense of equipping the flat, so the small amount of savings they had accumulated went in one swoop on pots, pans and cutlery. Ernie's wage at that time was thirteen guineas so furniture was bought from Ashfield's in Stretford for £200 on hire purchase and the gain from the ending of the saxophone debt was immediately gobbled up again. Ernie revelled in his new home and was determined to make it into something that would for ever expunge the childhood memories of Cooks Row. For the next week or so he spent every available mlnute decorating, painting, fitting floor coverings and hanging curtains. He was, he remembers, "real chuffed"!

The "Come Dancing" broadcasts ended and, once again, the attendance at the ballroom began falling. The management tried an experiment of having a "record night" when, instead of the live band, gramophone records were played over an amplifier. This was a new idea at the time and the novelty brought the crowds in, so much so that it was decided to make the "record night" a weekly attraction. Some members of the band welcomed the venture and were gloating at the idea of having a regular night off with no loss of pay, but Ernie was very worried,

"Can't you see what's happening?" he asked them. "It's one night now, then it will be two - soon it will be seven nights a week, and no need for a band!"

His forecast was, of course, to prove correct. The "Disco" was on its way, even if in an embryo state. It too would reign supreme for a while until its own demise would come and the Locarno become extinct, giving way to a Bingo Hall.

But that, for the moment was in the future. During that summer of 1957 the band was still an attraction and their wages secure. As secure as they could be, that is, from the way they were paid. Ernie could never understand how or why but Eddie Shaw's bank seemed to be his trousers pocket. On Fridays they would go up to his office cum dressing room for their wages which he would dole out to them in turn. There were no wage packets, he would delve deep into his pocket and bring out a handful of notes each crumpled into a small ball which he would then smooth out individually on the table top, counting as he went on. When the correct figure was reached he'd bundle the lot together again and hand them over.

The first real sign of the coming collapse was when it was decided to dispense with the services of the trio that had for years filled the intervals between sets of dances. The gap was filled by Eddie Shaw himself, on piano. As the band played its interval signature tune, "Lovely Lady, I'm falling madly in love with you . . ." the stage would now revolve to reveal a grand piano. Eddie, who had stepped off the revolve, would then sit at it and "tinker" for half an hour, stunning the crowd with sheer charisma. He was no great pianist, he was a pure showman. Ernie says it was uncanny how he could mesmerise an audience, time after time.

Eddie introduced another idea to maintain audience interest - a "Talent Contest" and he had no shortage of aspiring stars from the floor. The bait was a prize of ten pounds and dozens of would-be vocalists, comedians and instrumentalists would turn up hoping to be "spotted" - by whom no one ever seemed to ask ! For about a year Ernie had been visiting the home of a thirteen year old boy named Roy Buxton to give him clarinet lessons and since getting his own flat had been inviting the lad to his own home, where the sessions would go on for hours because Ernie could see the boy was keen and had talent. In a way, he felt he was acting something like George Garside had with him at Kneller Hall, willingly giving his time to a genuinely keen pupil.

He suggested to Roy that he should attend one of Eddie's talent contests and one night the boy nervously stepped on to the stage. He was so small he couldn't be seen so someone lifted him up and stood him on top of the grand piano. Ernie had written him a special arrangement for the occasion and, in front of his first large audience, that little lad in short trousers played "Memories of You" in true Benny Goodman style and brought the house down! The crowd raved. Even the band applauded. There was no doubt whatsoever who was the winner of the ten pounds that night.

At the end of the evening Eddie Shaw presented the money to him and asked,

"What are you going to do with all this money?"

"I'm going to buy my teacher a record," he said.

"What record?"

"Mozart's Clarinet Quintet."

"And who's your lucky teacher?" Eddie went on, "milking" the situation.

"Mr. Waites."

Ernie was as proud as a peacock, not only for the acclaim given to his pupil but for the humble attitude the boy adopted on winning.

Roy Buxton grew up to become a successful musician in his own right but went into the theatrical branch of the business, playing in pit orchestras for big shows in Manchester and London theatres.

That was not the only time when Ernie saw a band burst into unrestrained applause, though another instance involved professional performers. It was at a Sunday recording of "Variety Fanfare". For the recording of the radio show the orchestra was permanently on stage and on this occasion tall rostra blocks had been erected behind it to position a choir over the heads of the instrumentalists. The stage was, as usual, covered with a mass of cables leading to the large number of microphones needed - several dotted amongst the musicians plus some on very tall stands to pick up the choir, these stands were some eight feet tall. The programme was nearing its end and the penultimate item was the Vernons Girls Choir who did their act on the platform to the rear of the orchestra.. The choir item ended and Roger Moffatt announced the star of the show who happened to be Ted Lune. Ted's act always commenced with a long "letter from my mum", not a new idea by far, but he had managed to make a reputation with it.

He started "reading" his letter and had almost finished it when there was a "Crash!" - one of the girls of the choir, creeping off in the background, had slipped. She fell, dragging others with her, the microphone stands toppled and fell into the orchestra, a tall one catching Ernie a glancing blow on the head. He recalled a similar fiasco in Suez and, for a second, wondered if Salome had turned up again! The recording had to be stopped and there was a long break while the engineers repaired the damage and the orchestra sorted out its music. Ronnie Taylor, the producer, went on stage to re-start the recording and had to make a request to the audience, that every comedian dreaded

"In order to maintain continuity we'll have to re-start the recording at the beginning of Ted's act. Of course, you will have heard it all before, so may I ask you to pretend you haven't and try to laugh where you laughed before the accident."

Ernie, like the rest of the orchestra, knew that Ted faced an up-hill struggle - to tell the same jokes again so soon and hope to get a natural reaction was inconceivable. They played his signature tune, Ted came on for the second time - and "read" an entirely different letter! During the short break he had got together with his script-writers and had produced a brand new script in a matter of minutes. The band spontaneously applauded with the audience, appreciating such professionalism.

That night was memorable - Ted Lune got the acclamation, Ernie got a headache and lump on the side of his head!

Meanwhile, on the domestic front, a small hiccup had developed at home. As has been said, when first he saw the flat, Ernie was pleased to see the space at the back for a washing line, an essential piece of equipment for Frieda, and one of his first jobs was to fix one, complete with clothes prop. What he wasn't told, and could in no way be expected to anticipate, was that Jimmy Brewer had an old oil drum there in which he burned all his old wallpaper. When he did this, of course, the air was filled with tiny bits of charred and burning paper which floated about due to the heat of the fire, spreading all over the garden, and Frieda's laundry! Seeing that Frieda did washing every day of the week there was bound to be a clash of activities but Jimmy had to dispose of his scrap paper. An unofficial rota was subsequently agreed, albeit reluctantly by Frieda, specifying the days when he would do his incinerating and no laundry would be hung out. Like Queen Victoria, Frieda was not amused!

Ernie continued to be astounded at times by Eddie Shaw's audacity. It was natural that due to sickness or the like there would be times when he would have one or even two deputy players in the band but on one occasion he sent in a complete band of "ringers" while he took his own group to play a lucrative engagement at the Gaumont Cinema, Manchester, to play in the pit in front of the huge screen for the premiere of "South Pacific". Recognising the occasion could be a golden opportunity for valuable publicity he thought he could get the band noticed by playing a new version of "The Queen" and promptly put the idea to Ernie,

"You know what I mean," he said, "loads of big chords and fanfares." There was, of course, no mention of any fee for doing the arrangement!

Ernie dutifully went to work and wrote out the necessary band parts which, to the accompaniment of much unnecessary gesturing from Eddie, the band played. Two separate newspapers reported the event and, after reviewing the film, one critic remarked along the lines that "The Eddie Shaw Band played a version of the National Anthem that did nothing for the status of the Monarchy!", while the other made special comment on the "Fresh, sparkling arrangement of God Save the Queen". Such are the whims of critics!

In August the predictable occurred. The Locarno closed its doors as a ballroom and The Eddie Shaw Band ended years of association with Sale. Ballroom dancing was by then declining fast in popularity and giving way to the era of "Rock and Roll" and the venues where dance bands were needed were growing fewer. "The Palais" in Bolton, however, was still tenuously hanging on to its image and Eddie Shaw and his band took over there in August. This caused Ernie a major problem, how to travel from Sale to Bolton and then home late at night. Public transport was not available at those hours, he certainly couldn't afford taxis and the idea of cycling fifteen miles each way was out of the question. Once again Jimmy Brewer was his saviour, he had just bought his first car and offered Ernie a lift -a small gesture it may seem, but it prevented Ernie finding himself out of work.

The band they replaced had played in Bolton for over twenty years. Phil Foster's band had been resident at the "Palais" throughout the war and many a war-time marriage had its roots on the Palais dance floor. The ballroom held memories for most of the local residents and the post-war modernisation and loss of its established band made it a hard act to follow in those inhospitable times when the public seemed totally disinterested. Eddie Shaw thought they were fighting a losing battle from the start and he was correct - the engagement lasted only to the end of the year when the Bolton Palais, like the rest, succumbed to the Discotheque and Bingo.

They found a new appointment in Manchester as resident band at The Plaza Ballroom which had a new and dynamic manager by the name of Jimmy Saville. The regular band, which played every night of the week consisted of only eight members but they were augmented on Saturdays to create a "Big Band". By this time Ernie was writing all the band's arrangements as well as playing every night yet was still receiving only his basic wage of thirteen pounds a week, but he could see no way of rectifying the injustice due to the general lack of opportunities in the dance band sphere. Reports came in daily of ballrooms closing all over the country.

It was clear, however, that if a ballroom could survive amidst the torrential tide of change then the Plaza would be the one to do so. Jimmy Saville was a dynamic character who expected his staff to be likewise, constantly urging and exhorting them and always demanding the highest of standards. He was a fanatic for keeping fit and chose to ride a cycle in preference to using a car. Ernie remembers him arriving at the hall on his bike and then later appearing in the foyer in full evening dress - tails, high wing collar, carnation and sporting a monocle. He was the epitome of a man who was going somewhere. He oozed charisma and his message was plain - while he was a manager he was going to be the best manager. He insisted on all members of the staff being smart and set an incontestable example.

In May 1958 the Plaza was chosen as the venue for the annual Press Ball. It was an occasion where the "Big Band" format was required and it involved Ernie in much extra work writing the special items that Eddie Shaw demanded for such a prestigious event. Personalities from the newspaper world were there rubbing shoulders with stars of show business and the mayors and dignitaries from boroughs all over Greater Manchester. The band took the stage but did not begin to play because the ballroom floor was being ignored. The guests were standing around in huddled groups talking animatedly while others rushed to and fro both inside and outside the room. It was evident that something had gone seriously wrong but what it was, was a mystery until Jimmy Saville stepped up to the microphone,

"Ladies and Gentlemen," he announced, "news is coming in that the plane carrying the Manchester United football team has crashed on take-off from Munich. We understand it is a major disaster and there are many fatalities. Out of respect, therefore, it has been decided that the Ball should be cancelled." There was a dreadful hush, the crowd quietly dispersed and the band packed up to make its way home. It was another night that will for ever be imprinted on Ernie's memory.

The Eddie Shaw band lasted until July 6th. By this time it was apparent to everyone that its time had come and its members found themselves seeking work in a contracting market. Eddie himself went to the Oxford Cinema under the title of "Musical Director", running a trio from the balcony and playing between films, for the rest it was purely a matter of seeking what crumbs of work were available.

Forcing the spectre of unemployment to one side, Ernie attempted to turn the situation to his advantage and use the enforced idleness to rejuvenate his flagging marriage. The gregarious demands of show business were readily met by Ernie's extroverted character but were in direct conflict with the introverted life-style that was indigenous to Frieda. They had no common interests and had

had no mutual contacts outside the home, even with their own families, from whom they were slowly drifting apart, so he suggested they should go to Scarborough and spend a fortnight at his mother's, on holiday. Frieda overcame her reserve and reluctantly agreed.

It was a disaster. They arrived to find that Ted Stockell was in the midst of another bout of malevolent languor and Edith spent the first two days of their visit trying to keep the topic of any sparse conversation away from wars, the army or Germany, which turned out to be an impossibility. They were deprived of the intervening presence of Les Stockell because he, like Ernie, had signed on for regular military service, though he had joined the Royal Air Force. In the town all had changed, particularly around the area of the Harbour, where the places he knew and, in a way, loved, had long been demolished. His old friends had dispersed; he had a sensation of not belonging there any more. Some of the buildings were familiar but he was a stranger, a mere visitor to what should have been a welcoming hometown. He realised that time had intervened, Scarborough no longer offered him anything, he no longer belonged to Scarborough. He therefore sought refuge among the holiday makers, subconsciously begrudging them the carefree abandon they were so obviously enjoying. He longed for Frieda to be able to relax her forbearing disposition and to join in some light-hearted distractions but her self-assumed role of inferiority seemed to be immovable.

The family rapport he'd hoped for did not materialise either, in fact the outlook seemed to deteriorate even more. One afternoon during their second week they were left alone in the house while Edith accompanied Ted on a hospital visit. Ernie watched television and was pleased to hear Frieda pottering around in the kitchen, he assumed she was at last attempting to bridge the gap and was making some Austrian delicacy for them all for tea. Edith and Ted arrived back and Edith went into the kitchen,

"What are you doing?" he heard Edith ask.

"I've washed your dishes."

"But I'd already washed them before I left."

"They were'nt clean, they needed correct rinsing."

"Are you saying we're dirty?" Ted intervened, "because if you are I can't see why you're prepared to stay here sponging on us.

Ernie had no alternative but to pack their bags and catch the next train back to Manchester.

"I'm not going there again, ever." Frieda said on the way home. Nor did she. The journey home was made in silence.

It was a very downcast Ernie who again began searching the pages of "The

Melody Maker", wondering where his next job would send him. He was not happy at the prospect of having to uproot again as he had settled in Sale and had made many friends in the area, both within and outside the world of music. One day he made an unnecessary visit to Johnny Roadhouse's shop, purchasing reeds he did not need, purely as an excuse for kindred company. Without much encouragement he poured out his predicament and, much to his surprise and relief Johnny said,

"There's a way out, Ernie, one which solves my problem too, if you're interested."

"I've got to be interested, Johnny, I'm desperate!"

"In that case how do you feel about packing in playing full time? I need a manager for this shop, and I can put you on to session work at the same time to keep your hand in."

It was not just a temporary answer, it was a permanent solution to all his problems and on July 27th, Ernie "hung up" his saxophone to enter the commercial world of the music business. His new wage, as manager, was to be ten pounds a week but there would be many opportunities for him to do part-time work with the B.B.C. to supplement his income. It also meant he would no longer be committed to work every evening, practically every day of the year. He did not know it at the time but the move was to have far reaching consequences for his future, because it introduced him to the world of the "session" musician, playing for radio and television. It was also to be the start of his launching himself seriously into teaching.

CHAPTER FIFTEEN

Johnny Roadhouse's shop was on the ground floor of a long narrow building whose windows looked out onto Oxford Road. The foot of the staircase was situated at the far end of the shop so that anyone entering met the underside of the stairs, below which was a small counter. The business was a shop for musicians rather than a music shop in the accepted sense and was more of a warehouse than a retail outlet - an untidy Aladin's Cave of music, with haphazardly piled boxes holding all manner of items taking the place of an elaborate display designed purely to attract passing trade. In Manchester it was the recognised source of anything the professional musician might require and many famous names, over the years, used its services - Count Basie, Lew Stone, Acker Bilk, Dizzy Gillespie, Ronnie Scott and countless others. Any orchestra or band appearing in Manchester would visit the company for their needs, mainly because of the professional reputation of Johnny himself. Ernie therefore found himself dealing with musicians who, up to then, had been just well known artists; soon he was to be on first-name terms with most and a friend and colleague of many.

At the rear, up a few stairs, was an office and on the first floor, above the shop, a small recording studio which was the responsibility of "Pop" Roadhouse. This was a room divided by a wood and glass partition separating the "studio" from the technical area. The studio held a solitary grand piano and its walls were covered with egg packaging to prevent echoes; in the other section were the recording apparatus which produced as its end product a coated metal disc. The surface of these discs was very fragile and the record had to be played back using a special soft needle as the standard metal needle of the time would have ruined it immediately. Ernie decided to test it out and recorded his own composition "Clarinet Concertino", a disc that Pop kept as an example of his work.

Like every "new broom" Ernie set about trying to improve the business and suggested numerous changes, partly to justify his appointment as manager but mainly because, as a fresh pair of eyes, he saw inadequacies which had been overlooked through familiarity. In the evenings they set to work and redecorated the shop; fixing a false ceiling, building a long counter with a red formica top and creating a more elaborate display area. Within a few years they had taken over the shop next door, had a new large window fitted and equipped a full drums showroom. A new office was equipped on the first floor and run with ruthless efficiency by a newly appointed secretary, Mrs. Reid. The evenings were also taken up by tuition. Rooms upstairs were used as practice areas and many aspiring pupils would come to be taught by masters of their art, such as Denis

Newey (Guitar), Ernie Watson and Freddie Kelly (Trumpet), Johnny Roadhouse himself (Saxophone) and, of course, Ernie. When the lessons concluded pupils would inevitably need things from the shop, reeds, music and tutor books so Ernie would serve behind the counter again before they eventually closed, at no set hour, and adjourned to the "Griffin", the pub behind the shop, for a last-minute drink before closing time. Johnny would then give him a lift and it was rarely that Ernie got home before midnight.

Due to the lateness of the hour very few people ever witnessed his arrival at the flat which was a pity because it was certainly impressive - Johnny Roadhouse drove a vintage Rolls Royce. At least, Johnny called it vintage, Ernie just called it old - he recalls that its radiator had horizontal bars which dated it to the days before the design changed to its present vertical format..

Frieda was usually fast asleep when he got home but one night in September he was surprised to find her waiting up for him. This was so unusual that he braced himself for bad news - it was quite the opposite,

"I've seen the doctor today," she told him, "and he has examined me - I'm going to have a baby."

Ernie was stunned, shocked, overjoyed and excited, all in one great sweep of emotion. They had been married for four years and the idea of having children had gone out of his mind. Now, suddenly, he was going to be a father!

"What are we going to do, Ernie?" Frieda asked.

"What do you mean, what are we going to do? We're going to celebrate! One thing's for sure, we can't stay here, it's not big enough to bring up a baby. We'll have to find a house of our own.... the only snag is going to be how to pay for it, but we'll manage somehow."

Within a week Ernie, the eternal optimist, was house hunting, without capital - a task he found more difficult than he had expected.

The search for a suitable home had to be made at the rare times he was away from the shop. It was a strictly family business with Ernie and Mrs. Reid the only non-family members. Mary, Johnny's sister, was undoubtably the organiser and prime mover. She was a warm-hearted woman who gave all her enthusiasm and flair in spite of the handicap of suffering from a serious back complaint which, at times, left her permanently stooped. Pop ran the recording studio and brother Bill was the general handyman. Johnny, although the name behind the business, was absent most of the time fulfilling engagements with the N.D.O. but made himself generally useful when the opportunity arose. It was Ernie, therefore, who became the face behind the counter and the contact with the public.

They had only just completed the refurbishment of the shop when, one morning Ernie was pleased to see Kevin Kent come through the door. Kevin was an old acquaintance, he had been a member of the "Kordites" singing group and later the vocalist with the Syd Lawrence Orchestra. He was accompanied by a then little known Les Dawson and to Ernie's surprise they merely passed the time of day, walked straight through the shop and disappeared up the stairs. After an hour or so they came downstairs, walked past the counter, said "Cheerio" and left the shop. This happened time and time again and Ernie was fascinated by their strange behaviour. Eventually he was so intrigued that one day, after their enigmatic entrance and departure upstairs, he followed them - to find Mrs. Reid busy typing out scripts. It appeared that Kevin was Les's manager at the time and they were using the shop as their office. Not only for writing, however, for further enquiries showed that the phone number on their business paper was that of the shop! This early episode in Les Dawson's career was a long standing source of amusement for both him and Ernie in future years.

Among the other distinguished visitors during the early days was Carl Barriteau who was browsing in the shop when Pop decided to play the recording he had made of Ernie's "Clarinet Concertino". To Ernie's surprise the famous band leader said,

"What's that?"

"It's something I wrote." Ernie answered.

"And who's playing it?"

"I am."

Barriteau looked perplexed for a moment and then added,

"Then what are you doing behind a shop counter? You should be playing professionally."

"It's a long story." Ernie said. Barriteau made his purchases and left the shop.

A similar incident occurred a few weeks later, this time the customer was an American music publisher, David Gornston. He listened to some of Ernie's work and had a long discussion with him about methods of teaching music. The result was that he asked Ernie to write a set of study books which were eventually published in the United States. This was Ernie's first venture into the publishing world and he gained very little from it financially but he obtained valuable experience and, with the shop, useful publicity in America.

They found the house in April, it was a three bedroomed semi-detached in Winstanley Road, Sale, with a large garden at the rear and a very adequate one at the front. The owner was Jim Wallace and he must have been impressed with his erstwhile purchasers because he kindly offered to lend them the necessary deposit of two hundred pounds. Ernie thankfully accepted the offer and they moved in to number 71 on June 5th, 1959. It was the first home they had had which was not on rent and they were faced with repayment of both the mortage and the loan for the deposit as well as the expense of the coming family.

The baby was born on July 3rd at Withington Hospital and they named him Edward. As soon as possible after Frieda arrived home with their son he was baptised at St. Joseph's Church, Ernie thereby fulfilling the promise he had made at the time of their marriage to have any children baptised in the Roman Catholic Church. Their one problem was finding a godmother as they had no close friends who were Catholic. Frieda remembered their old landlady from Sibsen Road, Mrs. Harms, and it was she who finally did the honour.

The washing line in the back garden was soon festooned with terry nappies and Ernie grew concerned at the endless amount of hand-washing to which Frieda now subjected herself. He decided it was time she should adapt to more modern methods and in spite of her protestations bought a washing machine. It was a twin-tub, an advanced model at the time and when he would arrive home and see all the laundry it had done he felt justified in having laid out the money to buy it. It was a few weeks later that, on one of his rare days off, he was present in the house to see her use it. She loaded the soiled nappies into the first tub, switched it on and left it boiling away. Then, to his complete surprise, she dragged out the washing, carried it to the sink and began scrubbing away on her beloved wash-board before starting her ritual of dozens of rinses, all by hand. The second tub was never used as Frieda was adamant that the only real way to do washing was to wash it, no matter how much labour was involved. Ernie admitted defeat.

The return to professional performance came suddenly. He was in the shop one afternoon when Mrs. Reid called down to say he was wanted on the telephone. It was Johnny Roadhouse,

"Ernie," he said, "I'm at the Playhouse, we're short of alto sax. Grab a taxi and get your arse round here, quick."

The Playhouse Theatre was back-to-back with the Hulme Hippodrome and had been taken over by the B.B.C. as a studio. The early television broadcasts from the North had been made from a converted Methodist Chapel in Dicconson Road, now the theatre was taking its place as a permanent studio for both television and radio programmes. Within half an hour of the phone call Ernie was recording with the N. D. O.

He swears he will never forget the experience of playing with the N.D.O. for the first time. He was astounded by its quality and precision - a standard which would have overwhelmed a player without his grounding. When the recording was over Johnny said,

"Well, how was it? How did you go on?'

Ernie's reply has also been remembered by many,

"I felt as if I was going into an operating theatre wearing a boiler suit!"

The snowball gathered momentum and from then on, day after day, the calls would come - "Bring your clarinet", "Fetch your tenor sax", "We're short of an alto" - Ernie found himself in permanent demand, and not only by the B.B.C.

The Halle Orchestra would call him when they needed a saxophone player. A symphony orchestra does not usually feature the saxophone but some works demand one. Ernie would be recruited to play pieces like "The Threepenny Opera", Ravel's "Bolero" or "An American in Paris". He remembers his first excursion to the domain of symphony music, sitting on the high stage of the "Free Trade Hall" and feeling as if he was playing in a goldfish bowl!

Some of these engagements provided great satisfaction both psychologically and financially. One night he found himself at a concert being performed by the Liverpool Philharmonic Orchestra, where one of the items was William Walton's "Facade Suite" which demanded a saxophone. He had travelled to Liverpool during the afternoon but, after his arrival, a heavy fog descended on the area. The clarinets were seriously undermanned due to the appalling weather and, after hearing Ernie's rehearsal of "Facade" the conductor, John Pritchard, asked him if he could play clarinet. Ernie humbly said he could, failing to mention that the clarinet was his major skill. He could sense the attitude of some of the classical musicians - amused at the idea of a "danceband" player attempting to play their kind of music, especially as the score was written in the key of "A" and Ernie was using a "Bb" clarinet! This would demand the player not only to sight-read the music but to transpose it to a different key as he did so. Once more, Ernie did not mention that such an exercise had been his staple diet under George Garside and one for which he had received merit at Kneller Hall. The conductor called on the orchestra to begin and Ernie played - immaculately. He left Liverpool glowing with self-satisfaction and the double fee the conductor had insisted he accept.

The spectre of George Garside also reared when he was asked to work with the Lew Stone Orchestra for a week. He was asked to run through his part at rehearsal, once again on clarinet. As he began to play he was aware that Lew Stone had left his place and was standing in front of him listening intently to every note. To Ernie's amazement, as he reached the end of the first page of music Lew Stone's baton flicked under the music and, with a sudden flourish, flipped it to the next page. He did this all the way through, reading what Ernie was playing even though, for him, the music was upside down. Ernie says it was an experience just like the Kneller Hall days, when George would stand over him snapping "Play, lad, play!"

His absence from the job while fulfilling these now regular engagements threw the load of the expanding business back onto Mary and Bill so Ernie recruited extra hands to serve in the shop, but before they started work he made a point of warning them not to be surprised at anything that might be in the shop on their opening it. It was quite normal to unlock the shop, go in, and find a gearbox on the counter or the front end of a mini on the floor. Johnny had a hobby of rebuilding old cars and would often leave bits in the shop overnight. It must have been a strange experience for a cellist from the Halle to come to Manchester's top music shop to buy a new string and find a back axle complete with propshaft blocking the entrance!

The "regulars" were used to it but even they were surprised when the news broke that Johnny had swapped his Rolls for another. So was Ernie when he brought it back to the shop - he looked out of the shop window as Johnny drove up .... in a hearse! That hearse became famous in its day as any musician of the era will testify. Johnny modified it, it is true; he removed all the fittings from the back and painted it grey but its true purpose could never be disguised. From that day on Ernie, while being grateful for his ride home, was glad he got back in the dark.

Many trips, however, were made in daylight and it is impossible to describe the reaction of the guests at a wedding reception when they saw a hearse draw up at the hall, the driver emerge, lift the back door and a band emerge to play for the dancing.

This band of Johnnie's was normally a quintet comprising piano, bass, saxophone, trumpet and drums and it was popular at many functions in the Greater Manchester area, from Weddings to Barmitzvahs. They used no music and had no set programme, the members were all experts who could literally play anything required on the spot and could busk all night if requested. The trumpet player was Bert Brown and he and Ernie were so used to each other they could play completely together. They developed a technique, quite accidentally, of both playing exactly the same melody in unison - the saxophone mellowed the trumpet while the trumpet gave the alto a "bite", producing a sound that was unique and which became a popular attraction.

In 1960 the B.B.C. presented another season of "Come Dancing" from Manchester, this time from the Ritz Ballroom where the band was under the direction of Phil Moss. Ernie was invited to augment the band and play saxophone and tells the following story with a wide grin splitting his face: "Phil had a set of jackets made specially for the television show and they became the criteria for selection - if you didn't fit the jacket you didn't get the job!" He recalls struggling through the broadcasts in a jacket that was cutting him under the arms and Phil's solution to the problem - "Ernie, you look uncomfortable. It's not fair on you, struggling to play in that jacket. We'll have to do something about it - you'll have to lose some weight!"

Losing weight, however, would have been a difficult task for Ernie. Over the years his work within the Roadhouse organisation had changed and he had became more and more involved in running it. He was now booking musicians, paying their wages, submitting invoices to T.V. companies and acting as timekeeper at recording sessions. For the first time in his life he felt secure and settled. His wage had risen to twenty-five pounds a week which, coupled with the very lucrative fees from "session" work meant that he was at long last on a more than adequate income, his debts were paid off and, at last, he had savings in the bank.

Domestically, unfortunately, things had remained static. His work took him away from the home in which Frieda even more imprisoned herself with young Eddie. She now had no desire at all to mix with other people, make friends or socialise. Her preoccupation with "cleanliness" now stretched over the house with much of the furniture and large areas of carpets being covered with old towels and curtains, which greatly discouraged Ernie from bringing visitors to the house. This he found very embarrassing as he was constantly enjoying social and business meetings at the homes of his colleagues and found he could not return their hospitality. By the time Eddie started school he had given up all hope of Frieda joining the exciting circle of Northern showbusiness and had adapted to being alone in the company of couples. The situation did not auger well for the future.

This was the time when "The Shadows" and "The Beatles" had heralded the meteoric rise in popularity of the electronic guitar. Demands for these instruments caused a flood of business in the shop, extra staff had to be engaged and hundreds of guitars were sold, the vast majority on hire purchase. Ernie himself hardly did any work behind the counter, he was now involved in administration and performing in every branch of music. His versatility seems to have had no bounds and he would go from one extreme to the other. One moment he would be playing "Porgy and Bess" with Arthur Fiedler of the Boston Pops Orchestra and the next he would be accompanying for a Ken Dodd show. He would be with the B.B.C. Symphony Orchestra playing the "Facade Suite" one day and then change abruptly to augment "Dr. Crock and his Crackpots" in a series for television. All this, of course, could not take place without hilarious interludes. He recalls being in the orchestra for a Ken Dodd show at the Oldham Coliseum when, for some reason, a live lion was involved. The lion was kept in a cage in the wings and it was to make its way on stage via a wooden tunnel constructed behind the band. Something went wrong -the wooden slats of the tunnel must have broken, for the lion suddenly appeared behind the trumpet section. The leading trumpet took one look at the mane peering over his shoulder and shot off stage like a rocket, followed by the rest of the orchestra, none of whom were comforted by the trainer calling "It's all right - he's got no teeth!"

Dr. Crock and the Crackpots were an entirely different experience. The "Dr. Crock" band normally consisted of seven members but for the T.V. series this was augmented. The regular band had rehearsed their mayhem and knew just what to expect, Ernie and the other "extras" did not. They were playing "Light Cavalry when Ernie was amazed to see Dr. Crock produce a pair of garden shears and chop an end off one of the clarinets! The tympani were apparently covered with pure white drum-skins - until the percussionist hit one. It was filled with milky-white water and the band were drenched. There would be a squeal of a Swanee Whistle and one of the trumpeters (a dummy) suddenly shot up into the flies! As the music changed to "The Blue Danube" jets of water would gush out from the vibrophone and Ernie would be trying to play while sitting under a fountain! The following evening he would be in evening dress on the stage of the Free Trade Hall playing Vaughan William's Symphony No. 9. under the baton of Sir John Barbarolli. Life could never become boring!

When commercial television had first come to the North most of its live light programmes were broadcast from the A.B.C. Cinema in Didsbury but the policy was that whenever a band was required the musicians would travel to Manchester from London under the misapprehension, perhaps, that northern musicians weren't good enough! One day Ernie got the customary call for his services - this time to Didsbury, where he was handed an Eb bass! All they required him to do was to sit in the band and mime to a recording which had been made in London. As they were about to start a message was handed to the conductor who then said,

"It seems the recording is duff - play it live."

Ernie played the part required and was thankful for his "play" sessions with Ray Pinkney at Kneller Hall.

The musical director of the A.B.C. Showband was Bob Sharples who, although based in London, originally hailed from Heap Bridge in Bury and he saw no sense in the needless and expensive practice of transporting the showband and did not need convincing that northern musicians were as good as those from the south. Ronnie Taylor, meanwhile, had left the B.B.C. and was now producing shows for the new network so Bob Sharples asked him to do something about it. So it was that Ronnie approached Johnny Roadhouse to ask him to form a band for Independent Television "that is as good as the N.D.O." This put Johnny in an impossible position - he worked for the B.B.C. and could hardly produce a band that was in direct opposition, yet, as Ronnie well knew, he was in the best position to do so. Johnny refused the assignment out of loyalty but suggested that Ernie might be available. Ernie accepted the responsibility and a strange situation developed - he was to do all the administration for the A.B.C. showband, on behalf of Bob Sharples, from Johnny Roadhouse's premises, thus running one organisation from within another. In spite of what would appear to be serious difficulties everything ran smoothly.

This showband, subsequently famous under the title "A.B.C. Television Showband" and in which, apart from administering it, Ernie played alto-sax was the one which featured prominently in all the independent programmes of the sixties, including such shows as Holiday Town Parade where it gave live performances from various resorts, and "Big Night Out" which was also broadcast live from major holiday spots on Sunday evenings.

Although they played regularly for the benefit of holiday-makers they very rarely enjoyed a holiday themselves. Johnny would take a break from the N.D.O. but spend the time hanging round the shop displaying his famous braces. Ernie was intrigued by those braces as, long before he met Johnny, he had heard facetious remarks about them on radio programmes he had received in Malaya. When he joined the shop he discovered, first hand, that the Roadhouse Braces did exist! Not only did they exist, they were apparently indispensable. One day in the summer of 1963 Ernie said,

"Why are you hanging round here, Johnny, why don't you go away for a holiday?"

"I've never been away."

"Well, why not start? Tell you what, I'll go with you, let's go to Austria!"

It was said on the spur of the moment but Johnny seemed to like the idea. A fortnight later they were walking past the Opera House in Vienna - Johnny still wearing his braces with his rolled-up newspaper under his arm. Ernie took the opportunity of visiting Graz where to his great pleasure, contact was renewed with his Austrian in-laws and they spent a few days with the Lutz family who gushed over photographs of Eddie. Ernie left them with the promise that he would arrange for them to see the lad as soon as possible,

"Next year," he said, "at the latest."

These were happy days for Ernie but he could never hope to clear the hurdles that fate seemed perpetually to set up for him. His life seems to be a roller coaster of fortune, continually rising from the nadir of adversity to the peak of accomplishment and then plummeting back to the depths of despair. He was, at this time, riding a peak; his work was giving gratifying fulfilment, his financial difficulties had been left behind and he had purchased his own car, an Austin A40, so no longer was he dependent upon others to ferry him to and from his many engagements. The cycle of destiny decreed it couldn't continue but this time the decline centred mainly on those around him. With being forced to lead such a hectic life Ernie was not able to spend as much time with his young son as he would have wished although touring the resorts with the band did sometimes give him the opportunity to take Eddie with him, leaving him in the care of Grandma Stockell in Scarborough while he played the local venues. It became a regular event for Eddie and he enjoyed being spoilt by Edith as he had never known his maternal grandparents. Frieda did not accompany them as she kept to her vow of never visiting her in-laws.

Time and time again Ernie would have the enjoyment of meeting his mother tarnished by the inevitable question -

"Why doesn't Frieda come with you?"

"She's busy."

"Nay, Ernie, she can't be that busy, not every time you're booked over here. I know Ted's awkward at times but he doesn't mean any harm - and you have to make allowances for him. Now promise me - the next time, bring her with you."

How could he explain? He now fully realised that, unfortunately, Frieda had never completely accepted she was British. Sadly, she seemed to have an underlying conviction that she was regarded as a "foreigner" and that she lived under constant critical scrutiny. She worried about being observed as inadequate and the worry was rapidly turning into an obsession, sadly leaving her marooned on a desert island of her own imagination.

In 1964, a year after Ernie's visit, Frieda's family invited them to spend a holiday in Austria again. Ernie was fully committed with engagements but, remembering his promise, persuaded Frieda to go and to take Eddie with her. It was not a successful trip. Eddie developed tonsilitis and spent the first week in bed and for some reason during the second there seems to have been a family dispute which resulted in Frieda never repeating the event. All contact with her family seems to have ended from that time. Eddie, however, did come home with an Austrian Station Master's outfit!

Eddie started school that September. Ernie enrolled him at Springfield School and enjoyed the parental pride of seeing him grown up enough to wear school uniform - a purchase which gave him his first experience of "fame". The uniform suppliers was a shop called "Petites Modes" of Sale and Ernie went into the shop to see two ladies behind the counter, one middle aged and one in her early twenties. He left Eddie in the care of the young lady while he sat reading the paper.

"Don't I know you?" the older lady asked.

"I don't think so."

"Your face is familiar from somewhere."

"Did you ever go to the Locarno?" Ernie asked.

"Often, why?"

"I played in Eddie Shaw's band, though there's no reason why you should remember me from that."

"You're a musician! Where are you now?"

"Oh, all over - mainly television these days. I'm with the A.B.C. Showband now."

"That must be it! Hey, Karina! We've got a television star in the shop!"

Ernie was embarrassed. "Hardly a star," he said, "I'm only in the band."

The young lady joined them, carrying a pile of clothing, shorts, socks, school jersey and blazer. Eddie trotted behind.

"We'll have to keep an eye open for you, won't we?" she said and started making out Ernie's bill.

He paid and left the shop with some strange silly pride in that he had been noticed.

With Eddie at school, Frieda was left alone in the house again, spending the daylight hours with no company, an hour or so with her son before she put him to bed and then to sit brooding alone until Ernie arrived back in the early hours -or did not arrive at all if his work obliged him to stay overnight.

By late '64 a cause for concern also began to be noticed in the shop. Hundreds of their guitars and drum kits had been sold, many to misguided aspiring stars who, recklessly aping their idols on television, had committed themselves to huge debts under the impression that they would find themselves on the pinnacle of the entertainment Everest but, naturally, they failed even to reach base camp and the payments on the instruments could not be met. Bad debt after bad debt was creeping like a malignant growth through the company's account books. Attempts were made to recover the huge losses but money was not forthcoming, re-possessed instruments had to be sold off at further loss and finance companies were also demanding compensation. Johnny was becoming a worried man who and could see no way out of a serious cash-flow problem. The New Year saw no improvement and the crisis inevitably came after six months: the business went into voluntary liquidation, a victim of un-honoured hire purchase agreements.

The situation immediately involved the fate of the sub-business that Ernie was managing on behalf of the Showband. Bob Sharples made a hurried visit to Manchester.

"It's obvious we can't go on as we are," he said to Ernie, "it's an impossible position."

"What do you suggest?"

"I'll have to break from Johnny, that's clear. It's a terrible thing to have to do, but the powers-that-be can't work with a bankrupt company. As I see it, if things are to continue roughly as they are, I'll have to have a new company in Manchester to deal with our affairs in the north. Will you run it?"

Ernie was now in a quandary. Johnny Roadhouse was a great friend and, after all, the man who had really given him his start. Was he now to desert him at the very time he needed support?

"It would put me in a bad light as far as Johnny is concerned." he said.

"Don't I know that? But what's the alternative? It's the only way out, I'm afraid, and if you don't want to do it, I'll have to get someone else. There's not much time, let me know in a couple of days."

Ernie spent the next days in mental torment. Should he sink with his friend or go ahead alone? He then tried to think logically - if he did not accept the offer it would make no difference whatsoever to the Roadhouse's problem, he would just become another unnecessary sacrifice. He decided to accept, but his life had dropped into a trough again.

The decision brought disappointment to Johnny who, in his despair, saw Ernie's leaving as a form of desertion and the parting was not made on happy terms. Thankfully, as the years went by afterwards, understanding grew and the friendship restored. Happily, too, Johnny recovered, paid off all the debt that had been thrust upon him and re-built the business that still flourishes, with its old esteem, today.

The outcome was the formation of "Northern Orchestral Services Ltd." of Manchester, its directors, Bob Sharples and Ernest Waites.

Top:
The Eddie Shaw band 1957

Left:
"In full song!" 1959

Above:
Johnny Roadhouse's Shop 1958

Top:
Typical "gig" band, Grand Hotel, Manchester 1959
L to R Charlie Aspinall (Bass), Ernie (Clarinet), Pete James (Piano), Johnny Roadhouse (Saxophone), Kathy Lynn, Dennis Newey (Guitar)

Left:
Ernie 1960

Above:
Acker Bilk, Ernie, Johnny Roadhouse 1959

Top:
Sax Section, ABC TV Showband 1961

Left:
Ernie and the boys support Hughie Green c1964

Bottom:
Bob Sharples & Sax's 1963

Top:
Full ABC Showband c 1965
Front row, from right:
Bill Nickson, Maurice Davis,
Bob Sharples (Dark Suit), Ernie

Left:
Eddie Waites 1992

Right:
Golden garter 1972
Ernie (with Cilla Black!)

Bottom:
Les Reed and "Pop Proms"
Orchestra. Granada TV
(Ernie on sax)

CHAPTER SIXTEEN

Ernie's life was now centred on the Bob Sharples Orchestra, the administration of which took up a large proportion of his time. The orchestra had a basic complement of musicians which would be augmented by others as and when they were required, and he was now recognised as the "fixer" - the person who was responsible for booking the players and paying the wages. Ernie eventually teamed up with Nobby Clarke, the "fixer" in Jack Parnell's band, and they worked together, Nobby would have people ready to play in the Sharples orchestra when it arrived in London and Ernie, in turn, would have musicians that Jack Parnell might require when it appeared in the North. He saw no point in renting expensive offices but worked from both his own home and that of Mrs. Reid who, after the closure of the office in Oxford Road, became his full-time secretary. She would prepare all the invoices, contracts and other paper work and Ernie would visit her to dictate letters, deal with general matters and sign letters and cheques. The system worked very satisfactorily for years.

The amount of travelling Ernie was forced to do meant a reliable car was essential so in August 1965 he traded in the old Austin and bought a two-year old Mercedes, "TBR 567", a car which was to become his pride and joy. His life was reaching one of its peaks again.

Most of his work in those early years of ABC television was done at the Capitol Cinema at Didsbury although many outside broadcasts were made from the ABC Theatre on Church Street, Blackpool and it was there that he experienced a nightmarish situation that was subsequently reported in many issues of the musical press.

For the benefit of those unfamiliar with the production of the "live" variety shows of those days it should be explained that they were regular yet ultimate tests of the professionalism of artists, musicians and technicians alike. The show would be produced in one day. Rehearsal time was minimal, usually taking the form of a "run through" in the early afternoon, a break for tea and then the performance would take place in the early evening. The band would be given the artist's music and they would have time to try it out once before the live broadcast. Meanwhile the technicians would be scurrying amongst them arranging cables, cameras and microphones.

On this particular Sunday the show was "Blackpool Night Out" and the star was Eartha Kitt. The showband reported to the theatre to find the usual controlled confusion of scene shifters, stage staff and engineers all going about their tasks; the artists drifted in throughout the morning and Eartha Kitt arrived at noon - to break the news that her music had got lost somewhere between Copenhagen and

London. She had packed it in her luggage on a plane and the case had not been on the conveyor belt at Heathrow! The usual search was taking place but there was little hope of it being found in time for the broadcast, let alone for a rehearsal.

Bob Sharples rose to the unprecedented challenge. Bob Parsons, the theatre manager, gave up his office and Bob, Ernie, Maurice Davies, Freddie Platt and Eartha's musical associate, Art Day, got to work. While Brian Fitzgerald stood in as rehearsal pianist they were all scribbling away on manuscript paper upstairs. Bob Sharples wrote out the arrangement listening to Eartha's L.P., when he finished a page he handed it to Ernie who used it to copy out the woodwind parts, it then went to Maurice to write the brass section's music and finally the strings and rhythm sections were extracted. They had to repeat this for four separate numbers, working against the racing clock. They completed them, handed them out to the band with the ink barely dry, got changed into evening dress, sat down with the band and played. The band hadn't seen the arrangements until they actually played them for a live television audience!

After the show, which went without a hitch, Eartha Kitt said,

"Without Bob and his boys there'd definitely have been no show. They were simply wonderful."

Ernie's memoirs are full of such anecdotes and his scrap-books a treasure of contemporary show business history. It was also at the ABC in Blackpool that the showband first shared a programme with the then rising "Beatles". They did not accompany the Beatles, of course, they sat in the orchestra pit while the young lads rehearsed their part of the show. In a break one of them sat on the edge of the stage, feet dangling in the pit, idly strumming on his guitar. After a while he said,

"Mr. Sharples, I've got a tune I'd like to fit into the show, would it be O.K.?"

"I don't know," Bob said, "let me listen to it."

The lad played the guitar and sang his song. Ernie says there was unearthly silence while he did so, they were spell-bound. When he came to the end the whole of the band applauded.

"Hold on a minute." Bob said, taking some manuscript paper from his case, "Quiet, everybody!"

Fifteen minutes later he handed some hastily written parts out to the strings section,

"Right! Run through that again."

Backed by the strings the effect was unbelievable. The young man, of course, was Paul MacCartney and the occasion turned out to be the first ever full performance of "Yesterday". Such emotive moments could only really occur in "live" television - as could some of the most hilarious, which sometimes produced spontaneous comedy which could never be rehearsed, even though it taxed the performers to their limit. Ernie recalls a show in which Mike and Bernie Winters used a donkey in a sketch - and the warning cliche of "never work with children or animals" was undeniably proved justified. The donkey did nothing it was supposed to do and everything it was not supposed to do, including being incontinent, while Mike and Bernie intrepidly went on with the sketch, by then necessarily mostly ad-libbed, scrutinised by live cameras.

The Bob Sharples Orchestra was by now also regularly involved with "Opportunity Knocks", the renowned talent spotting show hosted by Hughie Green, which "discovered" such great names of show business as Russ Abbott, Freddie Starr, Les Dawson and Paul Daniels amongst many others. This show, like others fronted by Ken Dodd and Jimmy Tarbuck, originated from the Capitol at Didsbury and through them the ABC Television Showband acquired a national reputation.

Then ABC closed down, having lost the franchise to Thames Television. The new company had new ideas and adopted a programming schedule which presented weekday broadcasts from London with two week-end shows from the North. So it was that "Opportunity Knocks" left its Manchester origins and began its long run from the studios of "Thames" but as the Television Showband had become an integral part of the show Bob Sharples persuaded the powers behind Thames Television to allow him to keep the band as the entity it had become. Consequently the routine of the old days was now completely reversed - with the Manchester musicians travelling south to do shows in London. This satisfying acknowledgement of its quality, however, had its countering disadvantages - the motorway network had not been completed at the time and the journey to London and back seemed long and endless. It became monotonously routine, relieved only by a system of car sharing the musicians adopted in order to reduce the stress of driving.

Ernie's personal reputation as a professional musician was growing so rapidly at this period that engagements were coming from many quarters. In addition to his normal work he played background music for plays and shows for both Granada and Yorkshire Television. The Yorkshire venues proved a bonus - one of them, for example, an Eamonn Andrews Show from Newcastle-upon-Tyne, gave him the opportunity to visit his cousin Betty, whom he had not met since he was a young lad at Seamer Moor Road, and when they occurred during school holidays he would pack a bag and take Eddie with him in the car to leave him at Maple Drive in Grandma's care for short periods. Eddie became close to Grandma Edith and looked forward to his regular breaks in Scarborough and, on occasions, Durham.

It was on Yorkshire T.V. that Ernie made his debut as an "actor"! In a play called "Boy Dominic" he, together with Norman George on violin and a cellist, were dressed up in eighteenth century costume to play the parts of a performing trio - Ernie miming on an antique clarinet to a recording he'd made before the broadcast on his modern one! (Purely for the record, he was **not** nominated for an "Oscar")

These Yorkshire engagements gave him many opportunities to meet his mother and in the course of these visits during the latter half of 1966 he was forced to witness the rapid decline in the health of Ted Stockell. In spite of all that had occurred between them, Ernie was upset at the sight of a tragic old man still suffering from the effects of the Great War. It was a wonder he had survived fifty years with lungs damaged by gas and body punctured by shrapnel, and now it was clear that his wounds were gaining the upper hand. He had had bronchial difficulties throughout the whole time Ernie had known him, but now he was a pitiful figure, bedridden and gasping for every breath. The end came on January 8th. 1967. It was a Sunday and Ernie received a telephone call from Edith telling him that his step-father, mercifully, had died. He was seventy four.

It was about this time that Ernie began to experience a chronic weariness which he naturally assumed to be due to his way of life as the workload was by then becoming almost over-bearing. Apart from the regular Thames T.V. shows such as "Opportunity Knocks" he was booking musicians on behalf of Bob Sharples, as well as playing with them, for all the band's engagements - recordings for Decca, making film sound tracks, accompanying shows for Bruce Forsyth, Lionel Blair, Tommy Cooper and many others. One particular headache for him was the "Eamonn Andrews Show" because this was never the same any two weeks running. Bob Sharples had written the signature tune which did remain the same but the musical act which occupied the centre section of the show was different every week and there was no way of knowing what sort of band would be required for it. On Monday mornings Bob would phone Ernie with a message like,

"Next Sunday - Three brass, four woodwinds, two fiddles, cello and rhythm section." - and Ernie would have to find them. It was on such occasions that his association with Nobby Clarke was invaluable.

Early in 1968 Ernie heard that the Green Howards Band was in Colchester. He was booked for an Eamonn Andrews show in London that week so he decided to break his journey home and visit them there. Over the years he had been making arrangements of popular tunes that he thought would be suitable for military bands, as well as composing new music of his own and he took a folder of his work with him. He found the venue and was welcomed with much jocularity by the older members who remembered him from the past -especially by the Band Sergeant in charge, a totally reformed Brian Clancy who, by now, was adamant that the Green Howards was by far the best military band in the army. After a long and diverting session of reminiscing and exchanging news Brian suggested that Ernie might like to conduct the band,

"Go on, " he said, "show 'em what the old lags can do."

"Which number?" Ernie asked enthusiastically.

"Anything, they're good, these lads. What about some of your own stuff?"

Ernie handed out one of his compositions, "Puppet Suite", and got immense pleasure from hearing his own music played by what he still considered to be his band. He was so involved that he was not aware that another Bandmaster had arrived and was listening intently. When he had handed the baton back to Brian the newcomer approached him,

"I liked that," he said, "is it available from a publisher?"

"Hardly," Ernie answered, I've only just written it!"

"Would there be any chance of my borrowing it? I'll let you have it back in a couple of days."

He was true to his word and a few days later returned the music, adding,

"You should do something about this stuff. Why don't you drop a line to Des Walker?"

"Des Walker?"

"Captain Walker if you want to be exact. He's the Director of Music of the Royal Corps of Transport Band. He's just started a publishing company specialising in band music and he's looking for new stuff."

Ernie wrote to Des Walker and a week or so later arranged to meet him in London. There was mutual concord between them.

"Let me have as much as you can, as soon as you can," Des said, "- you know, short pieces as well as long ones."

"I've got a folder full already," Ernie said, "bits I've put together over the years."

"Right, let's start with those. By the way, are you a member of the P.R.S.?"

"No," Ernie answered, "never had need to be, nothing published so far to produce royalties."

"You'd better do something about that then, there'll certainly be royalties coming in from now on. Shall I use your own name on the copies?"

Ernie had never considered this aspect and had to think fast. He could imagine all his old friends looking at their music, emblazoned "Written by Ernie Waites", and for some unknown reason felt embarrassed. He could hear the banter - "Bloody hell! Look, it's Ernie!" - "This'll be a load of crap!" - "Souza eat your heart out, Ernie's at it!" - and so on,

"No." he said.

"Have you got a pen name? What shall I use?"

Ernie, of course, did not have a nom-de-plume but in an instant he realised he **did** have another name, the one he was born with. He would use his mother's name, but shorten it,

"Brien," he said, "Terence Brien."

Within months the name Terence Brien became a common sight printed on military band music published by Herald Music of Farnborough and on the sleeves of recordings of top military bands by numerous record companies. In January 1969 Ernie was elected a provisional associate member of the Performing Rights Society and in February he became Member No. 1263 of the Songwriters Guild of Great Britain. This afforded an additional income from royalties on over fifty compositions and he rewarded himself by buying his first brand new car, an Austin 3 litre, "LLG 713G".

His rapidly rising success brought penalties as well as rewards, however. He was spending more and more time away from home and his domestic situation was deteriorating even more. Frieda had become a very lonely woman and family disagreements were now a regular occurrence. When he was at home in Winstanley Road he also had to face disharmony with some of his neighbours. For example, Frieda strongly objected to them burning garden rubbish as the flying soot sometimes blemished her washing, she was upset when the man next door cut his hedge and pieces fell on her side of the fence. Her approach to rectify these events was, unfortunately, not exactly tactful and arguments would speedily arise. When Ernie tried to point out the triviality of the matter he would be accused of disloyalty and another fervent domestic quarrel would follow, ending with them going to bed in their separate rooms with an air of enmity that would carry over to the next day.

During the rise of Ernie's new career as composer and arranger he had also been approached by Derek Butterfield, the musical director of the Golden Garter, a popular night club in Wythenshawe, Manchester, to ask him to join the band there. Derek Butterworth was once a member of the B.B.C. Showband, led by Cyril Stapleton, and the band he had formed at the night club was of high standard. The Golden Garter, too, had a very high reputation in the Greater Manchester area and Ernie accepted the offer of thirty-three pounds a week to play there. To add this extra commitment to his already high workload would appear to be somewhat fool-hardy and, speaking in retrospect, Ernie fully accepts it to be so,

"But ....", he wistfully reminisces, "I still couldn't accept that I was secure.

Show Business was so precarious you grabbed every offer that was made."

Whether this was his motive or whether it was a subconscious attempt to escape from home is not clear but what does seem self-evident is that he was burning his proverbial candle not only at both ends but in the centre as well! He was now writing and arranging music for the Herald Publishing Company, managing the Bob Sharples Orchestra, playing at the "Garter" every night and recording television shows both during the week and at week-ends - and his feeling of being perpetually tired persisted.

It was at "The Garter" that he had a re-union with Eartha Kitt. She appeared there for a week and, naturally, there was much frivolous banter as to whether she had her music with her or whether it had to be made up on the job like making instant coffee!

Another frequent star at the club was Tommy Steele and, in the interval of one of his performances Ernie slipped out to the bar to grab a welcome drink. He was sitting at the bar with his pint of lager, chatting to another member of the band when he was jostled by a group of spirited young women who were obviously out for a night of celebration. One of them pushed into him just as he was raising his drink, making him spill some,

"Hey, watch it!", he said, "We only get time for one -and I want to drink it, not wash the bar with it!"

"Sorry," she said, "let me get you another."

He turned to her and there was mutual recognition.

"Petites Modes!" he said.

"Mother's T.V. star!" she replied, "Hey, girls, this is the chap we were telling you about - he's often in the shop for school uniforms - you know - he's the one who plays for all the shows on tele!"

"Not all," Ernie corrected her, secretly enjoying the obvious adulation of the group, "... just a few."

She ignored his correction, "You didn't say you played here."

"He plays every bloody where!" his friend added.

"I've not seen you here before." Ernie said.

"I've not been here before," she said, "But I like Tommy Steele, and this is my hen night - I'm getting married next week."

"In that case," Ernie said, "**I'm** buying **you** a drink!"

For the rest of the evening, particularly during the times allotted to dancing, Ernie noticed the young women of the group, whom he guessed were all from the Sale area, were smiling at him and giving little waves as they passed the band. He had a fan club! During the next few months, while walking around Sale, he found he was being recognised and greeted in the street by women whom he could only assume had been on the hen night. He did not like to admit it, but in some strange way it satisfied some hitherto unrealised feeling of vanity.

In mid 1969 there was a British Army exhibition which ran for four days at Belle Vue, Manchester. It was the biggest-ever exhibition and recruiting campaign to be held to date and it was opened by the Duke of Edinburgh on June 26th. One of the highlights of the show was a march entitled "Armex '69" played by the massed bands of over three hundred army musicians from Aldershot, Dorset, Liverpool, Reading, Woolwich and West Germany. It's composer and arranger - "Terence Brien". This work was done in between arranging the film themes of "Chitty Chitty Bang Bang", "The Great Escape" and "A few Dollars More" for a United Artists L.P. record for the Royal Artillery.

Meanwhile the "everyday" routine work still went ahead with his weekly playing for "The Bruce Forsyth Show" from Yorkshire Television and the dashing down to London for "Opportunity Knocks". Some of these meant even further travel when Hughie Green presented his programme as outside broadcasts away from the studios. The show would then journey country wide, from the Royal Air Force station at Finningley one week to the Royal Navy base at Portsmouth the next, where Ernie recalls playing the opening signature tune of "Op. Knocks" while rising on the lift of the aircraft carrier H.M.S. Bulwark. Obviously, it could not continue, although Ernie, a workaholic, did not seem able to see it.

The first to go was the engagement at the Golden Garter. After ten months Derek Butterworth, quite understandably, became disenchanted. He had employed Ernie as an attraction - the lead saxophone player of the Television Showband, but, due to his heavy commitments he found that, time and time again, "deputies" were arriving to take the place of the player he had engaged while he was performing elsewhere. Ernie accepted the criticism and fully understood Derek's justifiable complaint. He left the Golden Garter band in October 1969, with the agreement that he would be available to augment the band for special occasions when Derek required his services.

He wisely decided to take a few days off and stayed with his mother in Scarborough. She had now been a widow for nearly three years and Ernie was both pleased and relieved to see that she had rebuilt her life. She had been very depressed immediately after Ted's death but now she seemed to have started a new life.

"I've joined three clubs," she told him, "two of them for pensioners - it's hard to accept I've reached that age."

"And you don't look it, Mam," Ernie said truthfully.

"We go on all sorts of outings and excursions," she went on enthusiastically, "and I've started the regular meetings with Sarah again, just like the old days! Then there's the chapel - I still go to church on Sundays, mornings and evenings, I have to, I'm still in the choir. I'm never bored, I can tell you - in fact, I don't seem to have enough days in the week!"

"Everybody seems to say that," he said, "I hope I'm the same when my turn comes."

"Knowing you, Ernie, there's no doubt whatsoever!"

"How's Les going on?"

"Still in the R.A.F. He's a corporal now. As a matter of fact, you've only just missed him. He was on leave last week, he came round here with Georgina and the kids. I was thinking about the grandchildren only yesterday. Les has Stephen and John, you've only given me young Eddie - you've got some catching up to do, son! - and I'd love to have a grand-daughter."

He knew he could hold out no hopes of granting her that wish but didn't want to spoil her happiness with his own problems. His one great regret was that he had to maintain the pretence that all was well at home. The one thing missing in his life at that time was the lack of family intimacy. It was sad that she never came to stay with him in Sale and that Frieda never spent any time in Scarborough.

That unsettling thought was still in his mind as he drove over the Pennines on his way home. It seemed that fate had decreed that he was never to know the happiness of a really close family relationship. He had been handed over as a baby, lost a father as a child, failed to establish any ties with Ted Stockell and could not produce any affinity between his mother and his wife. He was also feeling so tired again. The outline of the narrow road over the hills started to blur and he realised it was imperative that he stopped for a rest. He shook himself out of his melancholy and pulled in at the first roadside cafe he saw. Sitting at a table with a cup of coffee he resolved to arrange a break as soon as possible, but it would have to wait until the New Year.

Christmas was approaching once again and this was one of his busiest periods of all. Every television company was preparing its programmes for the festive season and, consequently, instead of taking the rest he so obviously needed he spent the last two months of 1969 rushing, more madly than ever, from place to place fulfilling his engagements. The resulting stress made him determined to keep his New Year's resolution of taking on less work outside Bob Sharples' organisation.

But that, in itself, was a heavy commitment. He could not stop the routine clerical work of management and playing in the orchestra was a full-time occupation. January turned into February and still he had not arranged the holiday he knew he needed so badly. Then came March 1970, and more precisely

March 26th - the day when nemesis won the final battle.

On the evening of March 25th. Ernie and Frieda had had one of their now frequent squabbles, but this one continued long into the night. Ernie got up in the morning after a short spell of fitful sleep, dressed, packed his music cases and left without breakfast to go to the London Weekend Television studios in Wembley to play for a Tommy Cooper Show. It was his turn to drive so he called at Denton to pick up Maurice Davies, the lead trumpet player, with whom he had "paired" for the journeys for years, and they set off on the trip to London making their usual trivial conversation centred mainly on Henry Cooper's regaining the British Heavyweight title from Jack Bodell until Maurice said,

"What's up with you, Ernie? You don't seem your normal perky self."

"I'm knackered, mate. I've felt tired for months, now, and I had a barney with Frieda last night. I feel I just want to get my head down and sleep for a bloody fortnight."

"I bet you've had no breakfast."

"No."

"Right - we're in good time, stop at Coventry."

They reached Coventry within the hour and called at a cafe for a substantial snack. The rest did Ernie good and he seemed more lively on the second half of the journey. He drove confidently down the motorway to the outskirts of London while Maurice read the papers. They had tired of chit-chat and Ernie was quite happy to indulge in his own thoughts.

They reached Harrow and the end of the long trip was in sight. Ernie felt himself relaxing. He was fascinated by the rear of the car he was following. The back of the car seemed to blur and become two cars, drifting apart. Then they closed up together and became one again. The road ahead started receding and then approaching, back and forth, back and forth. He was drifting off into a peaceful sleep......HELL! He realised what was happening, shook his head vigorously, wound down his window and took several deep breaths of fresh air. He mustn't let that happen again! He was glad that Maurice was absorbed in the paper and hadn't noticed the incident. Concentrate now; they were nearly there and a welcome cup of coffee would be awaiting them. Keep your eye on the road. What was that sign? Missed it with watching the car ahead. He's gone! Where? Left! Round this sharp bend! Didn't see it coming! Turn for God's sake! Turn! No time! Wheel hard over! More! More! We're not going to make it! Oh No! Please, God, please!

They didn't make it - and a lorry carrying ten tons of steel was directly in their path. Ernie didn't feel anything, he was aware only of the screech of brakes, the lorry filling the windscreen and a sickening thud.

Then came blackness.

CHAPTER SEVENTEEN

By sheer providence a police car carrying four policemen had been driving behind the lorry and it was probably this incredible stroke of luck that saved Ernie's life. It was clear to their trained eyes that the driver, although seriously injured, was alive and they acted quickly and efficiently. After radioing for assistance, which saved precious minutes, they used a crowbar to open the car door and soon had him lying in the road, his legs strapped together with the seat belts from the car.

Ernie found this out later for at the time he was unconscious. Consciousness must have returned briefly however because he remembers looking up at a policemen who asked,

"What is your name?"

"Ernest Waites." was the weak reply as he relapsed into oblivion.

He remembers nothing more. He was unaware of the arrival of the ambulance that took him to nearby Stanmore Orthopaedic Hospital, he knew nothing of the urgent first aid given him in the casualty department. His first real recollection is feeling himself being pushed along a corridor, flat on his back and passing under a series of pipes and ceiling lights. He felt no pain.

He must have been a long time in the operating theatre because when he awoke into semi-consciousness it had gone dark and he found himself prone, looking up at the lights shining from the ceiling. He was in the corner of a ward and Jimmy Wallace, the friend from whom he had purchased his house and who still lived opposite in Winstanley Road, was sitting by the bedside. It never occurred to him until the next day that many hours must have elapsed to allow Jim time to get there. It transpired that the Sale police had visited his home and had informed Frieda of the accident. At a loss as to what she could do, she had run across the road to ask Jim for help. Without hesitation he had assumed responsibility.

"You stay here," he told her, "look after Eddie - I'm going down there straight away to find out what's happened."

Jim caught the next train to London and arrived at the hospital just as Ernie was being settled in the ward and waited there for him to recover from the anaesthetic. After what seemed ages a nurse came to the waiting room and said he could sit by the bed. Ernie's eyes opened and he glanced hazily left and right, he looked at Jim but it was some time before recognition dawned,

"Hello, Jim," he said, his numbed mind not questioning how or why he should be there, "what happened?"

"You've had an accident. Now, don't you worry about anything. We'll look after things at home, you get yourself right.

The doped mind began to clear, yet still did not weigh priorities, "Will I miss the show?"

"There's been a message from Bob Sharples - the band have got to stay in Wembley for the Tommy Cooper Show, but they'll be round to see you soon."

At the mention of the band Ernie appeared to comprehend, but his thoughts were obviously confused. Then, for a few fleeting minutes, understanding seemed to return and the question came that Jim had dreaded,

"Where's Maurice?"

"Sorry, Ernie, he was killed. It was instantaneous, he didn't suffer."

The whole world crashed down. Ernie relapsed into total silence, staring straight at the ceiling. A full minute must have passed, then his eyes closed and screwed tight. Jim waited patiently until he saw that Ernie had mercifully fallen back into sleep. A nurse had been watching the proceedings from the foot of the bed,

"Leave him with us now, and thanks for doing the worst job of all."

Jim Wallace set off back to Manchester on the midnight train, snatching what fleeting sleep he could. Such is friendship.

The following day Ernie was able to take stock of his position and the tally was horrendous. He had a broken pelvis, a dislocated hip, a broken arm, his chest had been crushed by the steering wheel, one of the levers on the wheel had impaled his forehead just above the right eye and his face and body were generally covered with lacerations and bruises. He was now lying flat on his back, his left leg, heavily plastered, was suspended in traction from a system of cords and pulleys and his right arm was plastered round a right-angled splint and supported on a metal strut from the side of his body. He was finding it painful to breathe and a mirror showed his face, where it was not covered by bandages, to be just a mass of scabs of dried blood. He hit the bottom of the pit of despair.

His spirit was somewhat lifted by the many visitors he received. The whole of the musical fraternity, famous and not so famous, were forever trooping in to wish him well. On the third day he received a comforting letter from Hughie Green, together with a huge box of fruit which was so large it had to be shared all around the ward. But, most of all, he was overwhelmed by the support of Bob Sharples and the rest of the Showband who were regular and welcome callers. One of the band, Ronnie Hazlehurst, brought Frieda and Eddie down from Manchester and, after their visit, put them up in his own home for the week-end before taking them home again. Such was the comradeship that he found he could count on, and it uplifted his heart by its unselfishness.

After a fortnight his breathing became easier and the pain was bearable. It was at this time he was visited by a police inspector. The officer was tactful and gentle with his questioning and his manner one of sympathy and kindness. He was, however, honest and did not try to gloss over the seriousness of Ernie's legal problems,

"You realise I had to come to see you," the inspector concluded, "and you must face the fact that there must be charges, but get yourself better and don't worry too much." He stood up to go, then leaned over Ernie and added, "If it helps, I can tell you confidentially that there's no question of alcohol or wilful action being considered, we're treating the affair as just a pure unfortunate accident case. You'll have to attend court when you've recovered, the charge is usually "Causing death by dangerous driving".

When he had gone Ernie laid back and considered the possible sentence, "Causing death by dangerous driving" sounded so grim and so impersonally gruesome, he had no idea what would happen to him and wondered if he'd leave hospital to spend years in prison. He suffered days of anguish, self-recrimination and self-pity until, on one day after the customary crowd at visiting time had left, he looked at some of the other occupants of the ward and put his worries into perspective; his arm was in plaster, the man opposite had lost one of his completely; his leg was in traction, the man in the next bed had been changing a wheel on the M.1. when a Danish lorry had run over his and there was no hope of saving either of them. His own problems started to slide into the background.

Manchester musicians were continually sending flowers and his London colleagues were constantly arriving with their own private panaceas. Musicians seemed to be under the impression that the best medicine for any ailment was either a bottle of whisky or gallons of Newcastle Brown Ale, smuggled in on every visit, and soon every locker in the ward was crammed tight with bottles and tins until they were at a loss as to where to hide them. As he reluctantly tries to recall those terrible weeks, Ernie repeats endlessly - "The musicians, and Bob Sharples in particular, were absolutely marvellous."

Bob Sharples also gave Edith the experience of her lifetime. She decided to come to the hospital to see Ernie, which, in itself, was an adventure for her as she had never been to London. She arrived at Euston Station and was met by Bob himself, waiting for her with his new maroon Rolls Royce to bring her to the hospital. She enthused for months afterwards- "I felt just like the Queen Mother!". She also secretly revelled in the fact that her Ernie must be very important for this man to meet her with such a posh car!

It was also fortunate that Les Stockell was stationed nearby at R.A.F. Stanmore, so Edith was able to take the opportunity of staying with one son while visiting the other in hospital. Les himself also became a regular visitor and it was an ironic fact that the accident had brought the step-brothers together again, as, due to their service lives, they had not previously met since their early youth. From that period they became closer than they had ever been before.

Another frequent caller was Des Walker, his music publisher, who often cheered Ernie by talking about the business side of music as opposed to endless trivia. Before the accident Ernie had been commissioned to arrange a considerable amount of the Beatles music in preparation for a long-playing record which was to be made by the band of the Royal Military Academy, Sandhurst, and Des was anxious to know how far Ernie had progressed before his enforced seclusion.

"They're finished, Des," Ernie told him, "about a fortnight before the crash."

"Can I get them? They're pressing me to be able to start."

Ernie looked crestfallen. "You could, Des, but I feel terrible about them."

"Why?"

"When they were complete I was so busy myself I hadn't got time to copy them all out, so I passed them on."

"To whom?"

"Maurice. Des - I just can't face Dorothy at the moment, least of all to ask for my music. He'd finished them, too."

Ernie doesn't know exactly how the approach was made to Mrs. Davies but on her second visit to him Frieda brought the folder with her. It was still on his locker, awaiting collection by Des Walker, when Bob Sharples next came to see him. Bob took one look at the bundle and said,

"Thank God, Ernie, you must be improving, I see you've started "moonlighting!"

Des Walker collected them and they were duly recorded. That was the last writing Ernie was to do for a long while, not only because he was in no creative mood but also because his right arm was still in a plaster cradle.

Ernie's bodily injuries took a long time to heal but his emotional damage was greatly alleviated by the support he was receiving from the hospital staff and his unusually large number of visitors. The main financial problems, too, had been eased due to the caring foresight of Bob Sharples. Frieda informed Ernie that, ever since his accident, a cheque for twenty pounds had arrived from Bob every week and it transpired that this was being paid by an insurance company on a policy that he had arranged to cover any of his band members for such an emergency. The cheques continued to be delivered long after Ernie was discharged from hospital, but that day was still a long while away.

Ernie was bed-ridden for six weeks until the day came when he was told he was being allowed to get up. His arm had finally been taken out of plaster two weeks previously but he had no confidence in using it to hold one of the crutches with which the two nurses arrived. They eased him to the edge of the bed and slipped his legs over the side; then, supporting him under each arm they encouraged him to stand and let his legs take his weight, which, by now, was considerably less than it had been before the accident. He obeyed their instructions. Ease out, feet on floor. Lift. He was upright again! The thrill lasted for seconds only, he fell flat on his back and the pain was excruciating. They tried again, with the same result.

"This is bloody impossible!" he said.

"It's not, leave it for now, try again later."

It was many days and innumerable falls afterwards that he finally managed to balance precariously on his crutches and it was then he realised what had happened to him. His left leg was permanently bent and, consequently, was about two inches shorter than the right. He now had to accept the fact that he would be lame for the rest of his life.

He was discharged from hospital on May 20th. still in chronic pain and unable to walk without sticks. When he did manage to move he was forced to adopt the stance which new friends, met since the crash, always associated with him -standing, and walking, with his left foot on tip-toe.

When the time came for him to find his way back to Manchester it was once again from the world of musicians that assistance came - they collected him from Stanmore Hospital and, in private cars, transported him back to Sale, and home. They left him sitting in an arm chair which was still covered by towels, staring out of the window watching the traffic go by along Winstanley Road, he was miserable, he was lonely, he was a cripple.

The period of melancholy lasted for weeks on end, mainly because he was inactive and cut off from the world of music. Even watching television became a nightmare, for inevitably the Sharples band would appear and this became a torment in itself. He found himself struggling out of his chair to switch the set off in order to ease his heartache. He grew tired of endless reading and he felt ashamedly ungrateful when he looked sorrowfully at the number of "puzzle books" brought by well-meaning visitors and which lay unopened in the corner.

In July, Eddie celebrated his eleventh birthday but circumstances even denied Ernie of the pleasure of that. While Eddie was opening his presents, Ernie was on the train heading for London. He had struggled on his sticks from Sale to Piccadilly Station, Manchester, and was on his way to Harrow Magistrates Court to face the charge of dangerous driving. The proceedings were a mere formality - he was remanded to appear at the Old Bailey in December.

It was Eddie who, unwittingly, started the long process of mental recovery.

He switched on the television one Saturday afternoon and sat glued to a "pop" record programme which Ernie would never have bothered to watch as the volume of repetitious chords often jarred on his musical ear. Eddie was obviously enjoying the programme so he suffered it while reading the evening paper. Suddenly something seemed to click and a seed of interest germinated in the mud of his bored mind.

"Eddie," he said, "do me a favour, son, fetch that tape recorder please - the one you got for Christmas. May I borrow it?"

Eddie went upstairs and returned with a portable recorder. Ernie switched it on and recorded the number one hit of the week.

The following day he was far from bored - he had found himself something to do. Sitting at the table, listening to the tinny sound from the recorder, he wrote the melody on to manuscript paper and, as he did so, his mind went back to the Eartha Kitt episode in Blackpool, when Bob Sharples was racing against the clock. But he was not in any hurry and, for the first time in months, was enjoying himself. He allowed the task to amuse him over a matter of days and, at the end of the week, he had an arrangement of the song - not for just guitars, but for a full orchestra, and, in his head, could hear it being played. The following Saturday he repeated the exercise, and his self-invented therapy became routine. Week by week, his collection of "pop" music, arranged for a full band, grew and it gave him great satisfaction to see the pile of folders growing.

One day, early in August, he received three visitors within the space of minutes and a buzz of conversation soon filled the room. They were all musicians, one being Roger Fleetwood, a prominent member of the N.D.O. It was he who brought up the subject of Ernie's hip. There was a long discussion about the long-term prognosis until someone said,

"I think they can stop the pain by cementing the joint permanently."

"Then I'd have to use crutches all the time!" Ernie said in horror, "I'd be immobile!"

"Forget it, Ernie," Roger said in his gruff way, "I've heard they can fit artificial hip joints these days."

"Come off it, Roger!"

"It's true, I tell you. You insist on it, Ernie - go and see the quack - and I'll buy you a pint if I'm wrong!"

"If you do, it'll be the first bloody time!" Ernie said as, for the first time, a faint glimmer of hope came into his mind.

"What are you doing with yourself? Doing any playing?" somebody asked.

"I've not touched my sax for months," Ernie replied, "what's the point, I can't go anywhere to play it."

"So how do you pass the time?"

"I've been experimenting - pass over those folders." he pointed to his "therapy" piled on a chair. He explained what he had been doing.

"At first it was just for amusement," he said, "but since I started I've had an idea. You all do these gigs at weddings and so on - How many times have the youngsters asked you to play the real "pop" stuff, and you don't know it? The days of "Anniversary Waltz" and "Who's Taking You Home Tonight" have gone, lads .... this is what they want."

For the next hour he was his old enthusiastic self, talking away while they browsed through his new music.

"We can't play this rubbish!" someone wailed.

"You can," Ernie said, "and you're going to have to -if you don't you can forget all the bread-and-butter gig work!"

One friend was studying a folder very intently,

"I think you're on to something here, Ernie. Look I'm booked for a twenty-first party next Saturday, a marquee job out in Mere, is there any chance of borrowing these? Better still, how about coming with us?"

"What would you need?"

"Piano, bass, clarinet, trumpet and drums - plus sax if you're coming."

"They're all there," Ernie said, "and if you can get me there, I'd be tickled pink."

"And you'll be twenty quid better off! I'll pick you up at seven."

So it was that Ernie started playing again. The event was a tremendous success. At first they had been met with hostile eyes when the customary guitars and amplifiers did not appear but when the young crowd heard "their" music, correctly arranged for the combination, they raved. The party went on into the early hours and resulted in the band being booked for two future appearances on the spot.

The news spread. "Ernie is back in business!". The telephone now kept on ringing - "Can you play with us on Friday?" - "We're at a wedding on Saturday, will you come?" Ernie found himself being transported here and everywhere, playing for many different small bands and on every occasion the request was concluded with "And will you bring your library?" He began to wonder whether they wanted him for his playing or his volume of arrangements!

In September Eddie started his secondary education at Ashton-on-Mersey School for Boys. For the first time Ernie was unable to take him for his new uniform so it was Frieda who accompanied him to buy the outfit he needed. She returned loaded with carrier bags and Eddie tried on his new clothes for his father's benefit. Ernie, like all fathers of that time, was both proud and surprised to see his son suddenly mature, now dressed in long trousers.

".... and the ladies in the shop send you their love," Eddie said, "they said they'd read about the accident in the local papers." Ernie was pleased they had remembered him.

Late in October he made an appointment to see his doctor and tentatively put the question,

"Is it true that they can fit artificial hip joints these days?"

"Yes, but the process is still in its infancy, and I don't know if yours could be done - it's mainly for arthritis. There's one way to find out - I'll see if I can get you to Wrightington Hospital, they're the experts."

On November 1st. he was in the consulting room of the Consultant at Altrincham Hospital after the long procedure of visits to Outpatients Department, waiting rooms and X-Rays. The doctor examined the X-Ray plates and told him that he had an osteo-arthritic hip and that the only treatment he could suggest was an operation. He would put his name down for surgery.

"I feel certain they can do something. There's a long waiting list, but you could do with time for the damage to heal properly."

Ernie returned home encouraged and decided to suffer the continual chronic nagging ache. The ray of hope he had received, plus the cameraderie of his frequent "gigs" all helped take his mind off the main approaching ordeal, at least for a few hours a week. Then came the summons to attend the Old Bailey for trial on December 17th. He set off on the long journey to London again, this time not knowing if he would be returning or whether he would spend Christmas in prison.

The Old Bailey was horrendous. He recalls waiting in a room, his stomach churning and his legs, already weak, trembling. His throat was dry to the extent that the act of swallowing was painfully sore. Of the room itself he remembers nothing, but the most unpleasant experience of all was to pass Maurice's widow, who sat, hands on lap, staring rigidly ahead. There was no greeting. Then his name was called and he was escorted along a long passage and had to climb some steps at the end. At the top of the steps were steel bars and he felt he was in prison already. He hobbled through a cage-like structure into the court. He was in the dock.

The rest is vague. It all took place in a haze, rather like a film scene where, to gain dramatic effect, the camera is deliberately out of focus. Time had no meaning. He felt as if he was on the set of a television drama - a familiar set where the central figure was a forbidding figure in red robes. A distant voice read the charge and, automatically, as he had been advised, he answered "Guilty". Men in wigs were orating. One went on at great length while Ernie was lost in his own thoughts, unable to concentrate on what was going on before him. The words were making him relive a nightmare, he was sitting at the wheel ......Maurice was reading the paper ....that car in front is starting to blur . . .

".... is a man of the highest integrity," a voice was saying, "with an unblemished record of service in the army,"

The road's looking strange .... wind down the window... there's a sharp bend

"....who rose to the rank of senior N.C.O...."

Turn! Turn! For God's sake, turn!

"....served for years in both the Middle and the Far East and left with meritorious references...."

You're not going to make it! Please, God! No!"

".... and is now a highly respected member of the musical profession."

His mind focussed and he realised his barrister was talking about him, appealing to the judge for leniency.

It seemed interminable. Photographs were being handed up to the judge. A policeman was in the witness box. There was more argument and counter-argument, and still Ernie felt more like a bystander than the central character. His fate rested on this cast of players who were creating a drama in which he was both villain and hero.

It ended. His plea of guilty was accepted and he waited for sentence to be passed. When it came he could do nothing except close his eyes, grip the edge of the dock to avoid falling, take a deep breath and blow the air from his lungs in a long slow sigh of relief:

"You will be fined the sum of ten pounds and you are disqualified from driving for a period of three years."

He hobbled back to Euston Station and, to the surprise of the ticket collector at the barrier, kissed the return ticket as he handed it over to be punched. He sat in a window seat on the way back feeling it was perhaps going to be a "Happy Christmas" after all - until he remembered the look on the face of Dorothy Davies in that waiting room. He was suddenly ashamed that, in his relief, he had completely ignored the fact that her Christmas was going to be dreadful and her youngest daughter Patricia would spend this third Christmas of her life without a father. He felt inadequate, he was powerless to do anything to rectify the situation.

Consequently, Christmas 1970 was certainly not a happy one, Ernie's self-imposed penitence being supplemented by the news that due to Ernie's physical incapacity to run the business "Northern Orchestral Services" was being closed down on January 1st. Bob Sharples had asked Mrs. Reid if she was prepared to carry on the business on her own but she had declined, and so another era ended.

Before him now there was nothing. He had no regular work of any kind and he was grateful for the few pounds he picked up when he was asked to do "gig" work, but even then he was totally dependent on the generosity of fellow musicians who offered to transport him to the various venues. Now he was playing purely out of necessity to earn money, the old thrill had gone and the spirit of innovation had been trampled into the dust of despair. His one solace was the certainty that things could not get worse - or so he thought, but fate had more cards to play.

On March 3rd he received a telephone call from Les's wife, Georgina who told him she had called at Maple Drive that afternoon and had found Edith lying on the bathroom floor, dead. Ernie's diary entry for the day says everything:-
"As I sit here at my desk the tears are never far away and I have never felt so desolate before. It seems a whole chapter of my life has disappeared and the only real contact with childhood has gone for ever. I have no feeling of belonging and when Eddie came home from school I had a terrible fear that even he would be taken from me and that I would lose the one remaining happiness in my life. Every time I look at him I see myself when young and feel the sadness and insecurity I felt as a child being transferred to him. I must try desperately not to pass to him the fear that dwells constantly in my own heart, as when I see Eddie I see my own childhood with all its memories ... all that remains now Mam has gone. Oh Mam .... Forgive me .... I miss you so much. R.I.P."

Ernie made the weary journey to Scarborough alone. Frieda maintained the break to the end and Ernie thought it best that Eddie should remember his grandmother as he last saw her. The funeral was on Monday, March 8th and the service was held at Falsgrave Road Chapel, where Edith had attended for many years. The choir of which she had been a member sang the hymns and when her favourite, "The Lord's My Shepherd", was sung to "Crimond" Ernie could take no more and collapsed in tears. Les Stockell and Georgina helped him back to the cortege which then proceeded to the crematorium where, as the curtains closed round the coffin, they said their final "Good-bye's".

All that remained was to clear up the legal affairs. Edith's will named Les and Ernie both as executors and beneficiaries although this was purely a technicality. The estate consisted only of insurance policies for the sum of one hundred pounds and the contents of the house which were of no value. As he watched the house being unfeelingly cleared by a dealer his heart sank again to see what little reward his mother had had for sixty-five years of struggle and unselfishness. He said farewell to Les and Georgina and boarded the train home, realising that the final break with Scarborough had come, and that the town no longer had any significance for him except in memory.

It may have helped him if he could have returned to absorb himself in his work again but this, of course, he was denied. Ernie Watson, the trumpet player of the N.D.O., became his main saviour of reason, uncomplainingly taking him to the few engagements he was able to accept.

Then fate played its ace of trumps. He received a message from Bob Sharples expressing his disappointment and annoyance. He felt he had been seriously compromised. The money he had been sending since the accident was being claimed on a group policy covering sixteen members of the band and the company had instructed him to cease paying it as they had had information that Ernie was working, making the policy invalid. The technicality had not entered Ernie's mind as the "work" had consisted of minor functions which he had undertaken to break the boredom and which had paid nowhere near a living wage. Legally, however, they were in order and Ernie made a hurried telephone call to speak to Bob personally and, he hoped, rectify the matter. He was told he was not available. On the 25th May he received a letter from Bob, the gist of which said that he was shocked that Ernie should have put him in such a position and that as far as he was concerned the end of the road had come. So ended a relationship which had lasted for six years. Six years which, up to that fateful day in 1970, had brought nothing but happiness.

His total regular weekly income was now £9.65 sickness benefit.

CHAPTER EIGHTEEN

The prospect for the future could hardly look blacker. He now had no work and, due to being unable to drive, could not commit himself to accepting any. Unable to walk without sticks he could not carry instrument cases on public transport, even if any had been available at the late hours to which he would be required to play. He was stuck on a roundabout of circumstances with no apparent way off. His only relief from frustrating boredom were the regular requests from Des Walker for more original compositions and arrangements for publication.

Day after day he sat by the telephone willing it to ring and occasionally his spirits would be lifted by a call asking for his services from someone who was also prepared to arrange to transport him. Ernie Watson was his salvation time and time again and he was grateful for work with Yorkshire Television, making sound backing for plays, and for engagements playing for the television programmes like the "Pop Proms". On every occasion a fellow musician would have to collect him, take him to the studio, carry his instruments, deposit him in his chair for the recording and then bring him home again. He began to dream of independence again, until then not having realised the tragedy of immobility.

July did bring a happy day. Des Walker telephoned to inform him that his work had been used at the Trooping of the Colour parade for the Queen's Birthday Celebrations in June. After the ceremony on Horse Guards Parade the massed bands of the Guards had marched to Buckingham Palace to play in the courtyard for Her Majesty. One of the items selected had been "Bell A'Peal" by Terence Brien. It was to be used from that day onwards.

In August came the letter he had been awaiting - an appointment at Wrightington Hospital for examination by the specialist hip surgeon and on the 27th he was interviewed by Mr. Charnley, the pioneer of hip replacement, himself. After many examinations and further X-Rays he was called into the consulting room.

"I've seen all your tests and records and I am sure we can make a great improvement and probably get you walking correctly again,"

Ernie's heart leapt,

"....but I'm afraid it cannot be done immediately. For a start there is a long waiting list and secondly your health is not good enough to proceed. Tell me, have you had spells of tiredness over the past years?"

"Yes, but up to the accident I put it down to overwork and since then I've assumed it was due to my struggling on these sticks."

"Only partly, Mr. Waites, our tests show that you are diabetic."

What next was life going to throw at him? In a way, however, he did find the discovery some slight relief in that it could explain the accident - maybe it was not due to his own carelessness. Perhaps he had blacked out ... but that was purely academic now.

"So what will happen?" he asked.

"We'll treat the diabetes and when that is under control we'll see about putting you down for replacement surgery. Meanwhile, is the pain bearable?"

"It has been so far, it's the sheer persistence that is wearing me down."

"Right, now you follow the treatment we're going to prescribe, keep to the diet you'll be given and I assure you I'll deal with your hip as soon as I can. I strongly advise you to wait for a couple of years as any undue strain, such as carrying heavy cases, would cause damage which would mean another operation very soon. So try to hang on but if the pain gets unbearably worse, get in touch with us and we'll give you priority."

He came home to adjust to another change of life-style in order to cope with his latest malady.

Towards the end of the year his fortune took its first upward trend, once again, due to Des Walker. Des was an associate of Ken Griffin, an ex-Guards musician who was now a producer with B.B.C. Television in London. He was responsible for a television version of Billy Smart's Circus and had asked Des for original music to use with the show. Des passed the request to Ernie,

"He wants all sorts of pieces," he explained, "half a dozen or so new fanfares to use throughout the programme, plus a couple of gallops for the horse riding acts as well as fresh arrangements for things like "The Man on The Flying Trapeze" and so on. Can you get them done and send them to me as soon as possible?"

Ernie was back in his own element again and spent the next weeks writing continually. His work was used on the Christmas programme and all those that subsequently followed.

Des, meanwhile, had left the Royal Corps of Transport and was now the Director of Music of the Welsh Guards. His successor was Major Bill Allen who contacted Ernie to ask him to continue to write for the R.C.T. for its tours abroad and its L.P. recordings. His association with the world of military bands was slowly being re-built.

The New Year of 1972 was marred by the news of the death of Mrs. Reid. Over the long years with the Bob Sharples organisation she had made herself Ernie's guide and mentor and the companionship had continued after the business closed down. He felt he had lost a close friend.

As the first months of the year went by Ernie realised he had got to make a decision about his future life. He was now beginning to face facts squarely and it was clear that he would, for a considerable time, be unable to earn a living as a performing musician due to his being unable to drive and due to his general physical incapacity. It seemed illogical, however, not to put the experiences of his life and his expertise to use and his mind began to linger on other possible outlets for his talents. Strangely enough, it was Eddie again who sowed the seed of an idea.

Eddie was by now becoming quite proficient on the clarinet, Ernie having encouraged him to play since he was very young. The new school he was attending had had no music department and it was therefore a rather excited lad who came home one evening with, for him, good news. The school had had a new headmaster since January and, at the first opportunity, he had appointed a teacher of music so the boring old days of "singing" periods were going to be transformed into music lessons. This gave Ernie the idea that perhaps he could use his skills as a teacher. He wrote to the Manchester Education Authority offering his services and was subsequently invited to meet Victor Fox, the Inspector of Music for the city's schools.

The result was another disappointment. He was told that the only way he could teach music in schools was by qualifying through a Teachers' Training College and obtaining the Teachers' Certificate. This was a three year course of training in itself but before he could even be considered for that he would need all the necessary "A" levels in general subjects in order to apply for a college place. His age alone ruled out that possibility. He could, however, become an peripatetic instructor of wind instruments but this would necessitate his travelling from school to school over a wide area. Lack of mobility tossed that option into the waste-bin of circumstances. He went home discouraged once again but still optimistic that, having got the idea, something might turn up.

It did. Only a matter of weeks later Eddie came home with the news that his own school had started a small group of boys playing instruments. He, personally, was disappointed because they had a teacher coming in for an hour a week but he was teaching the trumpet - there was nobody to teach the clarinet. That was enough! Ashton-on-Mersey School was within the Cheshire Authority and relatively near his home - Ernie made contact immediately and within days he was embarking on his new interest - giving individual instrumental instruction to children. True, it was for only two hours a week, but it was a start.

Fate started dealing him better cards from that day. He received news that the theme he had submitted for the Munich Olympics had been short-listed and was among the final six being considered and that the signature tune he had sent to the B.B.C. for "Come Dancing" had been accepted. His Olympic theme was eventually not the one selected for the B.B.C. coverage but it was used by German television.

The impact Ernie had on the development of music at Ashton-on-Mersey School is best summed up in the words of the headmaster, Wally Lindsay, writing some years later:-

"Two months after Ernie started teaching, Don Ezard, the teacher in charge of music, came into my office with a portable tape recorder and asked me to listen to a tape. From the recorder came the sound of clarinets, complete with base clarinet playing both very tunefully and accurately.

"Who is it?" I asked.

" Ernie Waites' group." he replied.

"It can't be, he's only had them for a few weeks, and not one of them could play a note!"

But they could by then, and Ernie had done it with only fourteen hours of tuition. Little did I know it, but at that moment I had heard the sound of the embryo of the Ashton Showband."

Ernie now had a real interest in life again and this encouraged him to make himself more mobile. He was still disqualified from driving so he bought himself a bicycle - a Moulton Bike, a small cycle with small wheels and no cross bar to impede the limited movement he had in his left leg. He rode it pedalling with his right leg only, his Sticks fixed to the handlebars with large bulldog clips. He was soon seen cycling around the streets of Sale, happily doing his shopping. There was only one major problem - he couldn't use the brakes! There was nothing wrong with the brakes, only the rider - if he applied the brakes he could not place his foot on the ground to support himself when the bike stopped and would fall into the road! He solved the difficulty by keeping a sharp eye out for lamp-posts and stopped himself by hooking his left arm round the one that was most convenient, rather like the old mail trains catching the mail bags suspended along the track!

Even this mode of transport had its hair-raising moments. One day, cycling through Sale centre, he was passing the library when a car hit him from behind and carried him for some twenty yards before it stopped and he slid off the bonnet to the pavement - right outside Sale Police Station! The back wheel of his bike was buckled but luckily Ernie suffered no damage, except to his dignity.

In January 1973 the medical powers decided that he should be fit for light work and he was consequently taken off invalidity benefit. He was therefore obliged to tackle the main Chester road on his bike to attend the Social Security Office in Stretford. Attending there did nothing to improve his newly-improving confidence. He spent hours waiting in queues in crowded sparsely equipped and barely decorated rooms among hundreds of others, some resignedly patient, some unsettlingly aggressive. When his time came to be seen the interview could have been made the basis of one of the television comedy sketches he used to accompany in the old days:

"What is your trade?"

"Musician."

"No call for that round here. What about a job on a farm?"

"I can't walk."

"What can you do?"

"Anything within my capabilities - I'm a professional musician. You know, theatres, radio, television, anywhere"

"Got no vacancies like that round here. What about a van driver?"

"No licence."

"What about a factory cleaner?"

"On two sticks?" "Hm. That's a point. Nothing for you. Come back next week."

He went back the following week - and the week after, suffering similar long queues and frustrations. He decided that the benefits would be far outweighed by the pain and discomforts, and took the risk of returning to the only real job he knew - playing. He contacted the Golden Garter again, was offered work at once and accomplished the seemingly impossible task of getting there and back on his bike. He would arrive home completely exhausted after playing for some four hours and then cycling, one-leggedly, for five miles with his sticks clipped to the front and his saxophone strapped to the back of the bike. He kept the problem to himself for three weeks until he was questioned about his mode of travel by fellow members of the band. As soon as they knew about it the cycling ceased - two of them, Roy Rich and Tony Whalley, arranged a rota system for collecting him in their cars which Ernie accepted gratefully but insisted on sharing petrol expenses.

Having returned to Show Business he was back among the people he knew and his past was forever being recalled. Stars like Ken Dodd and Frankie Vaughan would appear as cabaret artists and greet him with a jovial,

"Hi, Ernie! How's the leg?"

He began to feel he belonged again, except at home. He and Frieda were drifting further and further apart and were virtually living their individual lives, their only common interest being Eddie. His year of sitting around the house had done nothing to improve the relationship, in fact, if anything, it had strained it almost to the limit. They were getting on each others' nerves and Ernie's absence in the evenings was a boon in that it helped to relieve the mounting tension.

With working full time he could have stopped his two hours of teaching but, by Easter, he had developed a bond with the children he taught and it was a great pleasure to him to see their enthusiasm. Eddie had become one of his pupils - a situation which could have been embarrassing for both him and his father but such was the camaraderie amongst the youngsters that they encountered no difficulty. Ernie wrote special simple arrangements for them and, to everybody's pleasure, the group, now consisting of five clarinets, two trumpets, two saxophones and an Eb bass, played in public for the first time - providing the music for the hymns at the school's Easter Service, conducted by the music teacher with Ernie sitting with them playing the euphonium. This caused a greater interest to grow within the school, more boys began to request tuition and as the teacher of trumpet had left, the headmaster managed to persuade the authorities to increase Ernie's official teaching time to four hours a week.

As there were no spare classrooms the only place where Ernie could be housed was the school canteen. This was a small single storey brick building on the far side of the playground and it reminded Ernie of an army barrack hut! He therefore spent his time teaching boys to play instruments accompanied by the noises of rattling plates, pans and crockery coming from the kitchen. Being isolated from the main school building, however, meant that Ernie had little contact with the full-time staff of the school and it was due to this that his true value as a colleague was not at first fully appreciated as he would arrive on his bike, lean it against the canteen wall while he taught and then drive off again when he had finished. When the group played in the school hall it would be conducted by the music teacher who received the acclaim while Ernie maintained an unrecognised position in the background.

By the start of the winter term Ernie had the nucleus of a full band. He had moved from the canteen and was now ensconced in a stockroom in the main building which had been emptied for his benefit. It was just large enough to hold a cupboard, a small desk and two chairs (he felt he was back in a practise room at Kneller Hall, only now he was taking the part of George Garside) and his teaching time had been increased to ten hours per week. In December the band gave its first concert for parents in the school hall and, prior to breaking up for Christmas, it played all the carols for the school Christmas Service in nearby St. Mary's Church which was full of enthusiastic parents.

The tide seemed to have turned and he faced 1974 with renewed hope. By then he was managing with just one stick, he was working regularly at "The Garter" and, in the school band, he had discovered the most exciting and rewarding challenge of his life. They were only children, but, in spite of the public praise for their progress naturally being attributed to others, he considered they were **his** children and it was **his** band, born of **his** ideas, trained by **his** talent and ready to progress in **his** way.

The start of the New Year meant he had reached the end of his term of disqualification so he applied for, and regained, his driving licence. He accepted that he would not be able to use his left leg to operate a clutch pedal so he purchased an automatic car, a small white DAF. He was now fully mobile again, even though he was forced to pay a very high premium for his first insurance. Also within the first month he received word that he had now been elected a full Associate Member of the Performing Rights Society - the omens were all pointing to an improvement in his fortune.

More and more children were appearing at his stockroom door with instruments, many probably purchased as Christmas presents due to the reputation the band was steadily building, and it gave him great satisfaction that his influence was having such good effect. This reputation could be maintained only by hard work and continuous practice and Ernie gave his time voluntarily to hold band rehearsals in the school hall at the end of the day and from the start of the summer term they played for an hour or more three times a week. The enthusiasm was boundless, so much so that the girls' school asked to join in.

The Ashton-on-Mersey Schools were semi-detached, two identical schools, one for boys and one for girls, which, from the road, appeared to be one. A huge playing field stretched across them both at the rear but there was an imaginary line bisecting it and each school kept to its own territory. Due to the success of the band the headmistress of the Girls' School approached Wally Lindsay with the idea that some of her pupils could receive lessons from Ernie. She persuaded the Authority to allow her three hours of instrumental instruction and so, for the first time since the schools were built, female footsteps were regularly heard along the boys' corridors as the girls made their way to Ernie's little domain. Within weeks the band became the first permanent "mixed" enterprise.

By June he was so confident of the ability of his band that Ernie was ready to let them play for the general public. Don Ezard, whose relatives owned a caravan site in Ireland and could therefore provide accommodation, arranged for the band to take part in the International Music Festival which was held in Letterkenny, Co. Donegal and a "savings club" was established to pay for the trip to Ireland. Ernie, consequently, found himself, in a way, re-living his army days - organising music, programmes and transportation as well as playing professionally every evening. He was a contented man once more.

His happiness was clouded by the news that Des Walker had died. He received a telephone call from the Welsh Guards Band Office on July 27th to say that Major Walker had been found dead in a London hotel, having suffered a heart attack. He was fifty. Ernie's diary says:-

".....we shall have to see what will happen to his business, perhaps his wife Jean will carry it on. Des has been a very good friend to me .... pressure of life must have been just too much .... Guards' Director of Music, Music Publisher, A and R man for Recording Companies... Nature has called a halt ... R.I.P. Des."

Don Ezard left Ashton-on-Mersey School at the end of the Summer term, having been appointed to a more senior post elsewhere, but he accompanied the band on its first performance "overseas". This was an adventure for the youngsters, meeting musicians, both young and mature, from many foreign countries, all united in music. They played many concerts, one specially for the President of Eire, Erskine Childers. They were specifically invited to return the following year.

A week supervising a group of children cannot possibly go by without both worrying and humorous moments. Suffice it to record just one of the latter:-

One young lad, who played the Eb Bass, by far the largest instrument in the band, was notorious for forgetting his mouthpiece. At any moment Ernie would suddenly confront him and ask,

"Where's your mouthpiece?"

- and the lad would dive in his pocket and hold the item aloft. This became an amusing routine for the other children but Ernie knew it was essential for the boy's training. After a concert in Letterkenny they were all joyously singing in the coach taking them back to the caravan site where they were based when Ernie stopped the singing to say,

"Where's your mouthpiece?"

Up went a fist, clenching the mouthpiece.

"Where's your music?"

Up went the other hand, holding a music case.

"Well done!" said Ernie, and the singing recommenced.

About ten miles further on Ernie felt a hand on his shoulder. He looked round - it was the Eb Bass player,

"Mr. Waites - I've forgotten the Bass!"

The coach had to turn round in a narrow Irish road and returned to the hall where, after almost an hour, the Eb Bass, worth around five hundred pounds, was still standing on the steps.

At the start of the new term in September, Ernie's newly found enjoyment of life took another of its down-turns. The new music teacher was a young "brass band" man who did not seem very inclined towards woodwind. There was an immediate clash of personalities which was heightened when the teacher appeared as the band was preparing for an after-school rehearsal and, disregarding Ernie's presence, began to give orders. The children were nonplussed and, gazing from the teacher to Ernie and then back again, did not respond. When the teacher went on to explain that it was he alone, who was now in charge, Ernie felt belittled, his humiliation somewhat emphasised by the difference in their ages.

The newcomer produced his own band music which, in Ernie's opinion was both too difficult and uninspiring when compared to the "T.V. Themes" and popular classics that he had been writing for them since the band had been formed and through which their interest and enthusiasm had been raised as each child had had a part written specially for his or her individual ability. Within a short time the difference of opinion between teacher and instructor became obvious in the staffroom and the deputy head expressed his concern to the headmaster. It was a situation that obviously could not be allowed to continue and they were very concerned that the personal disagreements between staff members should not affect the children. Although the band had become an asset to the school and its reputation they were reluctant openly to support one against the other, hoping that, given time, a gainful partnership would evolve. The headmaster suggested that Ernie should contiinue to do what he was being paid to do, namely instruct instumentalists and, if he so desired, train his band voluntarily outside school hours, while the full-time teacher devoted his time to running the music curriculum within the school. It was a dichotomy that would survive on a knife edge, relying purely on goodwill. It did not last.

A few weeks afterwards the music departments of both the boys' and the girls' schools announced that they were co-operating to present a concert for the benefit of the parents, each school making its own contribution - the girls offering soloists and a choir, the boys, instrumental soloists and a band. This band, when formed, was naturally composed of members of the "after school" band trained by Ernie but as this was a "school function" would be conducted by the teacher. Band rehearsals for the concert were arranged after school and these, of course, clashed with the regular practices organised by Ernie. The children became confused and the relationship between the "conductors" again deteriorated, approaching animosity.

The band itself also faced the difficulty of playing a different form of arrangement and, due to the immaturity of the members, found some of the new music difficult to play. Although it was within the capabilities of experienced musicians some of it was in keys with which they were not familiar and included notes that some were unable to play. The teacher must have soon recognised this and, realising time was short, asked Ernie to provide some of his music with which the children were familiar. This Ernie refused to do unless he was allowed to conduct and rancour, bred from obstinacy, returned. Ernie packed his music in his car and took it away, sorrowfully deciding that the end had come.

The next day he went to see the headmaster to give his notice but was persuaded to stay until the end of term in order to allow his band to fulfil the concert he had planned for early December and to provide a short period to see if the school could resolve the dispute. Ernie agreed, in fact he could even understand the situation as it would be seen from the other side - a man is appointed to be in charge of music and promptly finds himself confronted by a group of children, passionately devoted to an unqualified peripatetic instructor! He sincerely regretted that the teacher, had not had time to study the background of experience and realise the reason for the band's staunch loyalty, and, indeed, it's very existence, as a more diplomatic approach might perhaps have allowed them to work together to their mutual advantage.

Ernie's diary, Oct. 9th 1974:-

"......I am left with a feeling that someone loaded the gun with bullets and the new music teacher and I pulled the trigger. What a sad end to two wonderful years. Despite the head's assurance that I would have complete charge of the band the music teacher seems to have other ideas. Perhaps I could form a Sale Youth Band somewhere, who knows, we shall see. Somehow, it seems that whenever I get attached to anything I lose it. Sometimes I'm afraid to love anything too much."

That same week Ernie read in the newspaper that in the High Court in Manchester the case for damages in connection with the accident of four years previously had been heard and that Mrs. Dorothy Davies had been awarded £35,000 "against the driver of the car in which her husband had been killed." Ernie had not been summoned to appear, the case having been dealt with by the insurance company. He felt some slight comfort in knowing that Dorothy and her children would now be secure.

CHAPTER NINETEEN

Ernie continued his instruction at school but with a feeling of pointlessness. Eddie was by now playing a leading role in the clarinet section and Ernie was reluctant to tell him that time was rapidly running out for the band. He therefore spent the next week or so in a sense of isolation - even, in a small way, deceiving his own son. He could not explain his feeling of loneliness to Frieda as, by then, all empathetic communication between them seemed to have gone and he began to yearn for the comradeship that he once enjoyed in his days of "Show Business". His relief came from the most unexpected quarter.

Wally Lindsay was a headmaster who believed in staff involvement in all major decisions and his office door was always left open for any member of staff to call in for a discussion of policy or just a general chat and rarely a morning break went by without at least one teacher joining him for coffee and exchange of ideas. Ernie, however, had never considered accepting the general open invitation, reckoning that his position as a peripatetic teacher precluded his using up the head's time and thus excluding full-time staff. With the prospect of the band giving his "swan-song" concert, however, and wanting it to be done to the highest possible standard of presentation, he thought he would put in some personal ideas to try to make it different from the traditional "School Concert". He carefully planned his approach to the head, anticipating that he would need all his subtlety to persuade the school to break with tradition. He soon found out he had worried unnecessarily as, to his pleasant surprise, he discovered that Wally had had professional experience of show business himself and they were on the same wavelength. He felt welcome as soon as he entered the office,

"Good morning, Ernie, nice of you to pop in, I thought you might have come long before this. We've only met when I've been playing referee!"

"I didn't consider it my place."

"Nonsense! When are you due to start today?"

"Not for half an hour yet."

"Well, let's make up for it, sit down, I'll ask Betty to fetch us some coffee."

Ernie settled down with some difficulty in one of the two small wooden arm chairs and Mrs. Betty Bolton, the school secretary, brought in the usual morning coffee.

For a while the conversation was idle chit-chat as the two men got to know each other. Ernie gave a brief outline of his days in the army, Suez and Malaya and they found some slight common interest as Wally had spent the war years in the Far East with the R.A.F., but when Ernie went on about the Bob Sharples Orchestra and the N.D.O., Wally's face suddenly lit up with interest.

"The N.D.O.!" he said, "When?"

"Oh, for as long as I've been in civvy street, why?"

"I worked with them for years in the fifties and sixties," Wally said, "I used to do script writing for B.B.C. shows from the Hulme Hippodrome. Do you remember Ronnie Taylor?"

"He gave me some of my early breaks," Ernie said, "when he was producing "Variety Fanfare", do you remember that show?"

"Do I remember it! I remember one particular one especially. You wont believe this, it sounds crazy. Amongst others, I used to write for a chap called Ted Lune, you may remember him with the "letters from my mam". Well, one day the Vernon Girls Choir were on just before he was and half way through his act......."

"They fell off the staging." Ernie laughingly interrupted, "Was it you who wrote the new script while the stage was being repaired?"

"You were there!"

"Not only there - I was the one who got hit by the jumbo microphone."

From then on it was an exchange of reminiscences until Ernie said,

"Look at the time! The kids'll be waiting for me."

"You must call in whenever you can - and as soon as possible. We've a lot to talk about!"

Ernie left the office feeling he'd gained a new friend, as indeed he had.

It was only when he got outside that he realised they'd never got round to the reason for his visit. He went back the following morning and broached the idea of a full concert.

"I don't want the usual school function," he said, "you know, parents lined up in rows staring at a platform lit by a sixty watt bulb and a backcloth of a bare wall."

"Neither do I," Wally said, "let's pull out all the stops we can, within our limitations. This will be my first major function since I came here, as well as yours. For a start, we'll hold it in the Town Hall."

Over the next few days they planned the maiden concert. Sharing a common interest in, and both having experience of show business they decided to attempt to produce a full show, centred on the band.

They arranged to print a programme, the cover of which was designed by the Art Department and which they hoped would be paid for by the inclusion of advertisements from local businesses. One of the obvious firms to be approached was the supplier of the school uniform so the owners of "Petites Modes" were approached. The answer was most encouraging, not only would they advertise but they would also sell tickets from the shop, which was just by

Sale Town Hall. From that day the proprietors, "Billy" Hardy and her daughter Karina became enthusiastic and staunch supporters of the band, never missing a performance.

Ernie had by then arranged a considerable number of popular classics, extracts from operettas and even "Glen Miller" items as well as some of his own original music so they devised a programme of wide interest and variety. They entitled it "In Concert". Assisted by other interested members of staff they decorated the banqueting hall of the civic centre and on a stage garlanded with flowers the children performed a two hour show attended by the Mayor and Mayoress of Trafford, local dignitaries and proud parents as well as the general public. It was an unqualified success, receiving revues in the local papers - unanimously expressing surprise at the standard achieved. The event had to be repeated six days later .... this time amended and under the title "In Concert Again".

Ernie's apprehension ceased immediately and he cast aside any idea of leaving. When the school broke up for Christmas he was full of ideas for the future and was confident that, somehow, he would retain his band.

Unfortunately the successful public debut did not bring about the end of the disagreement, if anything it fuelled it, as the teacher again insisted that as the person responsible for music he should be in charge. The headmaster re-stated his confidence in Ernie and the problem came to the notice of the Education Authority. A hurried meeting was arranged for all involved, together with the Education Office's Advisor for Music, the result was a repetition of the headmaster's previous solution - Ernie to run his band as an extra-curricular activity and the teacher to deal with music generally within the curriculum. It was all completely unsatisfactory and the situation, once again, explosive, but, having witnessed the joy of the youngsters before Christmas, Ernie was now not prepared to sacrifice the band because of personal differences and continued his after-school rehearsals.

He rapidly expanded the repertoire, introducing many of his old army arrangements, suitably amended for the youngsters' abilities and consequently by March the band was competent to play many marches and Viennese waltzes. He took another idea to the office and soon he, and other members of staff, were planning another major show - "A Night in Vienna". They toyed with many variations, from simple ideas to serving a full "Viennese" buffet or even hiring a stately home and driving guests from the car park to the hall in horse-drawn carriages! They decided to stick to basics and leave the more ambitious dreams to a later date. They began by making contact with the Austrian Embassy and Tourist Board for materials to decorate the hall while Ernie polished up the band.

The traditional "Sale Festival" was to be held in June and, following the publicity of the December shows, the school was asked to provide the concert for the final night. It was the catalyst that re-opened the controversy over the band leadership. The music teacher claimed his right to represent the school and started rehearsals with a band using his own music in school hours. It was a repeat of events of the previous year, culminating in the headmaster, who was by now getting rather exasperated by the whole sorry saga, expressing his disapproval of the general situation.

Ernie's diary: April 11th 1975:

"Today the music teacher said "In the event of my music not being suitable for the festival would you object if I used your arrangements instead?" I told him it was out of the question and that if he was going to prove himself he would have to do it without my help. Needless to say, all my plans for "A Night in Vienna" are held in abeyance until I have a decision from the Head as to who is in charge of the band."

The internal altercation continued for some weeks while, externally, all appeared to be going smoothly. Ernie was making arrangements for the return trip to Letterkenny for the 1975 Festival, this time with a far larger band. He therefore concentrated his rehearsal time for the items required for several concerts to be given in Ireland. Suddenly, his plans were changed:

Ernie's diary: May 27th 1975"

"The headmaster has asked me to take the band to the Sale Festival as it appears the towel has been thrown in and all appearances the school band were to make have been cancelled without notifying anyone. This leaves me a week to prepare the band."

The performance on the final night of Festival Week was an unqualified success resulting in the headmaster of the local Grammar School and the Head of Department of a school in Bolton both asking if the band would be available to play for some of their social functions.

Ernie was now in his element and his enthusiasm for the band became infectious. Its reputation grew with each performance and full preparations for "A Night in Vienna" went ahead. The show was presented at Sale Town Hall, this time with the building decorated with red and white bunting, trellis-works of flowers and dozens of large posters supplied by Austrian authorities.

Once again the local press enthused and, as a consequence more old contacts were re-made. One afternoon, just before band practice was due, Wally saw a man enter the school who was vaguely familiar and he assumed it was a parent of one of the band. Ernie, however, recognised him immediately,

"Fred!", he cried, "What are you doing here?"

"I saw the write-up in the paper and thought I'd see what you were up to." It was Freddie Hefferan, Ernie's colleague of the N.D.O. Freddie listened to the band and after a couple of numbers said,

"Clever arrangements, them, Ernie - the kids sound good. You're a musical con-man!"

Ernie smiled.

"You know that, I know that - but the public love them. I've written it all well within their scope ... and you can't see the join!"

"Do you mind if I sit in?"

"You're more than welcome."

So it was that Freddie Hefferan, a professional saxophonist, started to play in the band, increasing the interest and teaching. A few weeks later the incident was repeated, this time the interest came from Bill Nixon, the N.D.O. drummer. The band was like golf - anyone hearing it was hooked!

In August he took the band back to Ireland, this time there was a complement of about thirty players, accompanied by Freddie Hefferan, Wally Lindsay and Don Ezard, who had insisted on going again.

Eddie had left Ashton-on-Mersey school in July having been transferred to Sale Boys' Grammar School to study for his "A" levels but, like many others who had left school in July, he continued to attend band rehearsals. Ernie was now, in effect, running two bands, the band made up solely of current pupils and the augmented one which included the "old boys and girls".

In October, Ernie received an intriguing and challenging letter from Major Allen of the Band of the Royal Corps of Transport, part of which read:-

"....I am landed with large shows almost the size of tattoos for next year and having done the usual "1812" until I'm sick of it, am stuck for a show-stopper finale. Next year is the 200th anniversary of the Yanks throwing us out and I wondered if there is anything in the way of music that could be made into a sort of "1812", but nowhere near as long, with battle scenes etc. and the Yanks winning through ...."

It was a challenge Ernie could not resist and, in the short time he had available between ending rehearsals at school and setting off for his evening stints at the Golden Garter he composed a ten minute fantasia based on the history of America from the Mayflower to the War of Independence. He then arranged it for full military band. He entitled it "1776". It was difficult to play, demanding all the skills of the musicians, but it was received with great acclaim and later, in April 1976, he heard that it had been played by massed bands on the lawn of the White House itself.

In May, Ernie was in the head's office again with another idea - was it possible for the band to produce its own L.P. recording? This posed two main problems: How and where could they obtain the use of a recording studio and how could they find the money to finance it? Peter Pilbeam, a producer with B.B.C. radio with whom Wally had worked in the past, was still in Manchester and they telephoned him to tell him of the quality of the band. Peter was an astute man and, accepting their recommendation that it was something out of the ordinary, he invited the youngsters to the Playhouse Theatre for an audition. He recorded them for over an hour and subsequently used many excerpts from the tape in radio broadcasts. As a reward he gave them a copy of the full recording and so they had their "master". Within days a parent of a band member, Gordon Horsefield, phoned the school to say he had arranged the necessary finance and the first recording of the band went on sale within the month. To all appearances the venture had come to a successful end, but suddenly it turned out merely to be the beginning.

In June, Wally received a telephone call:

"This is Des Sissons of B.B.C. Television. Peter Pilbeam has just let me hear the tape of your school band. We're producing a series of programmes featuring school bands from all over the U.K., three bands will take part in each of six weekly shows and the top three will play in the final. The show will be called "Settle the Score" - we've selected most of the schools taking part by audition but in your case there's no need for another. Would you like your band to be included?"

Ernie took the band to the television studios on July 7th and judged by Larry Adler, Harry Mortimer and Bernard Keefe it gained the highest marks of the heat. Among many compliments paid by the judges was one from Harry Mortimer that was later to change its whole image:

"That band," he said, "is not a school concert band -it is a showband."

At the end of the month Wally got another telephopne call from Des Sissons - "The series is now over and your band's score was the second highest in the country. You will be in the final." When Ernie heard the news he was over the moon and hurried discussions began as to what they should play: Marches and Waltzes? No, Ernie decided, they were too ordinary; Glen Miller tunes? No, he said, others might do that...

"What I want," he said, "is to have them play something right out of the usual run - but what?"

"Could you write something yourself?" Wally asked.

"I could, but on what lines?"

"Something topical," Wally said,"what's in the news?"

A wicked smile crept over Ernie's face which widened into a grin,

"I wonder if the little beggars could cope?" he mused aloud. He sat silent for a while and then suddenly added "Of course they can - I'll make them cope, even if I have to rehearse them day and night!"

"What are you on about?"

"1776!" Ernie said, and explained to Wally about the speciality he had written for the army.

"Good God, Ernie," Wally said, "you're asking a lot of them, they're only kids."

"They're my band," he said, "they'll play it!"

Every night for the next fortnight he rehearsed them and when they were tired he rehearsed them again - and again. They arrived at the studios full of confidence and, at the end of the programme, Ernie received the trophy from Lady Barbirolli. They now had to face an agonising six weeks - the programme was not going to be transmitted until September and, until then, the result was to be kept secret and no-one told of the outcome! Luckily, two of those intervening weeks were to be taken up by yet another visit to Letterkenny which made it less likely that their pride and, by now, uncontrollable enthusiasm, would cause them to break their promise of confidentiality.

Before setting off for Ireland the band gave its usual "Au Revoir" concert, this time at the Garrick Theatre in Altrincham. Everything seemed quite normal until mid-way through the second half of the programme when Ernie, for the first time ever, apparently suddenly found himself facing a hostile band! He reached the part in the programme when the next item was to be the march "King Cotton". He raised his baton, brought it down and not one member played a note. He stood still, facing them in total silence - they, in turn, sat staring at him. He was totally perplexed. What had gone wrong? Then he realised that thirty or so pairs of eyes were not staring at him but at a spot above his head. He looked up to see a huge greetings card being lowered from the flies. As he opened it the band, and the entire audience erupted with loud applause. He reached for the card and opened it. It read simply "From proud parents" and attached to it was a magnificent pocket watch and chain. It was one of the rare times in his life when Ernie was stuck for words and he fumbled through a "Thank you" speech with tears in his eyes. That watch is still one of his treasured possessions and he never conducts the band without wearing it.

He was proudly showing it in the bar after the show when the two ladies from "Petites Modes" came to see it.

"You must be a proud man, Ernie." Billy said.

"I've played for the stars, I've played at great functions," he said, "but, for me, this must be the greatest moment of them all."

"We're having a bit of a party at my house after the show," Karina said, "do you fancy joining us?"

"I'd love to," Ernie replied, "but wouldn't your husband object to gatecrashers? I know I would."

Karina laughed, "That hardly applies, we were divorced ages ago. You come along - we'll celebrate with you. Those kids must be the best young band in the country."

Ernie found it hard not to tell her that in September they were going to be proclaimed so. He went to the party and enjoyed himself socially for the first time in many years.

When the programme "Settle the Score" was broadcast in September his phone started to ring with messages from people offering congratulations and others requesting the band play at various functions, amongst them being an invitation to play at the Golden Garter for Frankie Vaughan. It was clear that the success could not be allowed to pass unrecognising the work put in by the children and their parents so Ernie and Wally set about organising a fitting celebration which took the form of a formal dinner at a large hotel with the Mayor of Trafford and all civic dignitaries present. They also decided that the time had come to put the band on a more formal footing and, during the after-dinner speeches they invited the Chairman of School Governors, Councillor Ivor Hurst J.P., to become President of the band. Ivor was delighted at the surprise honour and accepted on one condition: ".... that I am not just a title. I will accept only if I can be a fully active participant." From that day Ivor has given his time and energy to furthering the progress of the band and has become another of Ernie's loyal friends.

It was through Ivor's efforts that in March 1977, Ernie received a mysterious request. Wally Lindsay came to him one day and said,

"Sorry I can't tell you more, Ernie, but will you prepare the band for "a big one" in July?"

"What sort of show?" Ernie asked.

"I can't tell you." "Where will it be?"

"I can't tell you."

"That's bloody silly! What the hell do I play? Marches? Swing? I can't prepare a programme without knowing the audience or the venue!"

"Sorry, Ernie, but you'll have to."

Ernie was both puzzled and somewhat annoyed. He had grown to regard Wally as a good friend and couldn't understand his sudden arcane attitude. He decided he could do nothing until he found out what was going on and continued constructing and writing his latest idea - a programme devoted to the music of the war years, from the popular marches of the time to the canteen songs and the sounds of the "big bands" of the '40's. By May this was ready and was launched at the Cresta Court Hotel in Altrincham under the title "The Warring Forties". The audience was successfully persuaded to turn up in costume and the hall was filled with uniforms, "land army girls", "factory workers" and "refugees". Children, parents and staff were intrigued to see the Chairman of School Governors, fully revelling in his role of Band President, arrive as a fully equipped "spiv", with pencil moustache and pockets full of nylons! Such was the camaraderie that the band engendered. Without the slightest doubt it was the most successful show the band had presented, the party went on into the early hours and the complete show was later recorded by Christine Prentice of Radio Manchester and broadcast under the same title. Once again, the reward from the B.B.C. was a copy of the master tape and so the second band L.P. appeared on the market. The first "pressing" of a thousand records sold out within weeks and thousands more sold over the following years. It is still the band's most requested programme.

On the Monday morning after the show Ernie was in Wally's office again.

"I've had an idea over week-end," he said, "what do you think of putting on a Festival of Remembrance in November?"

"That's strange," Wally answered, "the thought passed through my mind at the concert - we'd only have to expand it, add some sentimental items and get genuine military personnel and we'd have it."

They discussed the idea, on and off, for two weeks and finally decided it could be done. They were in total agreement on the format - nothing maudlin and with no religious bias of any sort whatsoever. Ernie promised to organise the musical content and Wally set to work on the script - each man thus concentrating on his own particular skill and ability. Their "meetings" for morning coffee became a daily ritual as the ideas and content began to co-ordinate into a full programme.

It was at one of these meetings that Wally said,

"Before we start, Ernie - about that special show I asked you to prepare. How far have you got?"

"Not far, to be honest - I can soon put a programme together when I know what numbers to include. How long will it last?"

"About four hours."

"What!? Who the hell wants a programme lasting four hours? The kids can't blow for that long!"

"Oh, they'll have breaks."

"I should bloody well hope so! But it's asking a lot of them. What's it all about, anyway? Why can't you tell me?"

"I can, now. I've told the powers-that-be that you must be put in the picture. They've agreed but have asked me to stress that, like I was, you must be bound to silence for security reasons - the kids mustn't be told yet, Ernie, but they'll be playing for the Queen."

"When? Where? How?"

"Well it seems that as this is Silver Jubilee year the Queen and the Duke of Edinburgh are going to attend a Royal Garden Party in Manchester and it's being held at Longford Hall on June 20th. Ivor Hurst and the Mayor nominated our band and it has been accepted. The Queen will be there for about four hours and the music will be provided by you and a military band playing alternately."

"What's going to happen next?" Ernie asked, "I thought "Settle the Score" was the limit - now we've gone well over the top. You'll have to excuse me - and we'd better leave the Festival for a month," he added laughingly, "I've got to get their music sorted out, the little beggars have got some tough rehearsals ahead of them!"

The band were allowed to know why they had been practising so hard a week before the Garden Party. It was a grand occasion. A special marquee had been erected for the sole use of the band in case of wet weather but luckily it was not needed but the top of the tent was used to display an enormous banner, kindly made and donated by Jack Delaney of Delprint, Manchester, proclaiming "Loyal Greetings from Ashton-on-Mersey Schools Concert Band". Elf Petrol Company donated the money to purchase special blazers for the band to wear and it was a very smart, and proud, group of youngsters who played, albeit stuffed with strawberries and cream, on a warm summer afternoon. Their greatest moment was when the Duke of Edinburgh stopped and said to them,

"Is it you who have been playing all afternoon? From over there I thought it was recorded music. How often do you practise?"

"Three times a week."

"When do you find time to do your school work?"

Ernie explained to the Duke how the band was formed and what it had done. The Duke congratulated them and rejoined the Queen who, by now, was the owner of a copy of the band's L.P. record, presented to her by Ivor. Ernie's scrapbook contains a valued picture of the band behind the Queen with her equerry carrying the record for all to see.

Top: A.O.M. Youth Showband 1976. BBC TV
Left: Ernie receiving BBC trophy from Lady Barbirolli 1976
Above: A.O.M. Showband, Liverpool 1993
Bottom: "The Band that played for the Queen" 1977

Top: N. W. Festival of Remembrance 1979
Above: Festival Organisers 1983 (From left: Peter Davies, Norman Whalley, Ernie, Ivor Hurst, Wally Lindsay)
Right: Ernie 1991
Below: "It's Great to be Alive" Free Trade Hall, Manchester 1983

Top:
The men who put Ernie back together! (Surgeons Bob Lawson & Mike Wroblewski 1993)

Left:
"Personal Thanks" Chester 1989

Bottom:
Ernie, Karina, Robert, Amy at Buckingham Palace 1993

Top Left:
Ernie re-united with Reg Lester 1988

Top Right:
Re-union with Freddie Hefferan 1993

Right:
Auntie Ethel, Cousin George, Margaret & Les Stockell 1993

Bottom Left:
Anice & Charlie Reynolds 1993

Bottom Right:
Kathleen O'Brien c1982

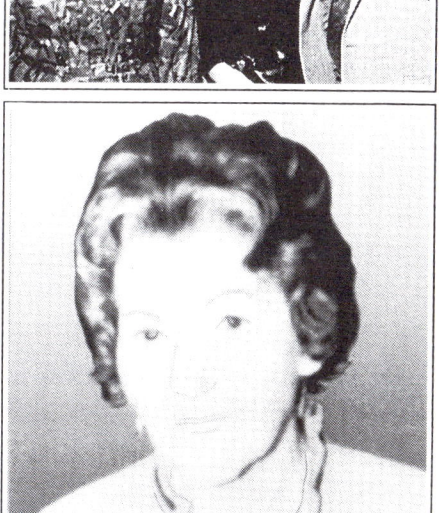

CHAPTER TWENTY

Ernie's lifestyle reverted to that of ten years previously except that now he was giving his time mostly in a voluntary capacity. He was teaching by day, holding band practices for both the school band and his "Concert Band" in the evenings, writing more music than ever to feed the band as it progressed and playing professionally at the Golden Garter into the early hours of each morning. He overlooked one important thing - he wasn't growing younger! His home life, like his social life, was at rock bottom and his only form of unwinding during this period seems to be the relaxing hour each lunch-time which he often spent with a sandwich and a cup of tea in the back of "Petites Modes" where the ladies always had a ready welcome for him. His visits there grew more and more frequent and he began to realise that his feelings for Karina were becoming more than friendship. It did nothing to improve the icy atmosphere that had developed at home.

In July more of the band left school and, as in the year before, asked to be allowed to continue playing. It was obvious that some permanent solution must be found for what was going to be an annual problem. A meeting was called for all those parents interested and the school hall was filled to capacity. The result was that the "Ashton-on-Mersey Schools Concert Band ceased to exist and a new band was formed. Recalling the remarks made by Harry Mortimer after "Settle the Score" the new title was an automatic choice - "Ashton-on-Mersey Youth Showband" - open to all young musicians in the area. Ivor Hurst was to be its Chairman and the band run by Ernie, Wally and another keen member of the teaching staff, Norman Whalley.

It was under that title that the band toured Yugoslavia during August and took part in the International Festival of Music in Dubrovnic. They took with them greetings and messages of friendship printed in English, Russian, German and French on the back of paper Union Jacks and, one evening, as they played in the beautiful square of the old walled city, Ernie was reminded of those long-ago days in Singapore - the lights were on all over the square and people were leaning out of windows, applauding and waving the paper British flags. It was a proud man who brought his beloved band back to England.

His happiness lasted only for a matter of days. In September, Eddie announced he was leaving home and going to live in France, where he had obtained a post as a sales representative for a publishing company. Ernie could not stand in his way but was devastated. His home life had evolved around his son and now the only reason he had for living there was going. About a week later he came for his "coffee meeting" to the headmaster's office but it was instantly clear to Wally that no progress would he made that day.

"What's wrong, Ernie?" he asked.

"I've had it," Ernie replied, "I've not had a wink of sleep. You know Eddie's gone?"

"Yes, I was pleased to hear he'd got the job. Has he run into trouble?"

"He's not - I have. I've just seen him off at the airport and it's made me realise the end has come. I can't take any more at home. I've packed a bag and left - it's in the back of my car."

"Where are you going?"

"I've no idea," he put his head in his hands and his shoulders hunched, "and I don't care. I'll find a hotel somewhere for tonight - I just can't face going back."

"Look," Wally said, "you're in no state to teach, you go and sort yourself out, I'll cancel all your lessons for today - and as long as necessary."

"No," Ernie said, "the kids look forward to their lessons, I'll have this coffee and carry on. It's the only way, really, you know that, the services taught us how to deal with emotional crises - get back to work! Good God, do you know we continued a rehearsal in Malaya after being told my best pal had died? I'll be O.K."

"Don't go off today without seeing me, Ernie - promise me that."

"Right." Ernie went to his stock-room and lost himself in his music. He got a surprise when he stuck his head round the office door on his way out.

"Oh, Ernie," Wally said, "I've been thinking. I've got a spare room - you're welcome to it until you make some permanent arrangements."

"Are you sure?"

"They taught us comradeship, too, mate - hang on for half an hour and you can follow me home."

Ernie moved into Wally's house in Stokesay Road, Sale, and from then on their evenings, until Ernie had to set off for the Golden Garter, were spent organising the coming Festival of Remembrance.

The Festival was held at The Odeon Cinema in November and, as expected, was a great success. Members of The Royal British Legion had been in the foyer selling poppies before watching the show and three days later Wally received a telephone call from one of them, Peter Davies.

"I saw the Festival on Sunday," he said, "and we're convinced you've got something new there. May we help next year and make it into a bigger event? There's nothing in the north-west to compare with the Albert Hall Festival, why not start one? I suggest the King's Hall, Belle Vue - it holds about five thousand."

"Five thousand!" Wally said, "how will we sell that number of tickets?"

"We will - think it over, have a word with Ernie and let me know how he feels."

It was obvious how Ernie felt as soon as he got the message. His eyes lit up. It was the challenge he needed to brighten up his life again as his mind was now on the future, helping him to overlook the present. The present could not be obliterated, however, as his relationship with Frieda had now turned to hostility. He continued to maintain the house in Winstanley Road and provide for Frieda until a legal settlement could be agreed but he went to see a solicitor and divorce proceedings were commenced on the grounds of irretrievable breakdown of the marriage.

In December he purchased a flat in Old Hall Court, Sale Moor and waited eagerly for the end of January when he would be allowed to move in. Wally had a long-standing arrangement to visit his family at Christmas and Ernie faced the prospect of spending the festive period alone. In a desperate attempt to find company he reluctantly booked in at a hotel for the holiday period when, during one of his lunch-time sandwich visits Karina invited him to have his Christmas dinner with her and her mother. He cancelled his hotel booking and the anticipated period of misery turned out to be one of the happiest Christmases he can remember.

The legalities of the purchase of the flat were completed in the first week of February and he set about redecorating it in the hope of moving in by the end of the month. He planned to furnish it partly with bits Frieda allowed him to take and with items given to him by Billy and Karina. His optimism proved to be premature as due to the small amount of time he had to spare the refurbishment took far longer than he had anticipated. He was still with Wally in Stokesay Road when he got the call he had been awaiting for years - to go to Wrightington Hospital for examination prior to hip-replacement surgery.

At Wrightington he was shown into the consultant's room and was greeted by a tall imposing figure,

"Good morning, Mr. Waites, my name is Wroblewski, sit down please."

Ernie, dressed in just a white towelling robe, sat uncomfortably on a plastic chair while the surgeon thumbed through his notes.

"I see you are a musician."

" Yes."

"Do you play regularly?"

"Oh, yes, but I get more pleasure teaching."

"Can you play the flute?"

Ernie began to wonder when he was going to be medically examined, this man seemed so relaxed and confident.

"Yes, but mainly saxophone and clarinet these days."

"I've always wanted to play the flute myself." He was perusing the notes and holding a conversation at the same time, "I think I can do something for your hip."

Ernie smiled. "I'll make a bargain with you," he said, "you fix my hip and I'll teach you to play the flute!"

Both men laughed,

"I'll hold you to that," Mike Wroblewski said, "now, let's have a look at you - lie down on the couch."

The operation was performed in April and after ten days in bed he was allowed up and, although balanced on crutches, he was delighted to see that his legs looked normal again. He was eventually discharged from hospital and returned to Stokesay Road because although his own flat was then ready he was in no state to fend for himself - particularly as, within a week, he went down with pneumonia.

His petition for divorce was unopposed and while he had been in hospital he had received word that his decree nisi had been granted and the terms of the divorce settlement finalised. After much acrimony it had been agreed that the house in Winstanley Road should be sold in order to provide a suitable flat for Frieda and that Ernie should pay her twenty-five pounds a week for life. Although his home life had been practically non-existent for many years the parting still affected him. Even after a month, when he was walking normally for the first time in eight years, he still felt a great sense of loneliness and the time he spent in the flat was disturbing. He would sit there, alone, gazing at the four walls, oblivious to the television or radio, his mind re-living the past. He needed a foundation, he needed roots, he needed to know who he really was. He was still on leave from his work so he packed a small bag and set off to Ireland, determined to find his natural mother and, with luck, the family to which he really belonged. Armed only with scraps of paper left by Edith he traced Kathleen back to County Kerry but there the trail ended and it was a very disappointed man who returned to England.

The divorce was made absolute on May 18th. It was the end of an era and he realised that having failed to find the past he must accept the present and concentrate on the future - a future he already dreamed of sharing with Karina but was wary of voicing his aspirations too soon. They met every day at lunch-times and at the band shows which he had soon re-introduced but with his evenings being committed to the Golden Garter any traditional form of courtship was impossible.

In August the band made a second tour of Yugoslavia, a visit made memorable because the area where they stayed was devastated by an earthquake only days after they had left. When he returned home he found himself thrown into the melee of the forthcoming Festival of Remembrance. Peter Davies informed him that all tickets had been sold, Wally Lindsay had completed the script and an excellent response from an appeal for advertisements meant that a forty-eight page souvenir programme was being prepared. The show was to be one of the biggest spectacles in the North-West for years. He began extensive rehearsals of the band's part in the show, which was by far the majority of its content. The date had been fixed of necessity for Sunday November 5th because on the official Remembrance Day, the following week-end, the throng of ex-service standard bearers would be occupied at the Albert Hall in London.

On Friday the third of September, in a moment of impetuosity, he proposed marriage to Karina. Although the thought of proposing had been in his mind for months he realised there was an age-gap between them and had never been able to summon up the temerity to voice his feelings for fear of rejection and a possible end of their association. He was in the shop for his habitual mid-day sandwich and Karina was listing a delivery of new stock when, for no reason he can recollect. He suddenly asked her if she would marry him - and, to his delight, she accepted. His state of euphoria on this occasion was not to last more than a matter of minutes! Billy returned from her lunch and they broke what they considered to be the happy news. To their mutual surprise Billy was completely antagonistic and broke into an angry diatribe about the age gap, Ernie's financial position and the apparent haste. The turnabout in her attitude towards him reminded him dramatically of the sudden change of Ted Stockell all those years ago when he had asked for a bike for Christmas - a transition which led to years of unhappiness. Was history repeating itself? He left the shop hoping that, in his absence, mother and daughter could talk things over rationally.

On the day of the Festival, Karina arrived at the King's Hall alone so it was clear to him that the differences had not been resolved but her presence, and her reassurance that the marriage would still take place, gave him the fortitude he needed to lead the band in front of the largest audience it had ever encountered. That afternoon over four hundred people took part in a spectacle that was received with tumultuous applause. The performance lasted nearly three hours and Ernie never had a minute's break. At its spectacular conclusion he was exhausted, running with sweat but exhilarated - and a cheque for three thousand pounds was subsequently presented to the Royal British Legion Poppy Appeal.

From then on the Festival became an annual event. Due to the demolition of the King's Hall two years later the venue was changed and eventually found a permanent "home" in the Opera House of the Winter Gardens at Blackpool, the donations to ex-service charities growing steadily greater as the years went by. Ernie and Karina were married quietly at Sale Registry Office on November 7th. Billy attended the wedding, albeit somewhat reluctantly, but her relationship with Ernie remained cool and disapproving. They settled in Karina's house in Hayling Road, Sale and Ernie's flat was rented out. The Hayling Road house was almost back-to-back with Wally's home in Stokesay Road and, from then on, both homes became meeting places for the organisation of both band and charity functions.

Amongst many others, two such events deserve mention. A show was produced with the sole object of raising the money to buy a specialist microscope attachment needed by Wrightington Hospital and Mike Wroblewski himself attended and accepted the cheque on behalf of the Hip Replacement Unit. The band magic worked once more - Mike Wroblewski, who had still not had time to accept Ernie's offer of flute lessons, became a stalwart supporter! The second venture was a show, inspired by Ernie's composition "1776", which they decided to entitle "Tribute to America". This was an exciting compilation of American folk music, Souza marches and "big band" swing in the styles of Glenn Miller, Tommy Dorsey and Charlie Barnet. They needed an American voice to link items but abhored the thought of anyone attempting to assume an American accent. It was a problem, until the obvious answer came to mind - use an American! A telephone call to the commanding officer at the U.S.A. base at Burtonwood was met with enthusiasm: An American officer recorded all the necessary passages, the personnel at the base heard the result, the programme was broadcast by Radio Manchester, a third L.P. record was issued, the Americans joined the annual Festival and the band gained its first regular "foreign" fans. More magic!

In May, 1979 Ernie was approached by Frank Slater, who sometimes augmented the Golden Garter Band playing trombone but whose main occupation was that of Co-ordinator of Music of Manchester schools, with the offer of a post within his department - a full time post with Ernie instructing in ten different schools. Ernie accepted and reluctantly handed in his notice at Ashton-on-Mersey - but with the agreement that he would be allowed to continue evening rehearsals in the school hall for the Showband.

The summer tour that year was to Belgium, playing many concerts at places as varied as the Opera House in Bruges to the open square by the Menin Gate. That performance at Ypres was memorable: When the band started to play the square was deserted, within ten minutes it was crowded to capacity - thousands of people appeared from nowhere, joining in "Tipperary" and raving to the Glen Miller numbers. They linked arms and swayed, they screamed for more, well into the night. One old man approached Ernie and, in faltering English, said, "They won't let you go - you're playing our liberation music."

The performance was interrupted by the traditional poignant playing of the "Last Post" at the Menin Gate at dusk and, afterwards, the cafes that bounded the square, closed up when the band arrived, all opened with the universal offer - "Drinks on the house for our English visitors!" Ernie had a very difficult task that night trying to shepherd the young musicians back to their coach.

During the tour the youngsters were taken to see the Flanders war cemeteries and Ernie was visibly touched when one lad, normally a "rebel", stared at the rows of gravestones and said softly,

"Chief - we now know what it's all about, we'll play better than ever for the next Festival."

Just one week after the band arrived home they read in the papers that the bandstand in Brussels, where they had performed, had been blown up by the I.R.A.

In September, Ernie began his new job with Manchester Education Authority and immediately recognised its drawback. His ten schools were distributed all over the city and he was forced to drive backwards and forwards through heavy traffic in order to fulfil his timetable. This made his daily commitment almost intolerable - he was now driving around Manchester, instructing at his schools, rehearsing his showband in the evenings and playing at the Golden Garter at night.

He arrived at the Garter one night late in the month to find his instruments had been stolen from the room where he stored them. He rushed home, borrowed an alto-saxophone from the showband, retrieved Eddie's old clarinet from his bedroom and got back to the Garter just in time for the show. He left the club well after midnight and, as he got in his car, he had a most unusual sensation of disaster. He suddenly felt extremely weak, his mind couldn't seem to focus on anything and he had a strange sense of impending death. It lasted for some minutes - he could do nothing but sit in the car; he couldn't call out, he couldn't move. He sat in the car park for about half an hour before driving home, weak and frightened. He did not realise it at the time but he had experienced his first heart attack.

Instead of seeking medical advice he plunged deeper and deeper into engagements for his showband. The concerts were now almost on a weekly basis and given for dozens of different causes; he read in the local paper that a deaf child was in need of a "bionic ear" - the band put on a show and the money was raised in one evening, there was an appeal for Guide Dogs for the Blind - he raised the funding for two, beds were provided for local hospitals and, through out all the activity, he was preparing the annual Festival of Remembrance. He reminisces today and constantly expresses the debt he owes to Ivor Hurst, the President of the band. Ivor is a practical man and a wise one - he pulled Ernie up in his tracks by pointing out he was becoming obsessed with success. Ernie had the common sense to listen to his counsel and began to limit his commitments. From that day on Ivor has been his steadying force, gently persuading him to slow down while at the same time encouraging his ambitions - but, on occasions, he couldn't be stopped.

Karina had her first baby on February 9th 1980. Ernie now had a second son and they named him Robert Kerry. Within a month Ernie had organised a special concert to provide equipment for Wythenshawe Baby Unit! They were proud of the baby, Ernie embarrassingly so, for he would regularly announce his latest parenthood at all bandshows, regardless of whether the audience even knew him - or cared!

In April he was surprised to receive a cheque in the post from the Festival Committee of Antwerp. The band had won third prize in the Antwerp Festival of 1979 - Ernie did't know they'd taken part! All he does remember is that they played, ad lib, for a few minutes in the town square while passing through the city the previous year during the tour based in Belgium.

Robert was eight months old when the band were booked for their annual **overseas tour** - this time to France, an opportune engagement as the visit **coincided with** Eddie's twenty-first birthday, and as Eddie worked in France **Ernie decided to** introduce him to his new brother and took the baby with him. **Karina therefore** faced the prospect of a six-hour coach trip to Portsmouth, a four-hour Channel crossing and another four hours on the coach from Cherbourg to St. Malo loaded with baby food, nappies and the hundred-and-one other items necessary to maintain baby life, plus a large birthday cake to present to her stepson!

The tour was the most immemorable in the band's history. They enjoyed **only two days** of fine weather throughout the fortnight, the accomodation was of third-rate standard and the facilities available at concerts almost non-existent. **Ernie quotes** one example which sums up the whole disastrous episode: They were due to play in the open air near Rotheneuf and arrived to find the place deserted and that no arrangements had been made for power for the bass guitar or lighting. Power was eventually obtained by tapping into the fuse box of a convenient kiosk while Ivor went off to find some local official. Norman Whalley somehow managed to rustle up a couple of light bulbs to give some meagre illumination but no-one could produce an audience. Nobody in the area had been informed of the concert and there was no publicity material within sight. Ernie had set the band up and was just about to pack everything away again when a coach of young people arrived. As he had an audience, albeit only about thirty, Ernie played and the group applauded enthusiastically. Eddie, had come from his work-base in Paris and used his command of French to thank them for their appreciation but it soon became obvious that his words were falling on deaf ears. Ernie tried in his limited German but was equally unsuccessful. He then reverted to English and was immediately understood - the group were a school party from Manchester!

It was early in 1981 that Ernie was suddenly seized by severe chest pain. The doctor diagnosed a coronary attack immediately and Ernie was confined to bed for a fortnight. He was advised to rest for three months. During this period the Golden Garter closed down and, for the first time in his life, Ernie received a redundancy payment. He was given a cheque for one thousand pounds but he realised he must now face the future with only his monthly pay from Manchester to live on. He was not deterred and, before he should, he began to devote even more time to the showband. The concerts began again in Radcliffe, Bury, Oldham, Whitworth, and Saddleworth and, before the end of the year, he had taken the band to Heywood, Atherton, Haslingden, Rochdale, Vale Royal and Stockport before the overseas visit to Gran Canaria. Even Ivor was beginning to despair about his insatiable appetite for work.

His daughter was born on June 9th 1982. Karina was to have had the delivery at hospital but the baby, probably inheriting Ernie's impulsive "get things done!" trait, decided otherwise and she made her entrance into the world in the back bedroom before an audience consisting of Ernie, Robert and a neighbour's dog! With memories of his early days in Scarborough and the girl who had meant so much to him in his childhood, he named her Amy. By now his acquaintance with Mike Wroblewski had matured into friendship and the surgeon gladly accepted the offer to be godfather to the new arrival, but she was not christened until January 1993, the delay being due to Ernie's medical condition. Following more bouts of chest pain he had been examined at the cardio-thoracic department of Wythenshawe Hospital and had then received a letter which at last brought his activities to an abrupt halt:

".. I therefore think it reasonable to offer you an operation which would involve probably two artery by-pass grafts........the chance of getting out of the operation would be somewhere in the region of 8/9 out of ten."

The operation was performed on July 1st, 1992 by the heart specialist of Wythenshawe, Bob Lawson. Ernie was now compelled to take proper rest and even after his discharge, he began a more sedate attitude to life - for a while. His thoughts again turned to Kathleen and he spent his enforced idleness making more enquiries about his natural mother and what had become of her. His notes say he had discovered that Uncle Bill, the only contact that Edith had had with her, had died in 1961 so, sadly, that avenue of research was closed and the trail had run cold. Once again he made telephone calls to various offices and contacts in Scarborough but, not knowing their surname, or the number of the house where once they lived, he could find no record of a "Tom" and "Frances" who resided in Princess Street so he had to assume that they, too, were no longer alive or had moved to an address which would be impossible to locate with so little information. Apart from travelling over to Ireland again, which was physically impossible, he could see no way of re-opening the search. He abandoned the idea and returned to occupying his time writing music.

Towards the end of the year he met Joyce Carter, a keen voluntary worker for the British Heart Foundation. She was the catalyst that set him off again. Within weeks the band performed at Radcliffe and raised over a thousand pounds for the charity. But this did not satisfy him and preparations began at once for a major "spectacular" to raise more. With Wally as co-ordinator and Peter as business manager, the "Festival" team, assisted by Karina, Audrey Halton and Norman and Elsie Whalley, set about producing a major show at the Free Trade Hall, Manchester. Entitled "It's Great to be Alive" and supported by people such as The Duke of Edinburgh, Sir Harry Secombe, Sir Jimmy Saville and Frankie Vaughan O.B.E., it was performed on September 30th and raised over five thousand pounds which was donated to the Wythenshawe Coronary Unit.

Even while this show was being prepared, preparations were also being made for the now established "North West Festival of Remembrance" in November and in spite of all pleas for caution from Ivor and general warnings from medical advisors Ernie was again totally absorbed - his task made even more difficult that year because Wally Lindsay suffered a major heart attack soon after the show at the Free Trade Hall and Ernie, on top of the vast musical contribution, assumed responsibility for the part that he would have played in the production of the forthcoming Festival.

By the end of the year he was fully involved again and was continuing his life as if nothing untoward had occurred. He was back in full-time employment by day, holding his band rehearsals in the evenings and, at the same time, suffering the usual sleepless nights experienced by parents of young children. His reward was in the band accounts - it had now existed for ten years and, during that time, had raised over fifty thousand pounds for charities.

CHAPTER TWENTY-ONE

Although Ernie was now in his mid-fifties he thrived on his new family and his life with Karina was one of happiness and contentment - which probably contributed extensively to the "second youth" he appeared to be enjoying. Life became routine: He saw Robert and Amy pass through the toddler stage and then came the day when he watched Karina fitting them for their first school uniforms. As she did so, he could not but recall the day they had first met when he had taken Eddie to the shop and he had been regarded as a "star".

Over the years he had evolved a method of teaching children to play recognisable tunes within a very short time and after five years with the Manchester schools he had amassed several folders full of simple music on which the youngsters thrived - because it enabled them to play as a "band" within a matter of weeks. He realised that this material would be of great value to other peripatetic teachers and band instructors so, after dividing it into appropriately progressive manuals, he submitted the work for publication. The set of booklets was published under the title "First Blow" and is in common use today.

1987 stands out in his memory because, in August, he realised another of his "impossible" dreams - he took his band to the United States and, as in every other country it had visited, it was received with acclaim and incredulity at its standard. They went to Florida where, amongst other engagements, the youngsters appeared as an attraction at "Disneyworld" and the Epcot Centre. As he played for the vast crowds milling round the huge complex he particularly noticed the blasé way in which the young band members accepted the challenge and his mind went back to the day when a terrified group of children had first played in the school hall for their proud parents - a group which had now been transformed into competent and confident musicians.

No sooner had they left Florida, however, than the area was devastated by a hurricane. Ernie began to wonder what sort of evil genie was following him, as over the years their appearance overseas always seemed to preface some kind of disaster! A tour of Romania had to be cancelled due to an earthquake, a similar catastrophe followed a Yugoslavian tour, a bomb blew up the bandstand in Brussels, a hurricane ravaged Florida and, when they played in the Canaries, a resort famed for 365 days of sunshine per year, no sooner had they set up their music stands under enormous sunshades than the heavens opened and they were drenched to the skin!

When they arrived back in Sale, however, he had another pleasant experience - he read that the Green Howards were holding a re-union and he drove over to Yorkshire where he found himself wallowing in nostalgia among members of the band with which he had played in Suez and Malaya. He was standing at the bar, re-living the past, when a voice behind him said,

"Watch it, Ernie, Salome's on the loose!"

He spun round and came face to face with Brian Clancy. Both men were older, and wiser, and a very happy evening followed as they related their respective post-army adventures and mis-adventures. A gap of thirty-five years disappeared in minutes.

His re-discovery of the Green Howards was a new interest in his life and, when it was possible, he attended meetings of the Green Howards Association. It was at one such meeting that he heard that the newly formed branch of the Association, in Barnsley, had no Standard and were trying to raise the money to purchase one - a difficult task as Standards are very expensive items. Ernie's response was predictable - part of the proceeeds from the pending November Festival would be allocated to purchase one. This was formally presented to the branch in March, 1988.

At the very first Festival of Remembrance Lord Kitchener of Khartoum had been invited as Guest of Honour and, every year since, it had become traditional to have an eminent guest. At the event held the previous November the Guest of Honour had been Brigadier Bob Long, the Colonel of the Royal Hampshire Regiment and Commander of the North West Division, Chester. In May he returned the compliment and invited Ernie to attend a ceremony of Beating of the Retreat at Chester. Ernie duly arrived and eagerly settled himself in the audience while the parade assembled. It was an impressive sight - the massed bands of three regiments gathered together for this one event. He wondered why he had been privileged to be given a seat on the front row and assumed it was because he was there as a guest of Brigadier Long. He was soon to be both surprised and (rarely for Ernie) scared out of his wits. During the performance Bob Long appeared, walked over to Ernie, led him to the bandmaster's stand and handed him the baton!

The Bandmaster, naturally, was perturbed and, quietly and unobtrusively, queried the Brigadier's action. Ernie stood on the rostrum and heard Bob Long whisper,

"I know what I'm doing - this man has conducted more bands than you've had hot dinners."

"What are they going to play?" Ernie asked

Bob Long grinned, "You'll find out when you start."

"This is ridiculous!" Ernie whispered hurriedly.

"Get cracking!" Bob said, ".....March tempo!"

Ernie knew he dare not keep everyone waiting. He took a deep breath, uttered a silent prayer, raised the baton and began. The bands followed him and, at the very first notes, he realised what Bob Long had done - they were playing the regimental march of the Green Howards! As the sound filled the evening air he experienced the greatest feeling of exhilaration he could ever have imagined. The incident was reported in the next edition of the papers, Bob Long became a friend and the magic of the showband had bewitched another victim!

For years, by now he had been repeatedly advised by his G.P. and hospital specialists to curtail his activities in general and to cease the stress of the endless driving through the heavily congested Manchester roads, so when he reached the age of sixty Ernie decided that he would heed their advice and retired from his post as instructor. So it was that from July, 1988 he had his days to himself. To rest and enjoy the leisures of retirement? No - to have more time to devote to his band and its work with youth and charities! He threw himself into more and more functions and more and more arranging of new repertoire. By then the amount of music he had written for the band had grown so large that he had to purchase an eighteen foot long shed and have it erected in his garden to house the bandparts! He purchased a photo-copier to speed up the production and Karina was appalled to find the machine taking up a large area of her dining room, the walls of which were already covered with shelving holding his record books, music library and band memorabilia. Ernie was a happy man.

In April, 1989 the band was asked to play at the Piccadilly Hotel, Manchester, the principal guest being H.R.H. Prince Edward, and in July it was invited to take part in the tercentenary celebrations of the Chester Regiment where the Guest of Honour was the Prince of Wales. Ernie's audiences were getting more and more elite! The engagement at Chester turned out to be one of the greatest challenges in the band's history. Ernie had been asked to play for about half an hour and, early in the morning, the band arrived by coach and began to set up their music stands. While they were doing so Ernie was approached by a frantic figure - the Bandmaster of the Cheshire Regiment. It transpired they were in deep trouble - the previous day the Regimental Band had played for the Parade of the Colours before Prince Charles but while they were doing so there had been a cloudburst and the ceremony had continued in torrential rain. As a consequence their uniforms had been drenched and were still unwearable and also some of the instruments had been affected by water and were unplayable. The performance had been arranged to last all morning, the Prince of Wales was going to be present and the band was out of commission - could Ernie take over? Ernie could, and did. The youngsters, who had come prepared to play for thirty minutes took over the whole show and played for three hours! They felt amply rewarded for their efforts when Prince Charles came to them to thank them personally.

This same period also saw the tercentenary of the Green Howards. Their celebrations were held at Catterick and, of course, Ernie went there to join in - this time without the band. His reputation had preceded him, however, and to his delight one of the first people to greet him there was Reg Lester, his first bandmaster.

"Ernie," he said, "when I think of that day when you, a lad of fifteen, came to me for selection, little did I know what I was starting."

Ernie laughed. "I remember it as if it were yesterday! What was it you said? .... Put your hand flat on the table and raise your fingers ...and then you allocated me to the clarinet!

"Well, was I wrong?"

"You were spot on .... and I'm grateful."

"Between you and me - I was lucky! But it all turned out for the best. I'm looking forward to the day when I can hear this band of yours."

He didn't have long to wait. In October Ernie arranged a special show for the Green Howards in the Royal Hall at Harrogate - and invited Reg Lester to be Guest of Honour.

It was becoming uncanny. Ernie's life seemed to be turning full circle as faces from the past were reappearing with such regularity. In a matter of months he had been re-united with Brian Clancy, Reg Lester and Les Stockell. The last was through a telephone call, out of the blue. The phone had rung at home one evening and Robert had answered it. He came to his father with a puzzled look on his young face,

"Its for you, daddy, it's a man called Les. He asked if you were a musician and were you in the army - should I know him?"

"If it's the Les I hope it is, son, he's your Uncle."

It was indeed Ernie's brother - they had not met since he had visited Ernie in the hospital at Stanmore. They had lost contact and he had been seeking Ernie for years, tracing him from 71 Winstanley Road, through Old Hall Lane and finally to Hayling Road. An immediate meeting was arranged and, while talking with his brother, Ernie disovered that his Auntie Ethel, Edith's sister, was still alive and living in Annfield Plain, Durham. The last time he had met his aunt had been when she attended his mother's funeral and, at the time, he had been astounded by the close resemblence she bore to her sister. He recalls that he had a shock as she entered the room - it was as if his mother had returned. As would be expected, he went to visit them and re-lived the days when he had gone to their home as a child when on holiday at his grandmother's.

His trip to Durham had a bonus - Ethel put him back in touch with his cousin Betty who was living in Newcastle. One by one he was being re-united with his family and the insecurity instilled by his childhood slowly disappeared. The only link still missing was, of course, his natural mother, Kathleen, but he had by now resigned himself to live in ignorance realising that by then she would have been over eighty and that the chain had most likely been broken by her death.

Another long-lost colleague with whom he was re-united was Les Dawson. In May, 1990 Ernie, seeing that the lovable comedian was then the compere of the popular television programme, "Opportunity Knocks", wrote to him reminding him of the nefarious activities above Johnny Roadhouse's shop in the late 1950's and, amongst other things, told him of the showband. Les replied in jocular mood and the outcome was that the band was later invited to attend Sachas Hotel in Manchester for an audition with a view to appearing on the programme. They passed the audition, of course, and were designated to appear at a future date. Three weeks later the show, for some reason, was taken off the air so the episode ended in disappointment for the band but Ernie found some compensation in the fact that he had re-established contact with yet another friend from the past.

When Ernie had first had his artificial hip fitted he had been told that it was expected to last ten years. He had been using his for twelve and had given it no quarter! When conducting the band he would swing about and gyrate like a man of half his age in perfect condition. On one occasion, Mike Wroblewski sat in the audience observing his actions with a look of total disbelief on his face,

"My God!" he exclaimed, "I don't mind my work being tested to any extreme - but this is ridiculous!"

It was not totally unexpected, therefore, when towards the end of the year, Ernie began to feel discomfort and the pain of arthritis started to manifest itself again. He was examined at Wrightington Hospital and the diagnosis showed the hip had deteriorated to such an extent that the only way to prevent his being totally crippled was for the operation to be repeated, but this time it would be more difficult because of the condition of his pelvis. Mike Wroblewski would perform the operation himself but there would be a delay due to the fact that his diabetic problem had also grown worse and Ernie was placed on an extremely strict diet for a matter of months.

Unfortunately, during this period of waiting he began to experience an ominous tightening of the chest and had more and more frequent attacks of angina. There was now a unanimous demand from Karina, Ivor and the surgeons that he curtail his activities immediately - he did so but only for a matter of weeks. As soon as the symptoms subsided he was off on his roller-coaster of life and, through it all, the band rehearsals were never interrupted and the schedule of concerts continued. The annual North West Festival of Rembrance was still his main item of the calendar but now that event had become even more demanding due to the sad death of Peter Davies who had been one of the most valuable members of the team. Ernie took more of the load on to his shoulders and, at the end of the festival, he was a drained man. It was patently self-evident that he could not continue for much longer.

By now the complement of the band had changed over and over again. Most of the original members were married with children of their own and hundreds of young people had benefited from his leadership over the years of the Showband's existence.

In 1991 he took them to tour Cyprus and it was there that he was rushed to a clinic after suddenly feeling ill. Following an E.C.G. scan he was told he had had a minor heart attack and must rest. The Cypriot doctors found that they had to accept the same response as their British counterparts had in the past - the band was committed to play, so Ernie carried on and completed the programme of events. To an onlooker his attitude may seem foolish, indeed, almost suicidal, but in Ernie's philosophy of life he was doing the correct thing in not letting anybody down.

He paid dearly for his irresponsibility. Within weeks of returning home he had two more attacks, the second culminating in his being rushed into the intensive care unit of Trafford General Hospital. He got out just in time to compere the Festival of Remembrance in November!

In December, following yet another examination at Whythenshawe Heart Unit, he received a letter, very similar in content to that of 1982 - he needed yet more artery by-pass grafts, and this time his chances were less. He was admitted to hospital in January, 1992 and the operation was again carried out by Bob Lawson.

The year had an horrific start for Karina, for, apart from Ernie being in the Intensive Care Unit, her mother Billy died on January 2nd and the funeral took place on the day following Ernie's life-saving operation. She therefore found herself emulating Ernie's life-style, rushing from the registrar to solicitor, from funeral director to church and then on to the hospital to visit her husband - and, all the time, running her business.

When Ernie was finally discharged from Wythenshawe Hospital he was, it appeared, a changed man. Both Bob Lawson and Ivor Hurst had given him serious lectures about curtailing his activities and, in any case, Ernie felt weak and frail. He behaved himself, he sat, although frustrated, reading, and writing music. As a way of counter-acting boredom he began collecting relevant information from his diaries and scrap-books and compiled a large folder of papers, legal documents and personal notes about his life with the idea of handing it on to his children for their interest. It is on the contents of that folder that his biography was eventually based. No one can therefore accuse him of irresponsibility at that time and yet, in his one long period of good conduct, sensible living and careful behaviour, his hip collapsed. Fate had played a cruel card and he was downcast. To Ernie, however, a challenge must always be faced. He had already made plans for the band to make a return visit to Florida, so he went - and the band played at Disneyworld again, with Ernie in a wheelchair!

By the time he returned he could walk again, with sticks, but every step was agony. He was re-admitted to Wrightington and, once again, found himself being prodded and probed by Mike Wroblewski.

"Well, Ernie, you've certainly given me a job this time, your hip is in a very bad state."

"Can you fix it?" he asked desperately.

"I can, but I can't guarantee a perfect job this time, the support will have to go much deeper. I'll have to have you in as soon as possible.... probably October."

"Can you make it later, after November?"

"What on earth for? This is urgent."

"I've got to do the November Festival."

"You've got to do nothing of the sort, Ernie, your health comes first."

"But there's so many people committed - I can't let them down. Come on, Mike - make it December - please."

"On one condition - that this is the last."

"It will be," Ernie said sorrowfully, "I know that myself"

At the Festival in November there was a sorrowful hush as, in a voice cracking with emotion, he made the announcement from the stage that he was compering the last Festival. The event had by then run for sixteen years and, during that time, had amassed some eighty thousand pounds for ex-service charities.

It was then he started his own personal appeal -"Ernie's Heart and Hip Fund". At every opportunity and at every concert since he has made an appeal from the stage for the audience to throw any loose change into a bucket on the way out from the hall. His aim is to raise a minimum of five thousand pounds to assist the work being done at both Wrightington and Whythenshawe Hospitals. He is not being disappointed.

As it transpired he could not be admitted to hospital in December and he suffered in great pain until a bed was available in January 1993 - when he was disappointed once again. His general condition was so low that Mike Wroblewski had to tell him the operation could not be done until he was fitter. He waited two more months while he was treated and the hip was eventually replaced in March.

Mike Wroblewski had been correct - it was more serious than the first operation and Ernie was on crutches for many weeks and, even after six months, still needed the support of sticks.

It was on crutches, therefore, that he joyfully resumed his band rehearsals in May and, on the morning after the first practice he found three letters on his hall floor; a gas bill, a personal invitation, written by computer, to win millions of pounds and an official envelope marked "Downing Street". He put the gas bill on the table, discarded the fortune in the waste bin and, with both perplexity and excitement, opened the third letter. It read:

"The Prime Minister has asked me to inform you, in strict confidence, that he has it in mind on the occasion of the forthcoming list of Birthday Honours to submit your name to the Queen with a recommendation that Her Majesty may be graciously pleased to approve that you be appointed a Member of the Order of the British Empire........"

He stood looking at it in disbelief for some minutes, examining it carefully to make sure someone was not pulling a practical joke, but then it dawned on him it was genuine and he handed it to Karina without a word. His mind was in turmoil as the meaning became clear. He was going to be Ernie Waites M.B.E. His thoughts were of gratitude - to the surgeons and medical staff, without whom he would not be there, to Reg Lester, who started it all, to the Green Howards, who made him a man, to the Ashton Showband and its officers, who had helped him make a dream come true, to the Festival Committee and, above all, to the millions of people who had attended the performances which had made it all possible. He spent the next weeks in turmoil because he could tell no one of the wonderful news.

Even by June, when the official announcement of his award had been made, he could not stand for any long period of time so he adopted the idea of conducting his band seated on a stool - because, through it all, he had maintained his rehearsals and his engagements.

By this time the band had become a regular attraction at functions arranged by Rotary Clubs. Following a major Rotary event at Southport, the Annual Ball, the previous year it had been in demand by club after club for their charitable work and, in summer 1993, was asked to perform at the International Convention in Blackpool where, for two consecutive nights, it played to audiences of over three thousand people. It was there he was asked to play at yet another Rotary function - in Scarborough. Scarborough! The wheel of fortune had turned again and he jumped at the opportunity of returning to his roots once more. The date was fixed for October.

His hip seemed to be taking an unusually long time to recover and he went to his doctor to check that such a condition was satisfactory as he realised that the weakness was not only in the treated leg - and he seemed to be perpetually tired. A few tests at hospital revealed the cause - it was not due to the latest operation, his diabetes had flared to new heights and muscle wastage had begun. He was told that the condition could no longer he treated by diet alone and that, from then on, he would have to start regular injections of insulin. It seemed he was going to be reliant on a walking stick for the rest of his life.

He had had no holiday during the year and, of course, the now traditional overseas tour by the band had had to be foregone for the first time so it came into his mind to combine the Scarborough engagement with a well deserved break and he invited Wally Lindsay and his wife, Edith, to share it with him. By now his biography was nearing completion and he suggested it would be an ideal opportunity to confirm local facts, taste first-hand impressions and take photographs that might be of interest.

They all duly arrived in Scarborough and on Saturday, October 23rd the hall in The Spa was crowded to capacity as Rotarians from far and wide ended their convention with a ball for which the band was providing the music. During the second half of the programme Ernie was interrupted by the District Governor of 1050 District who asked to be allowed to make an important announcement. Ernie stood to one side to allow him use of the microphone and assumed he was going to tell the members about Rotary business before they dispersed. Not being a Rotarian himself he therefore was not paying close attention to what was being said until he heard his own name mentioned and he was amazed to hear the reason for the break in programme:

".... our aim is charity and in Ernie Waites we have found a man who symbolises all we stand for. Although he is not a member of our organisation we have applied to headquarters in the U.S.A. outlining his work and I am pleased to announce that he has been awarded the highest honour the International Rotary Club can bestow - A Paul Harris Fellowship."

An embarrassed Ernie was then presented with a bound citation and a large gold medal as the hall erupted with applause. His acceptance speech was short, disjointed and delivered in a most abnormal manner - through humility, disbelief and bewilderment.

His few days in Scarborough were spent re-living his past and he escorted his willing friends round all the places of his childhood, particularly the Old Town. They saw St. Mary's Church and Anne Bronte's grave, they saw Church Street Steps where he had slid down the rail on a greasy plank; they were taken to the harbour and the spot where he had fallen into the slime, they saw Herbert

Waites' stable, still the same as it had been sixty years before and he pointed out the window of the room near Boyes' Store which had once been his home.

He drove them to Oliver's Mount, he walked them through Peasholme Park and gazed wistfully at the now overgrown open air theatre and he took them to Valley Bridge where once he had marched with the Green Howards to receive the freedom of the town. But the most poignant moment of all was when he parked his car on Sandside, displayed his "Disabled" notice and insisted on conducting a tour on foot.

Here his manner changed, as did his commentary. No longer did he use the first personal pronoun - from then on it was "She":

"She would have got off the tram somewhere around here," he said, waving his stick, "then she would have walked up this little hill and here, see, here is Princess Street. She would have walked along here to her auntie's house. See that small block of flats on the corner? That's where Bluebell Mission was - that's where she stayed with Edith and Herbert Waites before I was born. Look, there's St. Sepulchre Street, she would have walked up there on her way to the Balmoral Hotel where she worked."

He stood gazing around, as if seeking a face among the passing strangers, Karina took him by the arm,

"Come on, Ernie," she said, "we must give the children some lunch."

He followed his family and friends back to the car. At the end of Princess Street he stopped and turned round once more, he stared at the now smartly refurbished Georgian cottages, shook his head slowly and sighed,

"I wonder what became of her?"

CODA

Within days of the news of Ernie's M.B.E. becoming public, Ivor Hurst approached Wally Lindsay with the proposal that something special should be organised to celebrate the award and they met in Ivor's home in St. Annes to discuss ideas about the form of a celebration. They decided it should be arranged, as far as possible, without Ernie's knowledge - hoping to give him a pleasant surprise.

They realised that there was no chance whatsoever of Ernie committing himself to a firm date in the future for a private engagement so it was decided to cloak the function in the guise of a band show - but when he arrived to fulfil the "booking" he would find himself surrounded solely by friends from the past. While Elsie and Norman Whalley were asked to brief and advise the current band members of the deception, Wally and Ivor secretly set about the task of tracing the guests they wished to invite.

There followed months of letter-writing, searches in library reference sections, letters to the press, endless demands on "Directory Enquiries" and dozens of telephone calls - and by October they were satisfied they were ready to give him the surprise of his life.

The event was arranged for Sunday, November 6th and at 6.30 pm Ernie arrived at Worsley Old Hall, Manchester, to find the place almost deserted. Karina, who was in the conspiracy, took him to a large room and sat with him at a small table, keeping him in conversation to prevent him becoming aware of many people who were being spirited away to an upstairs room immediately on their arrival. The only unusual aspects of the reception room were that had been cleared of furniture apart from the table at which they sat, a large cut-out facsimile of the M.B.E. insignia had been fixed to a wall and, below it, was a small platform.

The main body of guests began to arrive and Ernie was soon overwhelmed by faces from both today and yesterday. Current band members mingled with members of the original band - most of these now in their mid-thirties and accompanied by wives and husbands. Band members of the intervening years were there, as were their parents; past benefactors turned up, helpers from the early days returned together with many volunteers who had performed at the Festivals in years gone by. The room was soon crowded to capacity and Ernie was visibly touched by the number of people who had come from all over the country at their own expense to pay him tribute.

Then, when the hall could apparently hold no more, he was led to the dais and seated on a tall stool. He was told there were some more guests whom he had yet to meet, guests who, unlike those in the room, were not mainly associated with the showband.

Surgeons Mike Wroblewski and Bob Lawson appeared, followed by Brigadier Bob Long and, from the B.B.C. days, producers Peter Pilbeam and Des Sissons. His old friend from the N.D.O., Freddie Hefferan, had travelled from Prestatyn and, from Yorkshire, who should appear but his old army colleagues Ray Pinkney and Brian Clancy. His life was being unrolled before him, going deeper and deeper into the past.

A fellow member of the Green Howards, Geoff Nalton, who Ernie thought was in Singapore, came to give him something he had been seeking for years - a Green Howards' cap badge and shoulder-flash. He was visibly moved when his Aunt and Uncle appeared, having travelled from Durham and they were followed by his schoolboy chum and fellow mischief-maker in the streets of Scarborough Old Town, Charlie Reynolds who had brought with him a special gift - a bible, dated 1907, which had been presented to Herbert Waites as a child, and which Charlie had discovered among his late father's effects. They had little time to reminisce about falling in the harbour mud when who should appear but his brother, Les Stockell with his sister-in-law, Margaret.

He was seated on the stool, shaking his head in disbelief, when a further shock was delivered. He was told that research into tracing his natural mother had been successful but, unhappily, she had passed away in 1988. He was absorbing this news when a framed portrait was handed to him - he was told it was Kathleen, the mother he had never known. He looked at it and, with tears in his eyes, clasped it to his breast.

He learned he was the member of a large family, he had a natural brother, sister-in-law and three sisters in Ireland. He had two uncles, eight nephews and a niece, all of whom, he was told, now knew of him and were eagerly awaiting to meet him.

He accepted an envelope containing their names, addresses and telephone numbers and gazed vacantly into the spotlight that was blinding his eyes. The spotlight was extinguished and, as his eyes accustomed to the normal lighting he saw hundreds of smiling faces, all happy on his behalf.

Then it came - the bombshell:

"Knowing you, Ernie, you'll either be on the first plane to Dublin tomorrow morning or you will spoil this evening for everybody by fidgetting - impatiently waiting to get to a telephone, so, to prevent our night being ruined we've brought them here...."

Five people, who had been observing from a far corner of the room, walked out of the shadows; his brother, his sister-in-law and his three sisters, the eldest bearing a startling resemblence to the face on the portrait. He rushed towards them and they met in a common embrace.

At the end of the dinner, well after midnight, the body of guests had left and the newly united family were huddled together telling him of their own past. His brother Patrick had been a professional musician, playing with major Irish showbands, his Uncle Archie had been a professional player of the double bass, two other members of the family had been musicians and Kathleen herself had been a singer and competent keyboard performer! Ernie had found his roots.

* * *

A taxi arrived to take his Irish relatives back to their hotel and, in the deserted car park, as Ernie said goodnight after making arrangements to meet them in the morning, Ivor turned to Wally and said,

"Well that's it, perhaps now he knows exactly who he is he'll slow down and lead a normal life for the remainder of his days."

"I'm sure he will. This is what he's needed - now he will take a rest."

The taxi drove off. The final "Goodnights" were said and Wally, happy at the success of the evening, walked towards his car. He was unlocking the car door when Ernie called across the car park,

"Are you coming to our house to meet them tomorrow?"

"We'd love to, if we're not intruding."

"Of course you're not. Anyway, I want to see you about something else. Next year is the fiftieth anniversary of D.Day - and I've got an idea..........."

So.....this is not **THE END!**